Fragments of the World

Uses of museum collections

Fragments of the World

Uses of museum collections

by

Suzanne Keene

ELSEVIER
BUTTERWORTH
HEINEMANN

AMSTERDAM • BOSTON • HEIDELBERG • LONDON
OXFORD • NEW YORK • PARIS • SAN DIEGO
SAN FRANCISCO • SINGAPORE • SYDNEY • TOKYO

Elsevier Butterworth-Heinemann
Linacre House, Jordan Hill, Oxford OX2 8DP
30 Corporate Road, Burlington, MA 01803

First Edition 2005

British Library Cataloguing in Publication Data
A catalogue record for this book is available from the British Library

Library of Congress Cataloguing in Publication Data
A catalogue record for this book is available from the Library of Congress

ISBN 0 7506 6472 X

For information on all Elsevier Butterworth-Heinemann publications visit our
website at www.books.elsevier.com

Typeset in Palatino-Roman
Typeset by CEPHA Imaging Pvt Ltd Bangalore, India
Printed and bound in Great Britain

Contents

Contents

Preface

... in 1851 the scanty collections ... occupied a length of 154 feet ... and three or four table cases. The collections now occupy 2250 feet of wall cases, 90 table cases and 31 upright cases...

(Augustus Franks, the noted curator, quoted in: David Wilson, The British Museum: purpose and politics, *BM Publications*, 1989)

... inadequate attention to methods of avoiding duplication and the implications for collection management have ... turned the dream into a nightmare

(S. Davies, Collecting for the 21st Century, Yorkshire & Humberside Museums Council, 1992)

... at an annual growth rate of 1.5% the size of the Nation's Collections will double within 47 years. A century hence it will have increased by almost 450%

(K. Gosling and T. Gill, The nation's collections: are we virtually there? *MDA Information* Vol 2, No 2, 1998)

For many years I have worked on the conservation and management of very large collections. In the Winchester Research Unit, these were the finds from ten years' research excavation. In the Museum of London there were the objects from the 1980s excavations that arose from the huge development boom at that time, and then the whole of the museum's varied collections. Quantified for the first time, we found that there were about a million objects in them. In the Science Museum there were the national collections of science and industry, in two storage sites in London and in Wroughton, near Swindon. There, we made access a collections management priority. Visits to the smaller objects store were popular but restricted; the large objects at Wroughton were a popular attraction – a very basic presentation, but on an enormous scale. Now, later, public tours of the store in London advertized in 2005 have been an instant hit.

Working with such large collections, one cannot help but reflect on how they could be a more useful resource. I hope that this book will helpfully review some of the issues, and provide some ideas for using the extraordinary resources of museum collections, at once inspiring and frustratingly intractable in their almost infinite scale and variety.

Suzanne Keene

The website complementing this book may be found at http://www.suzannekeene.info

List of figures

1 Introduction

'I suppose you use the objects to change the things in the exhibitions?'

'I suppose people come and work on the objects for research?'

'Why do you have collections when you can't display them?'

'Why don't you let some of the collections go to private owners who will appreciate them, then?'

These are questions familiar to many of those who deal with stored museum collections.[1] Currently, there are few convincing answers. In response to pressure to be relevant now, many museums have shifted their focus from their collections to their audiences. This leaves no clear purpose for collections, which are almost always vastly greater than any prospect of exhibiting them.[2] The strong consensus that museums are for people has given rise to a feeling that they are therefore not about objects at all.

The hope in writing this book is to show that collections can be, indeed have to be, a central focus in the new directions that museums are taking.

People who have not worked in museums may realize only vaguely that there are collections other than what is on display.[3] It is often stakeholders and those who provide funding for museums who ask these questions, and they do not perceive the collections as used or as relevant. Museum managers shrink from tackling such issues because they fear that the response will be calls to dispose off collections.[4] In fact, most museums have about ten times as many objects in store as are exhibited.

The collections range from a few hundred objects in a local or specialist museum to those that are the size of the collection of the Natural History Museum, London, with 70 million specimens. The concept of the collection, an assemblage of valued things, is almost universal.[5] However, in spite of this engagement with collections, there is no general view of how this potentially valuable resource may be exploited without being detrimental to it.

In truth, there is as yet no fully convincing answer to why collections that will never be displayed should be kept.[6] Of course, they are there as priceless cultural treasures, as the material record of societies, as the basis for research, for generating knowledge, or for lending to other institutions. All these justifications can be put forward, but in my own experience, and as has been publicly argued, most collections are little used.[7] In a climate where economic arguments rule the day, while museums obviously employ people, attract visitors to an area and offer various goods for purchase, the collections themselves do not give rise to any obvious economic benefits.[8] Voices are heard making the case are that cultural values are intrinsically important too, but they carry less conviction.[9] In the case of collections they do not address the accusation that the supply side, i.e. the museum, is determining demand by deciding to accumulate large collections that it cannot display, rather than by responding to a demonstrated user need for this resource.[10]

The purpose of collections then, is challenged. This challenge is fuelled in some countries, such as the UK, America, and Canada, by political demands for museums as recipients of substantial public subsidies to make an identifiable contribution to the public good. This inevitably directs attention towards an economic role, since it is notoriously difficult to measure cultural benefits. But it is not easy to point to economic benefits from collections (Fig. 1.1).[11]

It is argued in Chapter 10 (Values) that the collections constitute a store, a treasury, of cultural capital, which benefits individuals and also society more generally (Fig. 1.2). This is partly accepted: in bids for capital funding for premises or galleries, a supporting (but not the main) argument often made is that the museum has important collections.[12] It seems entirely justifiable to question why, if these collections are important, are they stored at considerable cost, undisplayed, and unvisited? If they are a store of cultural capital, where is the public dividend from them?[13]

Museum directions and perceptions

Museums, or rather, museum professionals, have been coping during the last 25 years or so with quite a few fundamental changes to their roles and organization, and to the museums in which they work. Stephen Weil, writing in America, encapsulated the change: 'from being *about* something to being *for* somebody'.[14]

During that same period the study of museums themselves and their functions became a much-visited subject of academic and professional study. There is an abundance of how- and why-to-do-it articles, conference papers, and books on every aspect of their operations, audiences, social, and political significance. One stone is little turned, and under it is the rather large issue of the purpose of the collections themselves. But there is an uneasy and widespread awareness among museum professionals of the need to tackle this issue.[15]

Photo: M. Thomson

Fig. 1.1 *The Réserves of the Musée des Arts et Métiers in St Denis, Paris (1994). The building houses the collections, including such iconic objects as a diving suit made to be displayed in the Paris exhibition in 1855, a wonderful object such as that which inspired Jules Verne in writing Twenty thousand leagues under the sea (1873)*

Photo: S. Keene

Fig. 1.2 *The Shôsô-in, in Nara, Japan. Built of close fitting cedar baulks, for 1200 years it protected the treasures stored in it: musical instruments, embroidered shoes, writing equipment, furniture, and many other wonders*

Concerns articulated

As a call for comment on international newsgroups confirmed, it is widely felt in museums that there needs to be a better foundation for justifying the non-displayed collections.[16] But attitudes vary between countries. Some countries have few museums with small collections and therefore little reason for concern; others, like the UK, have a large number of museums, many with extensive collections. In Romania and Scandinavia for example, it is simply accepted that museums have collections in store. In Argentina, concerns were raised in the mid-1990s about works of art kept in store (but not other collections), and in a current exercise referencing the public's attitude to services, museums identified access to collections as an important measure. Problems have not been identified there about other types of collection. Archaeological material does tend to attract attention: the large volumes of excavated material are of concern in various countries, including Australia and the UK.[17]

Two authors from the UK addressed the subject of collections in the early part of the twenty-first century. Julian Spalding's *The poetic museum* dealt in part with this issue.[18] Although Spalding says that collections are enthralling and fundamental to museums, he seems to feel that they can be too much of a good thing, something of an embarrassment to his view of the proper purpose of museums, inspirational communication. He calls for collections to be separated from museums and housed in collections centres dedicated to properly managing and preserving collections as a resource that could be drawn on by those wishing to access them. The main use that he envisages is loans: but this is an expensive way of dealing with what would still be a small proportion of the collections. When he was the Director of Glasgow Museums, Spalding set up the Open Museum project, a highly innovative means of increasing the use of collections.[19]

The second author, Keith Thomson, in *Treasures on earth*, argues that as museum collections increase, they become less beneficial as they are less accessible. Taking objects into public ownership is therefore not necessarily a good thing. But he puts a well-illustrated case for collections as the basis for research. The problem, he says, is one of funding: 'Museums have a product they cannot afford to "make" [*i.e. through the proper management and preservation of the collections*] and customers who do not pay [*i.e. collections access is expected to be free of charge*]. Museums are service providers without adequate subsidy'.[20] I am not convinced that they do provide much service: museums need better ideas on how to generate demand for and benefits from access to collections before they can expect more funding.

In 2001, a government-backed report in the UK, *Renaissance in the regions*, raised serious issues related to the funding and performance of regional UK museums. It found that collections were not only too little used, but also spelt out concerns about too little collecting, especially of twentieth century material. The *Renaissance* report was optimistic about the potential of collections themselves to be useful, for education and learning, and design and creativity, for example. But without more funding, said the report, serious improvement would be difficult.[21]

There has been a series of actions and policy statements in the Netherlands. The Delta Plan, which commenced in 1991, was a response to concern about the effective preservation of public collections as part of the national cultural heritage.[22] A national programme was funded to thoroughly take inventory and rank objects as nationally important, locally important, or not important at all. Following that, policy statements in 1999 and 2003 issued by the Netherlands Ministry of Education, Culture and Science called for much greater use of museum collections, for a view to be formed of the *Collectie Nederland* and also for a process of rationalization, that is, disposal or dispersal of some collections to more appropriate owners.[23]

Why the problem?

Why are non-displayed collections an issue? This is a question of the effective use of resources, usually provided from public funding. If the collections are not being used, why is public money being spent on storing, documenting, and preserving them? Is it still convincing to say that they are 'for the future'? Why will people then find them more useful than we do now?

Museums are organisms that ingest but do not excrete, as the well-known saying goes. The rise of the consumer culture, fuelled and served by mass production of items obtainable at ever decreasing cost, has made it very difficult to understand what to collect and what not to collect, especially for museums with history collections.[24] People living in London, Tokyo, New York, or Sydney have very similar possessions. Should museums start to ignore current material culture, collect only exceptional hand-made craft objects, or what? What about the *tsunami* wave of paper? At least photographs are now becoming digital: but preserving electronic material raises enormous challenges of a quite different nature.

There have been concerted national attempts to make collecting more rational. The SAMDOK programme in Sweden in the 1980s used working groups to develop an intellectual framework for what to collect.[25] Elsewhere, especially in the Netherlands, there are moves to adopt a 'distributed national collection' approach, facilitated by the ability to have a single view of diverse electronically digitized collections, catalogues, and listings.

Too much stuff?

The question is obvious: do museum collections need to be so large? Utilitarian, resource-based and commonsense views say that it is not economical for collections to grow in size indefinitely: neither the individual museum nor the general public can afford such a strategy. In some countries, the Netherlands and the UK in particular, there is an explicit view that museum collections are too large and out of control, and that the material should be reduced or at least much better used.[26]

Here again, the answer is not so simple. The collections are national assets and museums should be willing to relinquish objects if they could be better preserved, used, and enjoyed elsewhere. However, there are many difficulties in undertaking disposal on any useful scale. It is a costly process, and we should heed the lessons of past disastrous decisions resulting in collections that would today be considered priceless treasures being sold off – to make it worse, for far below their market value.[27] When disposal of collections objects is examined in any detail, it is hard to find any body of material to which it could apply without caveat.[28]

Individual museums have undertaken deaccessioning, but this is rare. In Canada, the Glenbow Museum found that a very considerable and increasing proportion of the eleven million Canadian dollar operating budget was being spent on simply maintaining their large collections. A grading exercise (expensive and demanding) was adopted and many thousands of objects were disposed off, mostly through sale. The substantial sums raised were spent on the better care of the retained collections.[29] The National Maritime Museum, Greenwich, embarked on a similar exercise in 2004. This built on a network of other maritime museums that it had established in the UK to explore whether some of its objects could be dispersed for wider benefit. In spite of these cautions, in some countries there are formal guidelines for deaccessioning which should result in fewer disasters – though at considerable financial cost.[30]

Museum collections: not a universal good

Museum collections are not an unmitigated blessing. Belk, in his book *Collecting in a consumer society* (a major root of the problem, this) joins those who argue that the museum plays an important part in glorifying material goods, reinforcing the idea that they are in some way inherently beneficial. Museums, he says, teach materialism.[31] He believes that if the public knew enough about them, they would judge many museum collections to be excessive. As a symptom of dysfunctional collecting he cites the rather wonderful example of a collection of air-sick bags in one of the world's greatest museums.[32] Many people will think of others. Collections, Belk and others argue, reinforce materialism, consumerism, elitism, racism, colonialism, and just to complete the indictment, sexism. Thomson says that excessive acquisition by museums removes things from private possession, where they can best be enjoyed, and spoils the fun for private collectors by inflating prices.[33]

In defence of collections

Do we need collections; aren't exhibits and participatory programmes what we really need? For an outsider, the museum is a point of entry to a society, providing as it does cultural keys; knowledge, artefacts, experiences, perspectives etc. For an insider too, the museum provides cultural keys – not so much as gateways into their own societies, but as mirrors to reflect back to themselves their existence and participation within their own culture.

Museums, but above all collections, where meanings have not been selected and imposed, are the places where insiders and outsiders may mingle in their use of cultural keys. Do we want an hygienic world where the complexity of human relations has been rationalized, loose ends tidied away, and discarded? Or do we want a world where the complexity of human relations is creatively articulated, where every person participates in those articulations, and where museums, theatres, and other cultural spaces are places where all are free to join in?[34]

We have an urgent need to maintain continuity with our past.[35] Social history collections, those which it is most often argued could be reduced through disposal, are some of those that particularly engage people. Collections build collective memories and public histories. A time of rapid social change is not the moment to embark on wholesale disposals.

About this book

The purpose of this book is to lay a better foundation for justifying museum collections – the vast quantities of objects that are never displayed (Fig. 1.2).

The scope is, boldly, worldwide. It would be arrogant and dull to concentrate on just one country – in this age of global travel and the internet, information can be found from every continent in the world. Sources and methods are outlined at the end of the book, *Method*. Of course, I am most familiar with collections matters in the UK, but good ideas for meeting the challenge are to be found everywhere.

The first part of the book reviews the raw material of the study: museums and collections. Museums have much in common wherever they are. Collections differ radically, from large or even enormous resources for research to highly mixed history collections or numerically small but very valuable art collections. Different uses are partly determined by the sort of collection. They also arise from the scale of the museum – from large national museums to tiny local or specialist ones – and from the political and social history of the country: i.e., who is represented, and how?

Five major uses of collections are discussed: research, education and learning, memory and identify, creativity, and finally enjoyment. I draw on theoretical studies to illuminate examples of present uses and suggest new possibilities.

Next, there is a great deal of synergy between digitization and the better use of and access to collections. Digital technologies are developing far beyond the keyboards and screens, and they could be exploited to assist with using collections. This is dealt with in Chapter 9, Digitization.

The value of collections has seldom been distinguished from the value of museums, but economists have investigated this (Chapter 10). It is easy to fall back on the economic value of museums in regeneration, cultural tourism, and so on. But cultural value is important, too, and this is what the collections especially embody. Museums could make a better case for it.

Finally, these threads are brought together to provide some pointers to the directions ahead. In the words of the ex-director of the Rijksmuseum, Henk van Os: The real problem is 'the unimaginative programming, failure of public relations or sheer lack of courage which prevent museum staff from making the best use of their stores and keep the public away'.[36] I agree: current attitudes and approaches to collections do not do justice to the potential of the collections nor do they result in a proper public return on them. Rather, as Spalding advocates, 'If museums could apply the highly entertaining, often inspiring new techniques of the science and heritage centres and children's museums to bring their own wonderful collections to life, they could capture the popular imagination once again, without ceasing to be museums'.[37]

I have included poems – the way that the words convey far more than their rational, prosaic meaning reminds me of museum collections, where a spade is seldom only a spade, and a crown is never just a circle of gold. James Fenton in the *Pitt Rivers Museum* could be describing the feeling of a collection in store (p. 12). The things that have lost the meanings that they had for their owner are exposed in the *Flea Market* by John Fuller (p. 82). Eleven or twelve hundred years ago the poem *Beowulf* explored the contradictions of treasure: jewels and gold that when they have been hard won turn to things eaten by rust (p. 119). Finally, Saadi Youssef questions, *Who broke these mirrors?* (perhaps by snatching objects out of their context and their world) and muddled them up – and who can gather the pieces together to preserve the memory? (p. 176).

Many kinds of collection, many uses and many possible answers. Hope for the stored collections lies in facing honest questions about their purpose, and in answering them, finding ways to make creative use of the

Fig. 1.3 *The Downland Gridshell (2002). An award winning building made of a grid of oak laths, it houses the collection, conservation, and teaching activities of the Weald & Downland Open Air Museum*

collections. Everywhere, there are people who feel that objects and collections are important in maintaining cultural identity and in helping people to be aware of their history and roots.[38] As this book will show, many individual museums, all over the world, have found imaginative ways of using their collections and making them accessible. It seems to me that there will have to be another revolution in museum attitudes and thinking. If they want to justify their collections then they must offer service to people to make use of them as the heart of their purpose. In the museum of the future, let us hope, the four questions that opened this chapter will never need to be asked.

Notes

[1]These are questions that I was typically asked of the stored collections of the Science Museum from 1992–2000. Similar questions are quoted in NMDC (2003). *Too much stuff?* National Museum Directors' Conference. p. 2. This is confirmed in conversations with colleagues from different countries and by correspondence on the international museum discussion lists, MUSEUM-L, 2004. November, Week 5; December, Week 1. http://home.ease.lsoft.com/archives/museum-l.html. INTERCOM-L (2004). 19 November – 2 December.http://susan.chin.gc.ca/~intercom/

[2]Keene, S. (2002). *Managing conservation in museums* (Second edition), Butterworth-Heinemann. pp. 13–5.

[3]For example, Gyllenhaal, E., Perry, D., and Forland, E. (1996). Visitor understandings about research, collections and behind-the-scenes at the Field Museum. *Current trends in audience research and evaluation*, **10**, 22–32.

[4]Responses to the UK Museums Association's consultation exercise, *Collections for the future*, 2004.

[5]Kreps, F.C. (2003). *Liberating culture*. Routledge. Chapter 6.

Simpson, M. (1996). Making representations: museums in the post-colonial era. Routledge. Chapter 5.

[6]See for example: Knell, S. (2004). Altered values: searching for a new collecting. In *Museums and the future of collecting* (S. Knell, ed.), Ashgate. Chapter 1, pp. 1–46.

[7]For example, Simon Jenkins, quotation in NMDC, 2003, p. 2. (See note 1)

Also Thomson, K. (2001). *Collections and Research.* Submitted to the Working Party on Renaissance in the Regions, May 15, 2001. Museums Libraries and Archives Council. URL: http://www.mla.gov.uk/information/policy/collectionrsch.asp.

[8]Pachter, M. and Landry, C. (2001). *Culture at the crossroads.* Comedia in association with the London Institute. pp. 71–79.

[9]Ministrie van OCenW (1999). *Culture as confrontation. Principles on cultural policy in 2001–2004.* Ministerie van Onderwijs, Cultuur en Wetenschap, Netherlands. Section 1.0.

van der Laan, Medy. (2003). M*ore than the sum. Cultural Policy Letter 2004–2007.* The President of the Lower House of the States General, The Hague, 3 November 2003.

[10]Throsby, D. (2001). *Economics and culture.* Cambridge University Press. p. 139.

[11]Weil, S. (2002). *Making museums matter.* Smithsonian Institution. pp. 75–80.

DCMS (2004). *Departmental Report 2004*, p. 14. Department of Culture Media and Sport.

Holden, J. (2004). *Capturing cultural value.* Demos.

[12]For example the Tank Museum's bid to the Heritage Lottery Fund for development funding, November 2004; many examples of cases for development funding to be found on the web.

[13]A question specifically put in 2000 by the Dutch State Secretary for Cultural Affairs van der Ploeg, R. (2000). *A fortune to display: a consideration of the profits in cultural terms from the Collectie Nederland.* Introduction from cultural policy statement. Dutch State Secretary of Cultural affairs, 1999–2000. April 2000.

[14]Weil (2002). pp. 28–52. (See note 11)

[15]Responses to the UK Museums Association's consultation exercise, *Collections for the future*, 2004. Also MUSEUM-L and INTERCOM-L, 2004.

[16]Members of the ICOM International Committee on Management. Responses from America, Argentina, Canada, Nigeria and Rumania. MUSEUM-L and INTERCOM-L, 2004.

[17]Interview and email correspondence: *Deakin University.* PhD candidate I. Schacht. Project: *Making room for the past: determining significance in archaeological collections from historic sites.* 21 October 2004.

Listed in Merriman, N. and Swain, H. (1999). Archaeological archives: serving the public interest? *European Journal of Archaeology* **2**(2), 249–67.

[18]Spalding, J. (2002). *The poetic museum*. Prestel. Chapter 7.

[19]RCMG (2002). *A catalyst for change: the social impact of the Open Museum*. A report for the Heritage Lottery Fund. Research Centre for Museums & Galleries.

[20]Thomson, K. (2002). *Treasures on earth*. Faber & Faber. pp. 63–65.

[21]Resource (2001). *Renaissance in the regions: a new vision for England's museums*. Resource (now the MLA). pp. 19, 40, 52; Section 3.5.

[22]Van Dijken *et al.*, (2001). *The Delta Plan for the preservation of the cultural heritage evaluated*. Ministry of Education, Culture and Science.

[23]Ministrie van OcenW., 1999: Section 1.0. (See note 9)

van der Laan, 2003. (See note 9)

[24]Knell (2004). Chapter 1, pp. 1–46. (See note 6)

[25]Steen, A. (1999). Samdok: tools to make the world visible. In Knell, 2004, pp. 196–203. (See note 6)

[26]For example quotations in NMDC, 2003, p. 2. (See note 1)

Thomson (2001). (See note 7)

Bergevoet, F. (2001). The Collectie Nederland in *Topics. Developments in Dutch Museum Policy*. Netherlands Institute for Cultural Heritage.

[27]Robertson, I. (1990). Infamous de-accessions. *Museums Journal*, March, pp. 32–34.

[28]NMDC (2003). (See note 1)

[29]Email correspondence: R. Janes, 23 November 2004. Also Ainslie, P. (1999). In Knell, 1999. (See note 6)

[30]See articles in *ICOM News*, 2003 no. 1.

[31]Belk, R. (1995). *Collecting in a consumer society*. Routledge. pp. 136–46.

[32]The Metropolitan Museum, New York. Belk, 1995: p. 147. (See note 31)

[33]Thomson (2002). p. 34. Also quotation from Simon Jenkins, UK political and arts commentator, in NMDC, 2003, p. 2. (See notes 20 and 1)

[34]I am grateful to Matthew Thomson for the thoughts in these two paragraphs.

[35]Toffler, Alvin. *Future shock*. Bantam, 1971. Chapter 1.

[36]Ministrie van OCenW, 1999: Section 1.2. (See note 9)

[37]Spalding (2002). p. 63. (See note 18)

[38]For a few of many examples, see several of the contributions to Ardouin, C. and Arinze, E., eds (2000). *Museums & history in West Africa*. James Currey.

The Pitt-Rivers Museum, Oxford

By James Fenton

Is shut
22 hours a day and all day Sunday
And should not be confused
With its academic brother, full of fossils
And skeletons of bearded seals. Take
Your heart in your hand and go; it does not sport
Any of Ruskin's hothouse Venetian
And resembles rather, with its dusty girders,
A vast gymnasium or barracks – though
The resemblance ends where

Entering
You will find yourself in a climate of nut castanets,
A musical whip
From the Torres Straits, from Mirzapur a sistrum
Called Jumka, 'used by aboriginal
Tribes to attract small game
On dark nights', a mute violin,
Whistling arrows, coolie cigarettes
And a mask of Sagga, the Devil Doctor,
The eyelids worked by strings.

Outside,
All around you, there are students researching
With a soft electronic
Hum, but here, where heels clang
On iron grates, voices are at best
Disrespectful: 'Please sir, where's the withered
Hand?' For teachers the thesis is salutary
And simple, a hierarchy of progress culminating
In the Entrance Hall, but children are naturally
Unaware of and unimpressed by this.

Encountering
'A jay's feather worn as a charm
In Buckinghamshire, Stone',
We cannot either feel that we have come
Far or in any particular direction.
Item. A dowser's twig, used by Webb
For locating the spring, 'an excellent one',
For Lord Pembroke's waterworks at Dinton
Village. 'The violent twisting is shown
On both limbs of the fork.'

Yes
You have come upon the fabled lands where myths
Go when they die,
But some, especially the Brummagem capitalist
Juju, have arrived prematurely. Idols
Cast there and sold to tribes for a huge
Price for human sacrifice do
(Though slightly hidden) actually exist
And we do well to bring large parties
Of schoolchildren here to find them.

Outdated
Though the cultural anthropological system be
The lonely and unpopular
Might find the landscapes of their childhood marked out
Here, in the chaotic piles of souvenirs.
The claw of a condor, the jaw-bone of a dolphin,
These cleave the sky and the waves but they
Would trace from their windowseats the storm petrel's path
From Lindness or Naze to the North Cape,
Sheltered in the trough of the wave.

For the solitary,
The velveted only child who wrestled
With eagles for their feathers
And the young girl on the hill, who heard
The din on the causeway and saw the large
Hound with the strange pretercanine eyes
Herald the approach of her turbulent lover,
This boxroom of the forgotten or hardly possible
Is laid with the snares of privacy and fiction
And the dangerous third wish.

Beware.
You are entering the climate of a foreign logic
And are cursed by the hair
Of a witch, earth from the grave of a man
Killed by a tiger and a woman who died
In childbirth, 2 leaves from the tree
Azamü, which withers quickly, a nettle-leaf,
A leaf from the swiftly deciduous 'Flame of the
Forest' and a piece of a giant taro,
A strong irritant if eaten.

Go
As a historian of ideas or a sex-offender,
For the primitive art,
As a dusty semiologist, equipped to unravel
The seven components of that witch's curse
Or the syntax of the mutilated teeth. Go
In groups to giggle at curious finds.
But do not step into the kingdom of your promises
To yourself, like a child entering the forbidden
Woods of his lonely playtime:

All day,
Watching the groundsman breaking the ice
From the stone trough,
The sun slanting across the lawns, the grass
Thawing, the stable-boy blowing on his fingers,
He had known what tortures the savages had prepared
For him there, as he calmly pushed open the gate
And entered the wood near the placard: 'TAKE NOTICE
MEN-TRAPS AND SPRING-GUNS ARE SET ON THESE PREMISES.'
For his father had protected his good estate.

2 Museums

Museums are the acquirers and holders of collections, and they control their use. Factors that determine the nature of museums have consequences for their collections, too. Such factors include the type of museum – national, regional, local etc. – which will be discussed in this chapter, and the type of collection, which will be considered in Chapter 3.

Museums exist within the context, different for every country, of social, political, economic and cultural history, and current circumstances. As well as country-specific factors, globalization has a growing influence. Even though museums as an international network contribute to globalization, they are also a means by which countries and regions respond to its influences, to maintain their cultural identity.[1] Then there are factors that are internal to the museum: its specific purpose, its organizational culture, and the attitudes and skills of its professional staff.

These considerations strongly influence and constrain what the collections represent and how they are used. In addition to these external constraints are the attitudes and training of the professionals in the museum, how they see their roles, how they allocate resources of time and money, and how they view their audiences and users.

Variety in museums

There is an array of different types of museums.[2] The museum may be a national museum; it may be a major regional museum, or a small local museum; or a university or an independent privately owned museum. Its governance, organizational policies, priorities, and purpose will vary accordingly. The collections may relate to a single subject or they may be local or place-based, with a variety of types of objects. The national context is also extremely varied, ranging from countries such as those in Europe, North America, and Australia where museums are a long-standing tradition, to countries where many of the museums in the Western sense are remnants of times of colonization, to places where museums are a response to recent conflict.

National museums

National museums and art galleries are symbols of national culture, knowledge, and pride. They are often showcases for other cultures as well: *'Showing Scotland to the world and the world to Scotland'*.[3] They are also storehouses of knowledge. Their collections often reflect historic colonial episodes or even conquests. Napoleon added to the collections of the Louvre as a consequence of his victorious campaigns (objects from this source that remain in the collection were subsequently purchased). Many national museums consist of clusters of specialist museums, for instance the sixteen German national museums, the Smithsonian Institution with nearly twenty constituent museums, and the UK national museums in London.

The collections of national museums are an expression of national culture and pride and part of every citizen's sense of self.[4] Very few have the whole collection on display – art galleries are those that come closest to this. It is more usual for national museums to have significant holdings, some vast, of collections in store.

Regional museums

Regional museums are important foci. Mostly publicly founded and operated, their role is not unlike that of national museums, but they have to uphold the region's specific identity and importance within the overarching identity of the nation. They also provide cultural experiences and services for people in the region, and their collections should play a part in this.

In the collections of regional museums, there may be less emphasis than in national museums on collections from other countries and more on the history of the region and its culture. The collections are more likely to be comprehensive than to have a specific subject focus, but of course there are many exceptions to this. There may well be a cluster of specialist museums, such as the Museums & Galleries on Merseyside in Liverpool, UK, or those in Melbourne, for the State of Victoria, in Australia. Often, a regional museum will have very strong particular collections arising from a local person, business, or activity. In particular, there will often be a separate regional art gallery, or art collections.

Local museums

These include a range of museums that deal with specific places, from large city history museums such as the Museu d'Història de la Ciutat in Barcelona, the Museum of London or the Museum of the City of New York, to tiny local museums. Some, particularly city museums, are funded publicly; small local museums such as those in many towns and cities in the USA may be set up and operated by societies or individuals. Smaller museums are often linked closely to local people; they may almost literally be the town's collective attic.

Local museum collections often reflect particular local industries, such as Reading Museum in the UK, which has excellent collections relating to the well-known biscuit manufacturer Huntley & Palmer. They may include, or be part of, local history centres, which encourage the use of collections, information, and knowledge. To cite an example from Burkina Faso, in West Africa, the thriving privately funded Bendrologie Museum in Manega was set up in 2001 to represent and celebrate local culture, displaying local habitations and cultural themes such as death, mysticism, African arts, music, and hunting.[5]

University museums

Owned and operated by universities, some of these museums are among the earliest to be founded anywhere, for instance those of the University of Bologna, and the Ashmolean Museum in Oxford. Many university museums were established in the days when collections constituted a foundation for understanding and knowledge, particularly of the natural world. Normally, university collections are subject-focused, being originally derived from academic activities, such as the Petrie Museum of Egyptian Archaeology in the University College London, which has collections from Flinders Petrie's excavations (Fig. 2.1). To some extent, the collections of university museums have been left high and dry, as many are no longer a major resource for research and teaching.[6] However, in Australia and the UK, national reviews have resulted in some improved funding and higher awareness in those countries. An argument sometimes used now is that they can promote the university and make some of its knowledge accessible to a wider public[7]: in displaying knowledge they are in a sense returning to one of the primary purposes of museums.

Specialist museums

Specialist museums deal with a particular subject, place, or geographical area, like the Norwegian Canning Museum in Stavanger, recording the important Norwegian fish-canning industry, or the Museum of Communism in Prague. Like local museums, they have often been established by an individual or by a society. Then again a specialist museum may be one of a cluster of regional or national museums. Specialist museums may also be provided to interpret an historic building or site. Many specialist museums are very small. Their funding can be precarious, and caring for their collections may not be top priority in the struggle for survival.[8] But even so, their collections may be of great interest because of the sharp focus. The Museum of Village Life in Argyropouli, Crete, is an example – see Chapter 3 (Collections and Figs 2.2 and 2.3).

Museums and conflict

There have been and still are, sadly, many conflicts to deal with in the modern world. Museums are a means to come to terms with the aftermath. Well-known examples are the Holocaust Museums in Berlin, Washington, and elsewhere.

A museum in Ho Chi Minh city (previously Saigon) reflects the horror of one of the major campaigns, the Vietnam war. The museum was first formed as the Museum of American War Crimes. Vietnam has since become a fashionable destination for cultural tourism, and the museum, renamed the War Remnants Museum, is much visited by Americans and international tourists as well as by Vietnamese people. One of the less distressing exhibits is a set of medals sent to it by an American veteran: 'I was wrong. I am sorry'. The museum shop reflects its international audience and its evolving role in the cultural tourism economy of the country. Mickey Mouse goods are jarringly juxtaposed with an exhibit of an American fighter plane (Fig. 2.4).[9] Another commemorative museum is in Kigali, Rwanda, the site of a mass burial place, dealing with the terrible

Photo: Petrie Museum

Fig. 2.1 *The Petrie Museum of Egyptian Archaeology, University College London. Almost the whole of the collections is in the museum. It includes extraordinary objects such as textiles: socks, dresses – a bead dress is from 2345 BC – household textiles, even soft toys*

Fig. 2.2 *The Museum of Village Life, Argyroupolis, Crete. A private museum set up by a family who have lived in the area for about 400 years. The collection is packed away each winter and a selection of objects is displayed during the summer*

Fig. 2.3 *The Museum of Village Life, Argyropouli, Crete. Part of the display with one of the proprieters. Visible are baskets for a variety of uses, the oldest object in the display (a strike-a-light), and one of the newest, an early cold box*

episode of genocide there in 1994. A museum and the National Genocide Documentation centre have been set up.

Museums from a colonial past

In countries where museums were part of the colonial era they may languish because they are not part of the culture of the country itself.[10] In West Africa, a number of attempts have been made to establish or revive museums in order to establish a post-colonial cultural identity and to provide a service for education, but in many cases these aspirations are not sufficient to ensure their survival.[11] In other circumstances, countries are proud of these splendid reminders of the past: in Kolkata (previously Calcutta), West Bengal, the Marxist influenced government is said to be developing a scheme to restore the many buildings constructed in the days of British colonial rule (though there is little current sign of this). They include the Indian Museum, built in 1874, the oldest museum in India.[12] The project is intended to assist the city's regeneration and to promote its cultural traditions.

Conversely, very large quantities of historic cultural objects from other countries are held in museums in the West, as ethnographic or anthropological collections. There are ongoing debates about whether this material should be returned or not if the originating country or people request it. The issues around such collections are explored in Chapter 3, Collections.

Photo: M. Thomson

Fig. 2.4 *The War Remnants Museum in Ho Chi Minh city. The museum shop sells iconic American merchandise such as Mickey Mouse puppets, with an American army plane exhibited alongside them*

Indigenous museums and cultural centres

Ecomuseums, community museums, neighbourhood museums, integrated museums, cultural centres, are modern echoes of indigenous practices such as keeping places or shrines that are useful to local people. Sometimes they are set up in order to transmit useful information through displays – farming methods that can help in times of drought or to encourage movements towards self-determination; sometimes to preserve things that the community values.[13]

These varieties of museums are very widespread. In the Pacific they began to be established in the 1970s. In Indonesia, many people no longer hold the traditional beliefs that surround certain artefacts, yet they are still concerned that the things should be cared for and that their meaning should not be lost. In Canada, New Zealand, America, and Australia they may house objects from indigenous cultures that have been loaned or returned from Western style museums. In such places cultural materials are housed with greater integration with cultural tradition than is sometimes the case in formal museums. Objects are more accessible and may be used in cultural ceremonies outside the place where they are kept.[14]

Museums, collections, and economics

Richer countries self-evidently have more and larger museums. It is interesting to consult the World Bank's lists of countries according to the size of their economy with their museum provision in mind.[15] The lower the economic bracket the country is in, the less likely it is to have an established system of museums on the Western model.

In contrast to the cultural centres and ecomuseums that are primarily for local people, museums can help economies develop. They can serve the requirements of cultural tourism, described in Mexico as 'an industry without chimneys'.[16] Examples abound in places as diverse as Vietnam, Ghana, Australia, India (the Madhya Pradesh museums are explicitly geared towards this – such as the Adivasi Gallery in Khajuraho: see Chapter 7: Creativity), and China.[17] China is planning a very large investment in Western style museums – 1000 by 2015 – for economic reasons and also as part of the government's wish for it to be seen as a fully developed country.

The museum established by the Ashanti people in Kumasi, Ghana, is another good example. It was set up not only to serve cultural tourism, to explain culture and traditional practices to the outside world but also to pass them on to the younger generation. Many of those establishing it had lived in the West and understood very well the uses of museums. It displays the court of the *Asantehene*, the King. It has no collections other than the objects displayed, since cultural treasures are part of community life and are therefore not shut away in a museum collection.[18]

In developed countries, too, it is argued that museums should be supported because they assist economic regeneration (see Chapter 10: Values).[19]

Professional attitudes

Margaret Mead is quoted here: 'we are not interested in the detail of what a Western museum is, but rather in its basic functions of storing objects of value, exhibiting ... being a structure that is itself of value'.[20]

However, these same basic functions can be the source of problems. Once a collection grows beyond a certain minimal size, it has to be documented and properly stored in order to be a useful resource. The location of objects has to be known, which means that procedures have to be enforced for controlling and recording their movement. The staff of the museum become accountable for the safe keeping of the objects, so security becomes an issue. Similarly, conservation and preservation measures have to be in place – or why keep the objects? In theory, these measures should enable a service to be provided for diverse uses of and access to the collections, but in practice the processes of the museum and the accompanying bureaucracies tend to be used as instruments of power and control.

The professional staff of museums traditionally act as gatekeepers to the collection and to information about it. Attitudes are slow to change. The idea is often resisted that the stored collections should become more widely and openly available, whether physically or electronically. People are quick to shelter behind the need for security, even when it is obvious that risk, if any, is minimal. Another frequent claim is that the collection or store is not in good enough order or is not documented well enough. The UK report on provincial museums, *Renaissance in the regions*, pointed out that the proper management of collections has been recognized as a basic museum function for over half a century – why, it asked, are museum staff still simply complaining about it?[21] As long ago as the seventeenth century, Dr John Woodward issued detailed instructions for the documentation and care of his geology collection (it is still kept in its purpose-made cabinets in the Sedgwick Museum, Cambridge).[22]

Museum professionals are coming to recognize that they need to be less exclusive about expertise and information. Curators are repositories of knowledge about objects in the context of collections, but others may know more about the objects' real world meaning – people from source communities, historians, anthropologists, archaeologists, scientists, members of specialist societies, the erstwhile owners or users of objects. The future lies in much more serious and wholehearted collaboration with those outside the museum. The curator of the future must be as much a knowledge broker as a specialist expert.[23]

Conclusions

Comparisons of museums in different countries point up the ways in which they are evolving. The Western model of museums grew out of aristocratic collections. It was designed to serve high culture, and knowledge of the natural world. The model was exported to many countries under colonial rule.[24]

This Western model is not good at preserving and working with local knowledge and culture, however. Now, ex-colonial museums are often found not to be relevant. The moves to establish indigenous museums may be showing the way for history museums to evolve. Ironically, it is the collections of local history museums in the West that are proving especially problematic as they grow without connection to local communities. Examples such as the Open Museum in Glasgow and the museum service in Tyne & Wear, UK, reconnect the museum with its locality in ways similar to indigenous or ecomuseums.[25] Key to these services is a much more open attitude to the uses of the collections by people outside the museum. It is these uses that will be explored in this book.

Notes

[1]Prösler, M. (1996). Museums and globalization. In *Theorizing the museum* (S. MacDonald and G. Fyfe, eds) Blackwell, pp. 21–44.

[2]Lewis, G. (1992). Museums and their precursors: a brief world survey. In *Manual of curatorship: a guide to museum practice,* (Second edition). (M. Thompson, ed.) pp. 5–21, Butterworth-Heinemann.

[3]For some years this was the advertising strap-line for the National Museums of Scotland.

[4]Belk, R. (1995). *Collecting in a consumer society,* Chapter 4. Routledge.

[5]Sanou, S. (2000). The private Musée de la Bendrologie, Manega. In *Museums & history in West Africa* (C. Ardouin and E. Arinze, eds), pp. 62–66. James Currey.
Website: *Manega Bendrologie Museum.* http://www.musee-manega.bf/ang/index.htm

[6]University Museums Group (2004). *University museums in the United Kingdom.* University Museums Group. p. 5.

Knoshita, T. and Yasui, R. (2000). University museums in Japan: a time of transition. *Museum International* **52** (3), 27–31.

AVCC (1996, 1998). *Cinderella Collections: University Museums & Collections in Australia* (with update 1998). Australian Vice-Chancellors' Committee, 1998.

[7]University Museums Group, 2004, p. 13. (See note 6)

[8]Resource (2001). *Renaissance in the Regions: a new vision for England's museums*. Resource (now the MLA). p. 75.

[9]Interview: M. Thomson and F. Keene. 22 July 2004.

[10]McLeod, M. (1999). Museums without collections: museum philosophy in West Africa. In *Museums and the future of collecting* (S. Knell, ed.), Ashgate, pp. 52–61.

[11]Several of the contributions in Ardouin and Arinze, eds, 2000. (See note 5)

[12]Rowe, M. (2005). Returning to former glory. *Museums Journal* February. 34–35. Interview: M. Thompson and F. Keene. 22 July 2004.

[13]Davis, P. 1999. *Ecomuseums: A Sense of Place*. Leicester University Press. Kreps, C. *Liberating culture*. Routledge. pp. 60–64; 120–121.

[14]Clavir, M. (2002). *Preserving what is valued: museums, conservation and First Nations*. UBC Press. 160–163.

Kreps, C. (2003). *Liberating culture*. Routledge. pp. 60–78.

Simpson, M. (1996). *Making representations: museums in the post-colonial era*. Routledge. Chapters 5 and 6.

[15]Website: *World Bank*. Country classification. World Bank. 2004. http://www.worldbank.org/data/countryclass/countryclass.html

[16]Vakimes, S. (2001). Indians in formaldehyde – nation of progress: the Museo Nacional of Mexico and the construction of national identity. *Museum anthropology* **25** (1), 20–30.

[17]Including in such disparate places as: Vietnam: Ho Chi Minh City (previously Saigon) – the Museum of War Remnants. Interview: Thomson and Keene, 2004. Ghana, in Cape Coast Castle, funded with US aid and in Kumasi, by the Ashanti people – McLeod, 1999. (See note 10)

Many Australian Aboriginal visitor centres described in Simpson (1996). pp. 132–133. (See note 14)

Casales, E. (2004). China's new cultural revolution. *The Platform*. **4**, 1, October. AEA Consulting. http://www.aeaconsulting.com/site/platformv4i1a.html

[18]McLeod (1999). (See note 10)

[19]The case of the Guggenheim Art Museum, Bilbao is frequently cited; for the UK, Travers, T. and Glaister, S. (2004). *Valuing museums*. National Museum Directors' Conference.

Evans, G. and Shaw, P. (2004). *The contribution of culture to regeneration in the UK: a review of evidence*. A report to the Department for Culture Media and Sport.

[20]Kreps (2003). p. 48. (See note 14)

[21]Resource (2001). *Renaissance in the Regions: a new vision for England's museums*. Resource (now the MLA). p. 74.

[22]Website: *Sedgwick Museum*. Exhibits: Woodward's legacy. http://www.sedgwickmuseum.org/exhibits/woodward.html

Keene, S. (1993). From junk yard to Aladdin's cave. *Museums Journal* (July), pp. 23–26.

[23]Discussion papers and responses to the UK Museums Association's consultation exercise, *Collections for the future*, 2004.

[24]Kreps (2003). Introduction and Chapter 6. (See note 14)

[25]RCMG (2002). *A catalyst for change: the social impact of the Open Museum. A report for the Heritage Lottery Fund*. Research Centre for Museums & Galleries.

3 Collections

Reserve collections, study collections, research collections, stored collections: all these terms are used for the collections a museum may have that are not displayed. All have overtones of second class, yet objects that are in the museum's collections store rather than in its exhibition galleries may be just as important, or more so, than those that are exhibited. The Science Museum's outstanding collection of astronomical instruments, for example, may be visited in store on request, but very few of these objects are exhibited in the museum (see Fig. 10.1). So I refer to this material as, simply, THE COLLECTIONS.

There is a variety of ways of making use of collections, but different types of collections can be used in some ways but not in others. This chapter will describe and discuss these differences. The national and cultural contexts for museums are also an influence. What is the effect of the attitudes, politics, and economics of the country on the perception of the collection? From a political viewpoint, collections are all too easily confused with museums, but they should be recognized as resources that are far more durable and valuable than the museum that happens to house them, perhaps temporarily.

Museum collections increased enormously during the twentieth century.[1] The Museum of London is one such example: in 1900 there were about 10 000 registered objects in the collections of its predecessor museum while by the year 2000 there were over a million. What are these objects; where have they come from? In modern society we not only want to make new buildings and roads but also want to save traces of times past; we use shopping as a major leisure activity; we want to know everything there is to know about the natural world so that we can exploit or protect it; and we generate gargantuan amounts of stuff on paper. So the increase in the number of objects can be attributed to the archaeological excavations arising from the rapid development of towns and cities; to the prevalence of manufactured goods and the consumer society; to our increased ability and motivation to catalogue the natural world; and to the arrival of typewriters, computer printers, print publication generally, and photography as a mass medium.

Collections vary greatly in size. The range is huge. In the UK national museums alone, the National Gallery has about 2300 objects in its collection; the Natural History Museum, over 70 million. In contrast, a small local or specialist museum collection may number just a few hundred objects. It is not only the type and size of museum that determines these variations: they are also due to the sort of collection and the purpose for which the museum has been formed and developed.[2]

In determining how a collection is used, the particular subject area is a major factor. Art collections may have nearly all their objects on display, while archaeology and natural history collections are mostly stored for research. The physical nature of the objects also constrains use. Costume and textile collections are very fragile and vulnerable to damage, while industrial objects may be large and robust. But use and attitudes are also shaped by political and cultural context. An archaeology collection in the UK may be used almost exclusively for academic research, but in Canada or Australia or Egypt it could be of intense interest to the people of the locality.[3]

The nature of collections

It is useful to see collections from four broad perspectives: fine art, functional objects, research archives, and place- and people-related collections. There are some fundamental differences: the purpose, the number of objects in the collections, the proportion that is on display, who uses them, and the major potential or actual uses.

One major purpose of collections is the aesthetic appeal: to be *visually enjoyed*. A paradigm for these is offered by the collection of 2300 paintings in the National Gallery, London.

Functional objects in collections engender an expectation that they will be made to work, and *demonstrate their original function*. Science and industry collections stand for collections of functional objects, such as the 350 000 objects in the collection of the Science Museum, London.

A third major class of collections is those that are primarily *archives for research*. The number of objects is often vast, such as the 70 million specimens in the Natural History Museum, London. An 'object' can be hard to define – is it a single potsherd or a boxful from an archaeological context? Is a sketchbook one object, or thirty?

The fourth type of collection is harder to pin point. In a way it includes elements of the first three. But collections *relating to places and people* – history and ethnography collections in particular – are a distinct type of collection with a different purpose.

However, even specialist collections usually include other sorts of objects – for example, photography collections in science and technology.

Objects for visual enjoyment

In art collections, objects are few and valuable. The National Gallery, London, only has just over 2000 paintings and frames in its collection. A very high proportion of the collection, or even all the objects, is usually on display.[4] Collections are restricted because easel paintings are expensive to purchase, and there are not many high quality works of art in existence. The value is great because private individuals and organizations compete with museums and galleries to acquire them.

Art collections are primarily for visual enjoyment: '... I could have spent a day with this collection. It is like walking into another world'. 'I loved the Japanese section. Their artwork is great – everything in such detail. For a time I forgot I was in Boston. It really felt like I was in a Japanese museum'.[5] A smaller proportion of the collection is likely to be in store, but on the other hand, any objects that are stored attract more criticism than most on the grounds that the museum is keeping treasures locked away and unavailable to the public.[6]

These collections are the basis for art history research by curators in museums and academics in universities and research institutions. It is difficult (for security reasons) to provide public access to objects not on display, but then, most usually are on public exhibition. Works of art are an inspiration to all kinds of creative artists working today. Art collections also have a very important function in establishing monetary values for the commercial art markets, which in many countries are economically quite significant (see Chapter 10: Values).[7]

Other collections that are primarily for aesthetic appreciation are those, such as many oriental collections, that are the subject of connoisseurship. Decorative art collections, which include ceramics, metalwork, textiles and furnishings, could also be said to come under this classification.

Functional objects

This type of collection includes vehicles, musical instruments, clocks and watches, scientific instruments, aircraft, and agricultural collections. In size such collections are intermediate: the Science Museum, London has about 350 000 three-dimensional objects, leaving aside archives and photographs (Fig. 6.1 shows one of the Science Museum's large-object hangars). High prices are sometimes paid for objects that are old and rare and therefore valuable, but the bulk of such collections may be acquired for only the cost of removing them from the business premises. The subsequent costs of storing and maintaining them are often not considered at the time they are acquired (Fig. 3.1).[8]

The use of functional objects is hotly debated. It is often expected that they will be seen working. It is difficult to disentangle ethics and purpose

Photo: Science Museum

Fig. 3.1 *Industrial storage: the Science Museum. Maximum use of environmentally controlled space through using heavy duty mobile racks that are
opened and closed by motors. Objects are fixed to pallets and retrieved
and put away using a forklift truck, which raises the store person to the level
of the shelf*

so as to decide whether they should be made to function or not when they
are part of a museum collection.[9] Some people very much enjoy seeing
such objects in operation, and some enjoy participating in using them. In
a sense the object is not complete unless its function can be fully appreciated, because the only point in originally making and owning it was to
use it. But to quote an aircraft enthusiast: 'somewhere along the way our
instinct to preserve got tangled up with our love for flying, and we started
preserving airworthiness instead of airplanes'.[10] This issue is discussed
further in this chapter.

Technological objects can be inspirational to engineers and designers,
since they demonstrate many ingenious solutions to design problems.
They should be a good basis for teaching and learning both history and

technology, but they are not greatly used for that or for research. The reasons may well be related: audiences and researchers lack experience of using this sort of evidence.[11]

Collections as research archives

Paper-based collections such as works of art on paper, ephemera and photography collections, technical drawings, are *de facto* archival. Some types of collection can be seen as archives, too – notably the many millions of objects in natural history collections and archaeology collections. Collections that are archives for research contain the largest numbers of objects.

It is not the function of these collections to be exhibited. A few colourful or large items may be selected for public display, but the destiny of the vast majority of objects is to be stored until needed for study or research (Figs 3.2 and 3.3). Natural history collections especially are a very important basis for research (Fig. 4.4 shows a store room in the Canadian Museum of Nature's Natural Heritage Building). The entomology collection of the Natural History Museum alone may have 175 000 objects on loan to researchers at any given time.[12] There is a project (the Barcode of Life) to develop a unique DNA identifier for every species of life on earth, linked to the representative museum specimen and to all the research information about it.[13]

Place- and people-based collections

This leaves the place- and people-related collections that comprise most of the objects in most museums: history and ethnography, military, and a large proportion of decorative art and domestic collections. These collections may be documented and stored by period, by place, by function (domestic

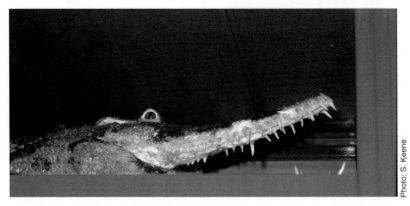

Photo: S. Keene

Fig. 3.2   *Storage on racks. An object in a zoology collection*

equipment, working life) or if they are extensive, according to a taxonomy of objects – costume and textiles, ceramics, metalwork, etc. Such collections are typically mostly in store. It is history collections in particular that prompt the question that lies at the heart of this book, 'Why are we keeping all that stuff'?

The uses of these place- and people-related collections are far less clearcut than are those of the three other types of collection. In indigenous museums the collections, ideally, serve the needs of the community to keep things safe and use them in their own cultural activities. In developed countries it is objects in history collections that individuals relate to, because they summon up memories, commemorate past achievements or events, or represent their cultural roots or presence in society (see Chapter 6: Memory).

But it is often these collections that are poorly organized and documented and therefore inaccessible. This is particularly the case when the collections have accumulated rapidly and resources of finance and staff have not kept pace. It may also be because collections in store have a lower priority than do museum exhibitions: but unless a balance is struck, resources will never be justified and the collections will not be a useful resource. In Sweden, the museum profession set up the SAMDOK programme some years ago in response to the problems of history collections, which has made the accumulation of history collections there both more rational and slower.[14]

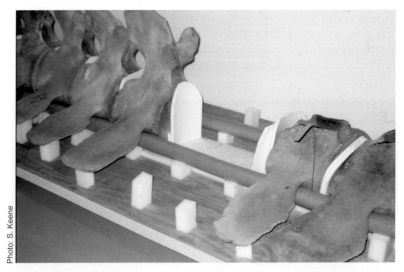

Photo: S. Keene

Fig. 3.3 *Whale vertebrae in the Canadian Museum of Nature's Natural Heritage Building. The enormous bones are supported on purpose-cut foam padding and boards. The storage is environmentally controlled*

The Museum of Village Life in Argyropouli, Crete, is an admirable example of a people- and place-based collection (see Figs 2.2 and 2.3). It presents the tools, domestic furnishings and possessions of a single extended family. They have traced their history back 400 years, and still live in the town. They had many things that they had carefully looked after over the years – it seemed a shame for them just to be stored away. A personal guide shows the museum – a member of the family, far superior to any digital personalization device – and explains the history of the objects, who had used them, and for what. The objects are from many different crafts – our guide's mother was a carpenter, her grandfather a shoemaker. Women in the family wove silk, wool, and cotton to make things for the household. Even in recent times, one member of the family had waited three years to be married, for her wedding dress to be made, starting from the raw silk thread. An early refrigerator or cold box was a comparatively recent addition to the collection. There is a large number of books, too, and some handwritten records. In museum terms, this is an admirably focused collection that represents a range of local activities – farming, keeping livestock, various crafts, and now keeping a village shop as well. The family intend to add to the collection but strictly from their own possessions.[15]

In some ways these collections have the greatest unrealized potential for more effective use, for research, in teaching and learning, and for enjoyment.

Virtual objects

These are yet another kind of object: computer software, computer games, and works of art. They are now being collected. Software objects can hardly be said to exist at all unless they are working.[16] Also, there is now a great interest in collecting the intangible heritage – capturing music, performances, and so on. The issues that will arise from collecting such material, and its uses, have hardly begun to be debated.[17]

Practical aspects

There are practical aspects of collections that constrain use. A museum may wish its collections to be fully accessible but these are still a public resource for the long term. A balance has to be struck between access and use, and preservation. The issues are security and safety, physical handling, storage environment, and information provision. Visitors cannot be left to wander around an ordinary museum store unaccompanied: it has to be specifically designed for that purpose, as is The Warehouse, the open store of the National Railway Museum, York (see Chapter 8: Enjoyment). Unfortunately, some of the people who are most enthusiastic about collections are just those who hanker after authentic parts of objects, or whole objects, to embellish their own collections.

The preservation needs of the collection are a strong constraint. If a collection is old or valuable, or fragile, this makes informal access and use difficult. Some types of objects, such as costume and textiles cannot survive much handling.[18] However, modern approaches to conservation are geared to finding ways of mounting or presenting objects to allow objects to be closely looked at without damage (Figs 3.4 and 3.5).

There are ways to work around all these problems, but they require proper building design, equipment and staff, with a more flexible attitude to balancing potential problems against benefits. Permanent public access to a collection or a store may not be feasible, but that doesn't mean completely banning everyone except museum professionals. The moving experience of the Yup'ik elders from Alaska visiting a collection in Berlin, where they were permitted free access to the collections in store, is described in Chapter 8: Enjoyment.[19] Making stored collections useful needs imagination and determination, but if museums do so they will powerfully aid the case for their cultural value.

Using functional objects

In a book about the usefulness of museum collections, the issue of operating functional objects arises time and again. Industrial machinery and vehicles are examples, but historic musical instruments sharply highlight the issues. Policies for these collections range from those (few) which are treated strictly as reference, not used for playing music, to those of which the main purpose is for the instruments to be played. A 1993 report on UK music collections warned of the rapid rate of attrition of unrestored instruments and pointed to 'a serious depletion of our record of knowledge'. Of 4000 early stringed instruments in the UK, it was estimated that at that time only 40 remained unrestored.[20] CIMCIM, the ICOM Committee on Musical Instruments in Museums, provides a number of helpful publications.[21]

The problem is that it is not possible to play musical instruments without altering them.[22] Then, the ability to make accurate reproductions of early instruments depends on reference examples still available, and this highly skilled craft is of growing importance. The Early Music movement, which began as early as the second half of the nineteenth century, but which has gathered many adherents and enthusiasts today, depends on the existence of unrestored examples of instruments contemporary with the music.[23] There is a great loss to research on early music: and, some people simply appreciate instruments in their original state. Many objects in ethnographic collections are from countries where examples of

Photo: Science Museum

Fig. 3.4 *Storage in drawers: the Science Museum: a medical collection. Small objects are often stored in this way. The doors of the cupboard are glass to allow some viewing. They are sealed to prevent pests and dust entering*

such instruments no longer exist, and it is questionable whether it is ethical for the current owners to restore them for playing.

On the other hand some collections, such as those of the Royal Academy of Music, were formed for the express purpose of using the instruments for performance and teaching. The instruments have already been altered considerably, if not in the nineteenth century when a lot of restoration was carried out, then more recently.[24] Using them to make music gives a lot of pleasure to musicians and audiences and there is no argument against this – they have already been modified.

Both approaches have great value for music, musicians, and audiences. The debate is not helped by the emotive depiction of objects as being in some sense alive. Policies of playing instruments may be portrayed as 'letting instruments live',[25] and there is an unsubstantiated view that the tone of instruments improves through being played.[26] I agree with Gail

Kavanagh that this is a form of fetishism.[27] Countering this viewpoint, Arnold Myers in 1985 wrote, 'How wonderful it would be to walk in Renaissance Venice, and build a collection of the instruments (humble as well as magnificent) being used in the churches and palaces ... The surviving instruments have, in fact, come to us by good fortune rather than rational decision'.[28] But many people have an animist belief that objects are, in some sense, 'alive'. I myself have experienced the pressure to bring an extremely rare, unrestored, and previously unrecognized keyboard instrument into playable condition (thankfully, it remains unrestored and unplayed).

Similar arguments are put for and against using other kinds of functional objects, and this issue will be returned to in subsequent chapters.

Collections and politics

At one end of the spectrum of attitudes to collections, it is accepted that they exist and there is no pressure to justify them. The Shôsô-in in Nara, Japan is truly exceptional. This wonderful timber structure was built in the eighth century to hold the Japanese imperial and religious treasures (see Fig. 1.1). This and its contents have been preserved ever since: musical instruments, domestic equipment, religious items, clothing and shoes – a wonderful panoply of exquisite things from over a thousand years ago. Until about 1950, the Shôsô-in objects were neither exhibited nor seen by the public, but there is now an annual exhibition of selected objects.[29] Cathedral, monastic, and royal treasuries are parallels in the West.[30]

Some other countries accept that museums have collections that are not displayed. In Scandinavian museums there was little concern about justifying stored collections: there are moves to provide better care for them. In Norway, there is a number of projects to construct new stores; in Denmark, museum legislation in 2001 includes requirements for proper documentation and accessibility for collections that are supported by public subsidy.[31]

In Romania, 'This was never an issue. Nobody is asking about the use of the objects that are not on display. It is obvious, [to] all the authorities, that they should stay in storage rooms.' In Argentina, only art collections not displayed had earlier been an issue; greater access to collections is now an objective. From Nigeria, there was a wise observation that a remedy may lie within the profession itself: 'The usefulness and justification of museum collections in storage is not endangered by their not being seen by the public, but by the fact that they are not "seen" by the museum curators'.

A report on the Natural History Museum, London, commented that museums in the US and France, approached for comparable statistics on attendance figures and expenditures, could not readily provide these and did not have to account for their activities in the same way.[32]

Archaeological collections, which in many countries are growing, can be a particular concern. This has long been the case in the UK (see Chapter 4: Research). It is so in Australia also and to some extent in the Irish Republic. In the Australian state of Victoria a research project has been set up to assess and report on this.[33] The National Museum of Ireland set up a system whereby regional museums may apply to be granted designated status. They can then retain archaeological objects on behalf of the state. It is also aware that the collections are a resource to be used, and is there-fore taking very positive steps to increase access to other types of collec-tions, especially the decorative arts collection in its Collins Barracks building (see Chapter 8: Enjoyment, and Fig. 10.2).[34]

In Canada, there are signs that the collections may be an issue, for instance a conference on the economic importance of culture, and also government consultancy reports on the value of the Canadian Museum of Civilization.[35] The Glenbow Museum in Alberta has drastically reduced its collections and now spends the savings on improved care and access for those remaining. However, it is helpful that CHIN, the Canadian Heritage Information Network, has for decades been making information about collections nationwide accessible.[36] Canadian respondents to my request for information put up a stout defence of collections: 'Museum collections are not gathered, preserved, or researched exclusively or even primarily, for exhibition, although this is obviously one of their more potent and public manifestations. … Why not describe an institution that exhibits its entire collection as an 'Exhibition Centre'? That's fine but let's not confuse it with a museum'.

And again:

> … there will always be a need for permanent collections, as they are a record of our species. There are also duplicate, poorly documented or poorly preserved objects which consume a great deal of scarce resources for little or no benefit to the institution. Dealing with these requires some common sense and a strong will, as there is still a belief that museums must keep everything-forever. That is ideal if you can afford to do it. In most museums, however, this belief is a sacred cow, and must be evaluated accordingly.

> Our loans run in the thousands a year, and although they only represent a very small fraction of the whole collection, it is the size and scope of the collection that makes it as useful as it is for this purpose. In a similar way, researchers do visit, and in slowly increasing numbers, but it is the critical importance of the collections to those that visit (e.g. First Peoples who are able to survey entire elements of their material cultural heritage that may no longer exist in their communities) rather than their numbers that is important.

Obtaining funding for the proper care and management of stored collec-tions was a very live issue in the USA, and it was considered difficult to justify them: 'you really opened up a great can of worms! … I'm sure more of us are going to be asked to quantify our reasons for increasing storage facilities'. 'My own opinion on this is that we as a *museum community* have done a poor job explaining what we do, why we do it, and the value of our organizations to the public'.

At the other end of the spectrum from the Shôsô-in in Japan, it is in the UK and the Netherlands that there is explicit government pressure to justify the large volumes of museum collections. Attitudes in these countries are discussed earlier in Chapter 1: Introduction. A question from the Public Accounts Committee in the UK House of Commons, 2001, was symptomatic: 'What percentage of the collection has not been on display during, say, the last ten years?' 'What sort of policy do you have for objects which are, in effect, never put on show?'[37] In the Netherlands, this is despite the ten-year Delta Plan to rationalize collections. In 2000, a ministerial statement there included: 'The shareholders of the Collectie Nederland – and they are the Dutch taxpayers – should be able to assume that the cultural entrepreneurs who curate the public cultural fortune (and this includes museums, archives, libraries, and other collection curators) attempt to gain the maximum profits from their input. Not of course for the sake of financial gain. But for the sake of the social and cultural returns that expresses itself for instance through an optimal accessibility and utilization of the Collectie Nederland for the whole of society'.[38]

Collections and cultures

Contrary to assumptions that non-Western peoples are not concerned with preserving their material culture, this practice is almost universal.[39] Many examples from Indonesia, Africa, the Pacific region, Australia, and America illustrate the argument that cultural items, sacred, and ceremonial objects have long been the means of transmitting and perpetuating cultural traditions and preserving or even sometimes reviving cultural practices. While they remain part of the local culture collections are not problematic: it is when they are separate from this, an end in themselves, that they become so.[40]

Collections from other cultures

There are many large, important, and historically very valuable ethnography collections from cultures world wide in the West, for instance those of the National Museum of Denmark in Copenhagen, the Royal Museum for Central Africa in Brussels, and the Pitt Rivers Museum in Oxford (Figs 6.3 and 6.4). Researchers from the museum holding the collections often work to establish links with the originating communities, and welcome access by individuals.[41] If the source community is not much represented in the country or the locality of the museum then links

Photo: S. Keene

Fig. 3.5 *Storage in drawers: fans. They are supported using acid free tissue to prevent warping. When the drawer is closed the darkness protects them from fading*

may be developed with people in the originating country, or countries, but the collections no longer play a part in the originating culture. (The repatriation of objects may, of course, be negotiated). The collections are not actively used as part of the indigenous culture that originally produced them as it exists today, although with determination and good-will the descendants of the originators can still gain much pleasure and benefit from them (see Chapter 8: Enjoyment).[42]

Belgium, with a haunting past in the colonial occupation of central Africa and the Congo, has returned part of its pre-eminent collections from the Royal Museum for Central Africa, near Brussels, to Rwanda and financed the establishment of the Rwanda National Museum in Butari to house them.[43] There are still magnificent collections in the museum near Brussels, where the displays in 2005 are as though frozen in time, in contrast to extensive collaborative research programmes. (A comprehensive redis-play programme is under way.)

In countries where museums have cultural objects from an indigenous population, it is increasingly common for significant objects to be returned to the source people. They may establish an indigenous museum or keep-ing place for their own purposes. Such museums still need funding to survive, however, and as time goes by the initial impetus for them may be lost, leaving a question mark over the collections. It is too simplistic to assume that every community wants its objects returned: there are many cases where they do not.[44]

Museums from a colonial past

If a museum in a country like Africa is a legacy from a country's colonial past, then there may be an understandably ambivalent attitude to it and its collections. The collections may be neglected and disregarded, even though they may be rare and valuable: perhaps more rarely, their survival may be welcomed.

> South Africa has a long museum history, dating back to the first officially
> proclaimed museum in Cape town in 1825. Our older museums are nineteenth-
> and early twentieth-century colonial creations, part of the attempted colonial
> intellectual conquest of Africa. They collected the scientific and cultural 'curiosities'
> of the subcontinent, and in many cases artifacts and cultural products of the African
> population were collected and exhibited along with stuffed wild animals in natural
> history museums. Works of art were collected from Europe to reinforce the cultural
> linkage between colonist and metropole. Until a very few years ago, African art was
> treated as 'ethnography' and 'ghettoized' in racially categorized collections.[45]

Other countries (or cities) have both a past as colonizers and a present population with substantial ethnic minorities. In many places, museums are making efforts to include those cultures in their collections. The UK is one such example. Multicultural populations are concentrated in certain regions such as the East Midlands, or London where nearly 30 per cent of the population is people of non-British ethnic origin.[46] Here museums are now much more positive towards their non-White population. For example, there are projects to identify objects in the collections that represent those cultures, to explore how ethnic populations wish to be represented in museums, and to use museum services.[47] Equal rights legislation assists these moves. But greater efforts need to be made to encourage and facilitate access to collections for everyone, especially for individuals or groups seeking traces of their cultural or personal history.

Collections in China

Collections in China are different again. China's artistic heritage is one of the oldest in the world: so is the international trade in its cultural objects. Museums such as the Shanghai Museum are now benefiting from donations of objects previously in the collections of private individuals. There are collections that reflect local industry as well, for instance in the city of Cixi, south of Shanghai, which was an ancient centre for porcelain manufacture.[48] Local museums reflect local history interests, too, such as the Guangxi Ethnic Relics Center in Nanning, which deals with the many different ethnic groups with distinct cultures in the Guangxi Zhuang Autonomous Region.[49] China plans a huge investment in museums – 1000 new ones by 2015.[50] Whether these museums intend to have collections or to simply be for interpretation, we can be sure that in due course they will accumulate.

Collections and conflicts

Museums of armed conflict are widespread; so are such collections. Preserving things that signify and provide evidence is a way of coming to terms with what has happened. For instance in Croatia, material from the war in the early 1990s is being collected, as well as that from pre-conflict life, to counteract complete cultural dislocation.[51] In South Africa, collections are being developed to deal with the apartheid era. In the Natal Museum there was a project to form the collection of the anti-apartheid struggle in Natal, as part of repositioning and development of institutions that would be appropriate to the new circumstances. The collection is particularly valuable because it can address the history of largely non-literate societies where the written record alone would be seriously incomplete.[52]

Collections: the dark side

The museum collection concept is not universally welcome and not solely beneficial. In an example of a museum in Côte d'Ivoire, the Musée Péléforo Gbon Coulibaly, Korhogo, is seen by some local groups as 'a sacred place where spirits hostile to man roam or as a place that houses masks which certain groups are forbidden to see'.[53] In societies that are the subject of ethnographic and anthropological collecting, there are very complex issues around the relationship of collections and people who owned the objects that have been collected and displayed. Human subjects can be objectified by the museum, which turns them, metaphorically, into dead animal specimens. In another example of a West African museum, some visitors are described as experiencing rage at seeing the royal family represented in the museum, or through being reminded that the kingdom of their birth had been conquered.[54] Alternatively, as Bourdieu has described in his well-known studies, collections in the museum may serve to promote the image of the powerful ruling class and denigrate by ignoring them the culture of others.[55] And some people find the memories conjured up by museum objects painful and unwelcome.[56]

Conclusions

Collections are often discussed as though they were uniform and can be discussed in generalizations. This review of collections has highlighted some of the many ways in which they differ. These differences have a very large effect on the purpose of assembling and holding them and on the uses that can be made of them.

   Attitudes to collections do not always follow assumptions, either. For example emotional reactions to issues of the repatriation of objects from other cultures often assume that the return of the objects is always what is wanted. This is not so. There are many reasons why people may neither want nor seek the return of objects. Rather, people may want to have free access to them while they remain in a place of safekeeping.[57] Contacts and joint research programmes with the source community and the host museum may be good ways of making bridges between nations and atoning for past wrongs.[58]

It is critical to realize that a collection is only as useful as the information that is available relating to it. Any museum can preserve objects and display them, but it has been argued that only museums embedded in local culture can preserve knowledge about them.[59] Writing in *The new museology*, Colin Sorensen called for museums, instead of amassing more and more things, to send those things they do acquire into the future fully equipped with as wide a variety of contextual materials for their after-life as any Pharaoh's tomb.[60] Usefulness may crucially depend on collecting context and information, not just object, but museums are some way off fully implementing this.

Objects that are in museums express by their presence in the collection and in the ways that they are categorized, the culture of those who collected them, and those who managed the museum. It is well documented that objects can powerfully affect people. But they are in fact passive mirrors for projected feelings: they can mean something different to each person who sees them. And values change. In Zanzibar the collections of the Palace Museum and the House of Wonders, established when the island was under Portuguese rule, were nearly destroyed, but these museums are now considered important elements in maintaining Zanzibar's identity within Tanzania and in raising the standard of education for its people.[61]

It is not the collections that are the source of colonialist messages of power and control, but the museum, in its buildings, systems, and displays. Unfortunately, too often the collection has been neglected or destroyed because it is implicated with the museum. Yet, the collection is a priceless record of culture, a way of pinning down and crystallizing memory, a record of the natural world. The purpose of a museum may radically change; it may be considered redundant; but the collections are a permanent record of our cultures.

Notes

[1]Keene, S. (2002). *Managing conservation in museums* (Second edition). Butterworth-Heinemann. p. 14.

[2]Keene (2002). p. 15. (See note above)

[3]Moser, S. *et al.* (2003). Transforming archaeology through practice: strategies for collaborative archaeology and the Community Archaeology Project at Queseir,

Egypt. In *Museums and source communities* (L. Peers and A. Brown, eds). Routledge. pp. 208–226.

[4]Keene (2002). p. 15. (See note 1)

[5]Walsh, A. (ed.) (1991). *Insights : museum visitor attitudes and expectations : a focus group experiment.* J.Paul Getty Trust. pp. 29.

[6]Discussion group: MUSEUM-L, 2004. November, Week 5; December, Week 1. http://home.ease.lsoft.com/archives/museum-l.html.

Discussion group: INTERCOM-L (2004). 19 November – 2 December. http://susan.chin.gc.ca/~intercom/

[7]Fisher, P. (1997). *Art and the future's past.* Harvard University Press. p. 28.

Throsby, D. (2001). *The economics of culture.* Cambridge University Press. pp. 122–124.

[8]Keene (2002). p. 15. (See note 1) Also author's experience when managing the Science Museum collections, 1992–2000.

[9]Mann, P.R. (1989). Working exhibits and the destruction of evidence in the Science Museum. *Museum Management and Curatorship,* **8**, 369–387.

[10]Anon. (1991). Tighar Tracks: a publication of the International Group for Historic Aircraft Recovery **7** (1), p. 1. Quoted in Clavir, M. (2001). *Preserving what is valued: museums, conservation and First Nations.* UBC Press. p. 63.

[11]Author's experience when managing the Science Museum collections, 1992–2000. Detailed figures were kept on access to those collections for research and study.

Interview: *Tank Museum.* David Willey, Head of Collections. 27 June 2004.

[12]Interview: *Natural History Museum.* Curator. 9 July 2004.

[13]Website: *Barcode of life.* Consortium for the Barcode of Life. http://barcoding.si.edu/

[14]Steen, A. (2004). Samdok: tools to make the world visible. In *Museums and the future of collecting* (S. Knell, ed.), Ashgate. Chapter 17, pp. 196–203.

[15]Visit to the Argyropouli Museum of Village Life, 29 August 2004.

[16]Keene, S. (1995). Objects as systems: a new challenge for conservation. In *Restoration: is it acceptable?* (W.A. Oddy, ed.) Preprints of a conference. Occasional Paper no. 99, British Museum, pp. 19–25.

[17]Keene, S. (2003). Preserving digital materials: confronting tomorrow's problems today. *The Conservator,* no. 26, pp. 93–99.

Keene, S. (2002). Now you see it, now you won't. (online demonstration) In *Museums and the Web 2002.* D. Bearman and J. Trant, eds. Archives & Museum Informatics.
http://www.suzannekeene.info/conserve/digipres/

[18]Interview: *Museum of London.* C. Ross, Head of Department of Later London History. 3 December 2004. There is considerable demand to study items from the Museum of London costume and textile collections. The Museum requires an appointment to be made and closely supervises users.

[19]Fienup-Riordan, A. (2003). Yup'ik elders in museums. In *Museums and source communities* (L. Peers and A. Brown, eds) pp. 28–41, Routledge. p. 40.

[20]Arnold-Foster, K. and La Rue, H. (1993). *Museums of music.* Museums & Galleries Commission, pp. 24–25.

[21]Website: *CIMCIM.* The International Committee for Musical Instruments in Museums. http://www.music.ed.ac.uk/euchmi/cimcim/

[22]Interview: Royal Academy of Music. F. Palmer, Curator of Collections. 9 June 2004.

[23]Goehr, L. (1992). *The imaginary museum of musical works : an essay in the philosophy of music.* Clarendon Press/Oxford University Press, p. 279.

[24]Interview: Royal Academy of Music. (See note 22)

[25]E.g. Dilworth, J. (2003). What to do with a Strad. *The bulletin,* Royal Academy of Music, September, p. 4.

[26]Arnold-Foster and la Rue (1993). p. 28. (See note 20)

[27]Kavanagh, G. (2000). *Dream spaces: memory and the museum,* Leicester University Press: p. 22.

[28]Myers, A. (1985). Conservazione, restauro e riuso degli strumenti musicali antichi: per una cara europea del restauro. (in English). Iaan *Anno Europeo della Musica: Covengno Internazionale di Stude, 16–19 Octtobre 1985, Venezia.*

[29]Website: *Shôsô-in.* Nara National Museum: Shôsô-in. http://www.narahaku. go.jp/around/shosoin_e.htm

[30]Lewis, G. (1992). Museums and their precursors: a brief world survey. In *Manual of curatorship: a guide to museum practice* (Second edition). (M. Thompson, ed.) Butterworth-Heinemann. pp. 5–21.

[31]Pressure to justify collections was discussed at a training meeting for museum collections staff and policy makers from Scandinavian countries, Soro, Denmark, 22 October 2004. A number of delegates were from Norway and were involved in new collection stores being built there. This follows the establishment of The Norwegian Archive, Library and Museum Authority (ABM-Utvikling) in 2003: Website: http://www.abm-utvikling.no/om/ english.html. In Denmark the Museum Act of 2001 includes requirements for proper documentation and acessibility for collections that are supported by public subsidy: Danish Culture Ministry (2001). Museum Act: ACT no. 473 of 07/06/2001.

[32]Travers, T. *et al.* (2003). *Treasurehouse and power house: an assessment of the scientific, cultural and economic value of the Natural History Museum.* NHM. p. 21.

[33]Website: *Deakin University: Cultural Heritage Centre.* Research and consultancies: Making room for the past: Determining significance in archaeological collections from historic sites.
http://www.deakin.edu.au/arts/centres/CulturalHeritage_Centre/ research/making.room.php
Interview and email correspondence: *Deakin University,* 2004. I. Schacht, PhD candidate. Project: *Making room for the past: determining significance in archaeological collections from historic sites.* 21 October 2004.

[34]Interview: *National Museum of Ireland.* R. Ó Floinn, Head of Collections. 6 April 2004.

[35]Gregg, J. (2003). Reframing the case for cultural. Paper to Accounting for culture: examining the building blocks of cultural citizenship. A colloquium marking the 5th anniversary of the Canadian Cultural Research Network and the 10th anniversary of the Department of Canadian Heritage. Canadian Cultural Research Network.
http://www.arts.uwaterloo.ca/ccm/ccrn/ccrn_colloq03.html
Outspan Group (2001). *The economic benefits of the Canadian Museum of Civilization: a case study.* Department of Canadian Heritage.

[36]Website: *Artifacts Canada*. Canadian Heritage Information Network. http://www.chin.gc.ca/English/Artifacts_Canada/index.html

[37]NMDC (2003). *Too much stuff? Disposal from museums*. National Museum Directors' Conference. p. 1.

[38]van der Ploeg, R. (2000). *A fortune to display: a consideration of the profits in cultural terms from the Collectie Nederland*. Introduction from cultural policy statement. Dutch State Secretary of Cultural affairs, 1999–2000. April 2000.

[39]Kreps, F.C. (2003). *Liberating culture*. Routledge. p. 60.

[40]McLeod, M. (1999). Museums without collections: museum philosophy in West Africa. In Knell, ed., pp. 52–61. (See note 14)

[41]Interview: *Pitt Rivers Museum*. Curator. 27 October 2004. Website: *Royal Museum for Central Africa*. http://www.africamuseum.be/

[42]Many of the papers in Peers and Brown, eds., 2003. (See note 29)

[43]*UCL Institute of Archaeology*. A. Reid. Seminar. 14 December 2004.

[44]For Australia, quinquennial reviews report on returned material: State of the Environment Advisory Council (1996). *Australia State of the Environment 1996. An Independent Report Presented to the Commonwealth Minister for the Environment by the State of the Environment Advisory Council*. Australian Government: CSIRO pub.

Department of the Environment & Heritage (2001). *Australia State of the Environment Report 2001: Natural and Cutural Heritage Theme Report*. Australian Government: CSIRO pub. p. 118.

[45]Dominy, G. (2000). South Africa: Collecting the material culture of apartheid and resistance: the Natal Museum's Amandla Project, 1992–94. In *Museums & history in West Africa* (C. Ardouin and E. Arinze, eds.) James Currey. pp. 5–17. p. 5.

[46]National Statistics (2005). *Ethnicity: regional distribution*. http://www.statistics.gov.uk/cci/nugget.asp?id=263

[47]Helen Denniston Associates (2003). *Holding up the mirror: addressing cultural diversity in London's museums*. London Museums Agency.

[48]McGregor, R. (2004). The long march home. *FT magazine,* 28 February, pp. 34–35.

[49]Interview: M. Thomson and F. Keene, 22 July 2004.

[50]Casales, E. (2004). China's new cultural revolution. *The Platform.* **4**, 1, October. AEA Consulting. http://www.aeaconsulting.com/site/platformv4i1a.html

[51]Vujic, Ž. (1999). Collecting in time of war. In Knell, ed., 2004. pp. 128–134. (See note 14)

[52]Dominy, G. (2000). South Africa: Collecting the material culture of apartheid and resistance: the Natal Museum's Amandla Project, 1992–94. In Ardouin and Arinze, eds, 2000, pp. 5–17. pp. 6–10. (See note 45)

[53]Ouattara, T. (2000). Côte d'Ivoire: material culture and its use in museum programmes. Musée Péléforo Gbon Coulibaly, Korhogo. In Ardouin and Arinze, eds, 2000, pp. 109–115. p. 113. (See note 45)

[54]Ouattara (2000). (See note above)

[55]Bourdieu's work is discussed in Merriman, N. (1996, repr. 2000). *Beyond the glass case*. Institute of Archaeology, UCL. pp. 78 ff.

[56]Kavanagh, G. (2000). *Dream spaces: memory and the museum*. Leicester University Press. Chapter 8.

[57]Fienup-Riordan, A. (2003). Yup'ik elders in museums. In Peers and Brown, eds, pp. 28–41. p. 40. (See note 3) The elders specifically did not seek the return of the objects from their historic culture.

For Australia, see Department of the Environment & Heritage (2001). (See note 44)

[58]Illustrated in a number of the contributions to Peers, L. and Brown, A., eds, 2003. (See note 3)

[59]Kreps (2003). pp. 40–43. (See note 39)

[60]Sorensen, C. (1989). Theme parks and time machines. In *The new museology* (P. Vergo, ed.), Reaktion. pp. 60–73.

[61]Sheriff, A. (2000). Zanzibar: Encapsulating history: the Palace Museum and the House of Wonders. In Ardouin and Arinze, eds., pp. 155–163. (See note 45)

4 Collections for research

Collections in museum stores are for research or they are surely for nothing. Many museum professionals feel that collections are little, or insufficiently used for research[1], but is this the case? What can be learnt by comparing collections that are primarily for research with those for which this purpose is less clear cut? Who are the researchers and what sort of benefits do they seek? What can museums do to facilitate and promote research on their collections?

Archaeological collections offer a practical case study that illustrates some of the difficult issues for both museums and researchers. Natural history collections are a success story for museums in using their collections for research. Their use is intensive and widespread, and this can be compared with the use of archaeological collections. The use of other types of collection for research will be discussed.

In conclusion, some of the answers to promoting research – some proposed by others and some raised in this chapter – will be reviewed and further questions will be raised.

What research?

Research based on collections can mean analysing many objects to answer questions about an overall picture, or a few objects (or just one) can be studied in great detail and depth. Research may address the understanding of objects themselves – the dating of paintings, or the identification of separate species – or it may tackle questions of broader significance, using objects as evidence of history or cultural practices. Research is also at different scales, from international networks of scientists researching natural history, to university led projects with a number of researchers, down to local history societies and individuals interested in a topic, or in the history of their family or the place where they live. There is also research for commercial reasons: property development companies who need to know about possible archaeological deposits they might encounter (to their cost!); companies seeking to exploit natural resources; players in the international art and antiquities markets.

Some examples of research using museum collections are described here, to give just a flavour of the hugely diverse range of research projects that take place. Even subjects as well known as a painting by Vermeer, the expedition of Lewis and Clark to the American West, or a six or seven million-year-old humanoid skull can only be understood in the context of other, humbler things that are stored safely in museums, not for display, not for loan, not for use in handling and education sessions, but simply as the record of all our cultures and histories, unwritten as well as written.

Lewis and Clark's Indian Collection[2]

Lewis and Clark are, to White Americans, two of the heroic actors who opened up to White settlers of the American West. In 1804, they left St Louis to explore the Missouri River and the route through to the west coast of America. The centenary of their expedition was celebrated in exhibitions, documentaries, books, historical markers, and re-enactments. However, many Native Americans saw this rather differently: 'We Say No! to all entreaties to "celebrate" or "commemorate" the genocide of five hundred Nations and the theft of our history'.

During their expedition Lewis and Clark encountered many American Indian tribes and sent back consignments of objects and natural history specimens, sketches, and notes. This material has since suffered various vicissitudes, but some of the objects are now in the collections of the Peabody Museum of Harvard University. The research project took a team of researchers several years to complete – for just sixty objects. It is a complex task to reconstruct the histories and significance of objects in collections that may be poorly documented.

This material has recently been researched to see what light could be thrown on the Native peoples' side of the story by the objects themselves. From this viewpoint, the story is about the objects as elements of diplomatic exchanges between representatives of a new nation and the leaders of indigenous nations, a place of extensive continent-wide trade networks and intertribal diplomacy. (Indeed, American Indian tribes themselves had long been players in a complex sequence of migration, conquest and settlement.) Some American Indian people are now drawing on objects from this collection and others to rediscover and revive their own cultures.

Another example of ethnography collections being used in research – this time when a group of Yup'ik elders from Alaska visited an ethnography collection in Berlin – is described in Chapter 8, Enjoyment: 'My vision is this. Many of us have been in the dark for many years. And now, stories and information about our roots have emerged from this unknown, faraway place across the ocean'.

Attributing famous paintings[3]

Only thirty-five paintings exist that are firmly attributed to Vermeer. The notorious episode of forgeries by van Meegeren in the 1930s and 1940s threw doubt on some. The small painting, *'Young woman seated at the virginals'*, was considered a suspect and for ten years it had been the subject of scientific and art historical research by Libby Sheldon, in University College London, latterly working with a committee of experts. Following the death of its previous private owner and a confident attribution to Vermeer, it came up for auction in 2004 and was eventually sold for £16.2 million (Fig. 4.1).

Photo: L. Sheldon

Fig. 4.1 *The Rollins Vermeer, Young lady seated at the virginals (detail). The painting was sold in 2004 following its firm attribution to Vermeer by Libby Sheldon and a committee of experts*

A wide range of examination techniques enabled the production of the painting to be progressively well understood, and through comparison with other paintings, its likely authorship to be determined. X-radiography and visual examination showed the nature of the canvas: it is highly comparable to that in another Vermeer painting, *The Lace-maker*, in the Louvre, Paris and could well be from the same bolt of cloth. The pigments and paint were examined using stereoscopic microscopy of the surface, cross sections, polarized light microscopy and other instrumental techniques (Fig. 4.2). They revealed a warm buff/grey ground containing lead white, chalk, red and yellow ochres, lamp black, and umber; several lead-tin yellow shades in the shawl; green earth in flesh tints; and use of expensive ultramarine (ground lapis lazuli) in many areas. These pigments and the techniques of their use are found in other paintings by Vermeer – especially ultramarine to achieve the effects of light and luminosity that are particularly celebrated in his paintings.

Other techniques had been used that are typically found in his works. There was a lack of visibile underdrawing (there is evidence that Vermeer used chalk, which would not be visible), but underpainting, could be discerned. A mark for the perspective vanishing point can be traced.

This Vermeer was intensively investigated because its attribution had been in question. The project drew on research and knowledge of many other paintings, in the Louvre, Paris, the National Gallery, London, the Mauritshuis, The Hague, the Metropolitan Museum of Art, New York, and public and private collections. Paintings in museum or gallery collections offer the most valuable evidence because their provenance, the techniques of their production, and their art historical aspects have normally been thoroughly established. They remain permanently available for further study, with every physical intervention documented.

Famine, death, and evidence from teeth[4]

The Museum of London's collection of archaeological human remains is one of the largest in the world. This unique resource allows archaeologists to investigate past human biology. Dr Daniel Antoine, a Wellcome Trust Senior Research Fellow at University College London (with other associates), is currently using one of the Museum's assemblages, from the Royal Mint site, to study the impact of the Great Famine of AD 1315–1317 on the health and growth of Londoners.

This site, located near the Tower of London in East Smithfield, contained many individual graves, as well as two mass burial trenches and a mass burial pit, densely filled with several hundred well-preserved articulated skeletons. It has been identified as the Black Death cemetery that had been opened as an emergency burial ground in 1348–1349 by Ralph Stratford, the Bishop of London. It is the largest and most comprehensively excavated

Photo: Libby Sheldon

Fig. 4.2 *Using microscopy to analyse paint and pigments. Libby Sheldon in University College London*

Black Death cemetery in England and provides a unique assemblage of people who died in 1348–1349, at the peak of the Black Death epidemic in London.

Similar to the Black Death, the Great Famine is recorded as one of the greatest calamities of medieval Europe, but little is known about its impact on the people who survived it. The Royal Mint collection provides a unique opportunity to investigate this through analysing the teeth of individuals who survived the famine, but died during the Black Death in AD 1349. Those people buried in the cemetery who were in their thirties at the time of their death would have lived through the famine as children. Teeth form during childhood, and as a result any systemic disturbance experienced during dental development, such as episodes of nutritional stress, can create microscopic defects in dental tissues. Regular growth structures within these tissues – similar to the growth rings of a tree – are being used to build detailed growth records of the early years of their lives, including any period growth disruption. The timing of growth disturbances provided by the tooth record is being compared with the detailed chronology of the Great Famine. The impact of the crisis on skeletal development is also being investigated.

This will provide us with an insight into the effects of the famine on individuals who were children during this period, and will add to our knowledge of the overall health of fourteenth century Londoners. This research project is the more valuable because it is a collaboration between a historian, who can use documentary evidence to help develop the questions and interpretation of the archaeological research.

African cultural history from textiles[5]

Wood carving has for many years been the focus of attention on arts and culture in southern Africa because these works are analogous to sculptures of wood in the West and so are treated as an extension of that culture. Textiles are more functional and are generally seen as a form of decorative art. African textiles barely feature in research and publications. However, traditional songs hint at an ancient tradition of the importance of cloth and textiles. A study of textiles was conducted from the Université National du Benin, Cotonou, using museum collections in Benin and abroad.

The objects are from excavations and history and ethnography collections. There is a range of excavated evidence: the earliest, from the Niger delta, dates from the ninth to eleventh centuries. Depictions on bronze and brass artefacts, for instance those from Benin, supplement the evidence from textiles themselves. The preliminary assessment shows that evidence from textiles can supply information about many aspects of history and culture. In southern Benin, according to oral sources, weaving and cloth were unknown until the seventeenth century. Yet this is at odds with the evidence from archaeology, which appears consistent with accounts from Arab writers in the eleventh century, who wrote about woven clothing being worn inland. The date when weaving was introduced, where the technology arose, the kind of fibre and dyes that were used, and the cultural significance and use of textiles and clothing are just some of the questions that can be addressed. Not only textiles but also sculptures and depictions, oral and written history contribute to make up the picture.

In Africa, weaving and textiles are important evidence for history and culture, yet at present, they are insufficiently represented in museum collections, and there are plans to improve them as a basis for ongoing research.

Natural history: face to face with our past

It is claimed that 'Toumaï' (hope of life) is a human ancestor six to seven million years old.[6] A large number of comparable hominid remains were examined to reach the proposed conclusions. Extensive comparison of evidence of the ecology of the site and others, from faunal and other biological material, were required in order to infer a date for the remains. Analysis and understanding of the fragmentary skull depended on study of the collections of National Museum of Ethiopia, the National Museum of Kenya, the Peabody Museum and Harvard University, the Institute of Human Origins, and the University of California. Specimen series will be deposited in the Département de Conservation des Collections, Centre National d'Appui à la Recherche (CNAR) in Ndjame´na, Chad. Whether this skull and others do represent early hominids or ancestral apes is hotly contested. It is essential that evidence is retained in museum collections as the foundation for informed debate.

Who researches?

Researchers working on museum collections include both those who earn their living through research and also many people for whom this is a private or leisure interest.

A professional researcher may be an academic or a scientist, an author, or a researcher for a business. Archaeologists use archaeological and paleontology collections, designers and historians of design draw on decorative art collections and archives, buyers and sellers on the commercial art and antiques markets research the authenticity of possible sales and purchases ... the list goes on. Scientists conducting research based on natural history collections of all kinds constitute a very large, perhaps the largest, proportion of professionals using collections for research.[7] Much of this work is for commercial purposes, for example, mineral prospecting; court cases involving infestations; water pollution.

Amateur researchers include people researching family or local history. There is enormous interest in this in several countries, the UK, the USA, and Australia for example.[8] Local history and military museums in particular have collections that are of interest to these researchers. During the period 2004 and 2007 the Imperial War Museum, London, expects each year 103 000 – 105 000 users of its collections and enquiry service, both amateur and professional.[9]

There is a heavy demand for information from museums through enquiries. For example in 1998/99 the UK Science Museum, London handled 27 000 enquiries, and a typical small specialist museum, the Potteries Museum & Art Gallery in Stoke-on-Trent, 6500.[10] Many of the Science Museum enquiries (analysed in 1999) were about the collections or related matters.

What do researchers require?

Whatever sort of objects or collections they wish to study, researchers have some obvious needs.

Locating source material Where is the stuff? To research material, one must know that it exists and be able to locate it. Museum collections should be listed on the internet, so that information about them is freely available to all, yet many museums still dispute the usefulness of this. There are many listing initiatives: notable examples at a national level are CAN: Collections Australia Network, Artifacts Canada, run by the long-established Canadian Heritage Information Network; and Cornucopia, a developing database of UK museum collections.[11]

There are also listings of particular types of object, being compiled by academic or curatorial societies. These include natural history listings, European paintings in the UK and scientific instruments, among others.[12] To take just the latter, the Online Register of Scientific Instruments is an international database of these and related objects available freely to all via the internet (Fig. 4.3). So far, major collections from the UK, the Netherlands, America, Italy, Canada, and Belgium as well as a few items in private collections are listed. The Register is developed and supported by the Museum of the History of Science in Oxford in association with the Scientific Instrument Commission of the International Union of the History and Philosophy of Science:

> *The primary purpose of the Online Register is to provide an efficient, centralized, widely available register of historic scientific instruments and related objects that exist in dispersed collections of all kinds from around the globe. It is analogous to a computerized library catalogue in that it holds only a limited amount of key information about each instrument: the information most commonly used to allow an instrument to be located. It does not contain any detailed information about an instrument's form, use, or history. It is a gateway only – a stepping-off point to more extensive information that will be held by institutions themselves, whether on-line or off-line* (Fig. 4.3).

Locating material within the museum. The next challenge for the researcher will be for the museum to produce the material they wish to research: objects and also the documentation relating to them. This depends on the museum having compiled the basic collections management information: what is in the collections; to whom does it belong (loaned material may need special permission for others to access it, to loan it, even to conserve it); where is it?

Full documentation. Then, there is the issue of associated documentation. Even if the electronic documentation is in good order, a museum may not have got to grips with its paper records, yet these will often be crucial to serious research into an object or objects. An object is only the focus for a cloud of information about who – when – what – where – why. To be confident in using the object as evidence the researcher needs to know its provenance – how it was acquired, who used it, and how, whether it was

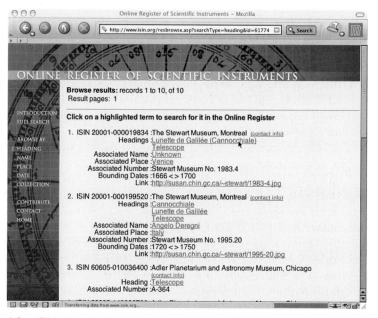

Fig. 4.3 *ISIN: the Online Register of Scientific Instruments. Objects from major collections in various countries are listed on ISIN. The database can be searched as one. It is a guide to tell the researcher where they can find the instruments to study*

new or old at the time of acquisition, and why it was considered significant at the time.

Object(s) in fit condition for study. Of course, object-based study depends on the objects being preserved well enough to be a useful source of information. In the case of large-scale vulnerable collections such as natural history specimens, this cannot be assumed. For example, specimens such as plant material and animal and bird skins are vulnerable to insect pests and fade from exposure to light; minerals and fossils, to unsuitable environmental conditions such as relative humidity. Other types of objects have similar problems of preservation.

Access to material. In practice many museums, not only small ones, may find it difficult to provide for collections researchers. Not all, perhaps few, have enough spare space for collections to be studied on any scale. There are security issues: unfortunately researchers sometimes succumb to the temptation to privatize selected items or parts (radiator badges from vehicles are popular). This means that an invigilating staff member must be present to concentrate on the activities of the researcher.

Some museums, especially natural history museums, are willing to send objects or specimens out to researchers. The Entomology Department at the Natural History Museum, London, routinely has a staggering 175 000 specimens out on loan. This is seen as part of the process of distributed knowledge building of the natural world through the collections.[13] As well as individual researchers and projects, there are many networks of scientists working on developing this understanding. For instance the National Geological Survey in the USA is facilitating building the National Biological Information Infrastructure in the USA, an electronic federation of biological data and information sources.[14]

Case study: archaeological collections of the Museum of London

This is a category of collections that is primarily for research and that exists in museums the world over. Issues arising from archaeological collections follow a predictable pattern. In the early days of archaeology, excavation is relatively small scale, conducted by archaeologists from universities often with unpaid volunteer excavators, or sometimes from central government agencies. As the economy grows and historic occupation areas are redeveloped or rural areas are intensively cultivated, the pace of archaeological discoveries and excavation increases greatly, but funding for proper storage and organization of the excavation archive does not. A museum that accepts archaeological material soon experiences problems in properly managing this large volume of material.

The UK has a long tradition of archaeological excavation. It is a country that has historically been densely populated; since the nineteenth century large scale development has been taking place.[15] Even in the UK, where the principle is largely accepted that excavations should be funded so as to cover the costs of proper finds preparation, there continues to be concern about the scale of the archaeological archive. This is mirrored in the USA and in Australia. In Australia, in the state of Victoria alone, since the heritage legislation in 1995, the number of consents to conduct excavations (as a result of development) has tripled and there has been a corresponding growth in the amount of material requiring storage. Heritage Victoria has set up a project with the Australian Research Council and the Cultural Heritage Centre for Asia and the Pacific, Deakin University, Melbourne, to investigate the issues.[16] In the USA, a familiar set of problems has been described: the archaeological profession does not value its collections nor has it managed its growth to form a comprehensive resource; planning and local policies insist that the products of excavations be kept without engaging with the resource requirements; archaeological curation has been consistently under funded by all parties; the costs of archaeological curation have been rising; collections are not used enough and so the case for their proper curation is weak.[17]

The London Archaeological Archive and Research Centre (LAARC)

In the UK, a series of official reports from 1975 onwards identified these problems.[18] In 1996 the Museum of London, recipient of perhaps the largest body of excavation archive and finds from anywhere in the world, closed its doors to further material because it was unable to fund their ongoing maintenance. Eventually the museum raised the funds to create the LAARC: the London Archaeological Archive and Research Centre, purpose built to house the London archive and staffed and operated as an accessible resource for those wishing to study the excavation finds and records.[19]

The LAARC brings together the material evidence and records from archaeological units and excavations in London. The policy is to manage the material within the available storage space for many years to come. Re-boxing into standard sized boxes and discarding material that has no valid archaeological context achieves large economies of scale. Diverse catalogues, which will be on line, are being developed by the MoL. This of course requires a continuing investment in staff and storage equipment. However, the cost of meeting standards for the preparation of incoming material has been shifted firmly to the excavators: 'We are committed to accepting archaeological archives relating to the London Boroughs and the City of London, *provided that* they conform to our published guidelines' (original emphasis).[20] Its Guidelines are a detailed specification based on the published national standards.[21]

The LAARC: an appraisal

The aim of the LAARC is admirable: to make the archaeological evidence from London fully available to all, whether professional or interested public. There is a comprehensive public website with clickable maps leading to excavation descriptions and other information, and there are arrangements for visitors to use the archive.[22] It is fully meeting all the targets agreed upon with its funders for its operation and use. However, use by non-professionals has been disappointing, in line with findings that most archaeological archives in UK museums are not extensively used.[23] The slightly out of the way location contributes to this. Experience in a different context suggests also that enthusiasts are put off by the formal surroundings of a fully managed museum storage environment rather than being able to use informal premises that are under their own control.[24] The whole subject of the use of museum collections by enthusiast societies would repay further research.

Formal relationships with higher education organizations are more successful. There are links with four universities: in the UK, University

College London Institute of Archaeology, Birkbeck College, and Royal Holloway College; and La Trobe university in Australia. Joint research projects and teaching are successfully exploiting the archive. Also, the MoL's own linked Museum of London Archaeology Service is a major user of the archive in planning and assessing current and future excavations and archaeological strategy.

The MoL's research strategy for the future is to identify parts of the archive which are of particular interest, and to positively encourage their research. For example, the early modern material (seventeenth century and later) was not previously a primary focus for study. Excavated evidence for the earlier history of London was more interesting to UK researchers because the historic record is less complete. But for researchers in Australia (La Trobe university) and North America, the early modern period was the time of early settlement, when many goods were brought from London, and many sealed and well-dated deposits are represented in the London archive. Medical research is another instance, with a project to analyse some of the human remains to assist research into spinal deformities.[25]

However, the LAARC is still experienced by some as difficult to use freely, with the museum wishing to control research that is proposed rather than to provide a straightforward service of access to an archive, as do record offices.[26]

Collections researched and less researched

Are some types of collection more used for research than others? Natural history collections, at least those in major museums, are an essential and much used body of material: archaeological collections should be, given the same interest in local history.

Natural history collections have an economic justification. There is a long tradition of good collections management and many good role models, there are good networks of scientists and curators. Hence these collections are much used for research. The contrary is true of archaeology collections on almost every point.

Archaeology collections lack the economic relevance of natural history collections and must instead rely on arguments of academic research and cultural value. Natural history museums are well aware of the status of their collections. The Natural History Museum's new Darwin Centre for its collections is being built in one of the most expensive real estate areas in the world (see Fig. 11.1), and the collections of the Musée National d'Histoire Naturelle in Paris are, similarly, housed in central Paris. The Musée National says of its collections:

Vivants ou non, rares ou répandus, les spécimens d'histoire naturelle conservés dans les différentes collections du Muséum sont toujours uniques et recèlent des informations précieuses pour la compréhension de la vie sur la Terre.[27]

(Living or not, rare or commonly occurring, natural history specimens preserved in the various collections of the Museum are all unique containers of precious information for understanding life on earth.)

The first type of collections to be systematically formed, the formation and management of natural history collections has been extremely well understood since the mid-sixteenth century if not earlier.[28] It is well recognized that a natural history specimen is only as valuable as its documentation. An exhibit at the Canadian Museum of Natural History invited the visitor to decide which of six varied specimens was worth keeping: those that failed did so on the grounds of lack of documentation or poor physical condition, while rarity could counterbalance these as a reason for retention.[29] Archaeologists have understood less well than natural history scientists the purposes of their archives.

Natural history specimens are mostly collected by scientists for use in science, while in archaeology the glamour of new discovery through excavation has outweighed the more thoughtful study of excavated evidence, though this is changing. Therefore archaeologists do not have the benefit of a tradition of using excavation archives and finds that have been created by others. Biologists and other scientists have well-established international networks and projects, in particular studying biodiversity,[30] that result in coordinated cataloguing across different museums. There is no such coordination for archaeological collections research, and there cannot be, since unlike natural history specimens they do not represent a myriad facets of a single world.

In the case of art collections, art objects are normally well documented and researched because of their monetary value. Art collections as a whole have important economic and also political relevance, due to the international art market and the long tradition of acquiring art, especially paintings, as symbols of wealth and social position.[31] Art curators in museums play an important part in setting saleroom values[32] (and see discussion that follows; Chapter 10: Values). Art history is well established as an academic discipline and art collections are extensively drawn on for research.

Decorative art and design collections in larger museums are widely used as reference material by artists and craftspeople as well as by private collectors and by the antiques traders. Such museums often have a tradition of partnership or association with a university or college, or the educational institution may have such a collection, as do the Surrey Institute of Art & Design and the Goldstein Museum of Design of the University of Minnesota.[33] Costume and textile collections are crucial material for historians of those subjects, and are also popular with designers.[34]

The study of scientific instruments is gaining ground as part of the interest in social constructs on the history of science. This perspective proposes that scientific advances are influenced by the materials and the technology available at the time to carry out experiments, and are not dependent on concepts alone (see Chapter 5: Ongoing learning).[35] Industry, technology and agricultural collections are less used for research, not so much due to lack of documentation and provenance – frequently this will be very well known as they are often acquired when local businesses collapse or machinery becomes outdated and needs to be disposed off – but because academic and other research based on material evidence is not well established. Here too there are exceptions for particular industries such as the railway industry – interest in the history of railways is widespread.

In the case of local history collections, those in small local museums can be well used: they are obviously relevant to local people and places and are not overwhelmingly large. Chippenham Museum and Heritage Centre attracts over 20 000 people a year to its museum and its archive, photographic, and objects collections by marketing outreach, school events, and other programmes. Research uses include comparing the past appearance of local features such as houses or the canal, research for books, for instance on poorhouses, and engineering students with an interest in Chippenham's engineering past on Brunel's first railway.[36] Norfolk Museums Service, UK, has three study centres for the costume and textiles, fine and decorative art, archaeology and natural history collections. They are open on particular days of the week. The website stresses that anyone can work on the collections (with due notice): 'Ever wanted to get your hands on real museum objects? Well here is your chance.'[37]

Research using ethnography collections is well established: there is political pressure on museums to justify having them. To cite two major collections, the Pitt Rivers Museum, Oxford, supports more than 200 research visits a year to its collections and has nearly twenty current research projects by staff and research students;[38] the Royal Central Africa Museum, near Brussels, is one of several museums to include a research institute with a large, active research staff.

Discussion

Nearly all museums eventually develop collections of significant size. Research then becomes a primary reason for holding them.

Judging success

How can successful research use be measured? Should a museum be aiming at ten visitors an hour, a day, a week, a year? Research is an activity of individuals, and user numbers will always be insignificant compared to visitors to museum exhibitions. Some figures are: 200 research visitors a year to the Pitt Rivers collection; 200–300 actual visits plus about 2000–3000 enquires to the Tank Museum in Dorset; 20 000 less formal users of Chippenham Museum and Heritage Centre (including visits to the museum). More research is needed to compile statistics on usage and to understand the conditions for success.

Success ought also to be judged by the outcomes of the research: the difference it makes to people's lives. It should not be forgotten that museum collections are culturally very important to many people, although to others they may be just a case of 'too much stuff'. In Australia, some indigenous communities find that academic knowledge of their cultural heritage is crucial to their survival. They can use the results of academic studies to gain control of land through Native Title claims and other processes. They also use the knowledge gained through academic research in educating young people and in generally raising awareness of Indigenous Australian culture. Economically it is useful to them as indigenous Australians increasingly run heritage tours and other tourist events. Academic involvement in research is thus a tool used by a community to strengthen its identity in its dealings with the outside world.[39]

Collections centres: the answer?

What about collections centres: off-site warehousing facilities where collections are kept separately from the museum, or museums (Fig. 4.4)? Should collections be moved out of museums into separate, dedicated facilities, as some advocate?[40] There is a growing number of examples, for a range of collections. One of the earliest, if not the earliest, is the Museum Support Centre of the Smithsonian Institution. This was built in 1983 at a cost of $29 million to house some of the Smithsonian museum collections, notably natural history and American history. Nearby is the recently opened National Museum of the American Indian Collections Resource Centre. The Science Museum, London, took on a disused World War II airfield in 1981, nearly 90 miles away from London, to store its large object collections and to enable it to collect aircraft. There is the LAARC of the Museum of London (the building houses the other museum collections as well as archaeology collections). For archaeology collections, similar central archives are the norm in some countries, for example Peru and Belize.[41] In the Netherlands the feasibility of a National Reference

Photo: S. Keene

Fig. 4.4   *Storage for research: the Canadian Museum of Nature's Natural Heritage Building. These natural history collections are stored in giant mobile racked cabinets, in an environmentally controlled store in an off-site collections facility. The specimens are protected from pests, fading and damage from heat and humidity*

Collection is being explored.[42] Other examples of dedicated storage buildings will be found in the chapters that follow (Fig. 4.4).

Collections centres clearly do work in some circumstances. They would rate highly for collections preservation, especially in the very long term. But I doubt if they are the universal solution. In my experience of being responsible for two off-site collections stores, a remote store little used by staff, with material in it that the museum does not itself exploit much, is a top target for savings in budget reduction rounds. This does not get easier if storage is shared: what if one party wants to stop paying, or won't pay for the standard of facility that the other partners want?

Locally focused history collections are often seen as a major problem area: but it seems to me that their usefulness depends crucially on their being available to people in the place to which they relate. Would members of the public who have an interest in the history of the place be prepared to travel to them? It would especially affect the elderly, for whom the museum and its collections are actually and potentially an excellent resource. A remote centre would make collaborative ventures with educational organizations local to the museum difficult.

When it comes to operating collections centres, there are management issues to be addressed. There can be quite difficult management problems unless the store is busy and staff are fully occupied. What about the expert staff – do they go with the collections, or stay with the museum? There is no tradition of running museum collections like archives, where much of the stock is very rarely consulted but where there is an acceptance that storage should be funded. Archives (in the UK at least) are heavily used. What source of funding will pay for seldom used museum collections, remote from the museum, year in year out?

It may be that there do need to be places where collections that are beyond the scope of the museum to use are stored. But the place where the collections could be used to the maximum is the museum itself. Otherwise, what is it – an exhibition centre? Perhaps, this is indeed the future for museums.

Conclusions

Research is the function that could potentially draw on more of the collections than any other use. There is a paradox. Many examples of research based on museum collections can be found in journals and by searching the web, and yet the experience of most of those managing museum collections is that any particular collection is used very little for research. For most collections in most museums it is the exception and not the rule.[43] But still, there are examples of collections, such as natural history and art and design collections, that are very intensively used by researchers.

If there were more collections-based research, it would justify more of the collections. Not only that: it would add to and enhance them immeasurably as a store of knowledge. Provision for research is expensive but then, so are other museum operations. If museums could point to extensive use of their collections for research at several levels, professional, commercial, and individual, the justification for them would be more convincing. For countries such as the UK where numerical performance indicators are important, these need to be broadened to reflect more than just visitor figures.

What could museums do to foster the research use of their collections? Most museums do not provide well for researchers. The requirements seem straightforward, but measured by cost per researcher they are expensive, requiring investment in staff, storage, documentation, and secure facilities for study. Without an assured demand it is difficult to justify expenditure on these. On the other hand, without this investment, will demand ever materialize? The examples described show that it is not necessary to be a large, well-funded museum to provide facilities for research: smaller local ones do too, and they can be very popular. It seems that it is more a matter of will than of finance.

If its collections are to be enthusiastically used for research, the museum must see services to researchers as a central function and not just as a secondary one. There need to be proper facilities – a place for researchers to work, with access to the collections database, staff to answer enquiries, assist researchers and invigilate, and facilities to work on collections objects. The facility needs to be marketed so that people know that it is available, and it needs to provide its services in a way that tells non-professional users that they have as much right to draw on the collections as anyone else.

Encouraging collections-based research is not a passive task. Museums need to be much more active in forging partnerships with universities or colleges. Nearly all the examples of striking research described earlier are the result of collaboration between universities and museums. It is encouraging that in the UK, the Arts & Humanities Research Council not only helps to fund university museums, but also offers grants for 'resource enhancement' – projects to prepare material for use in research and teaching, including museum collections. It funds collaborative research, such as the AHRC Centre for the Study of the Domestic Interior, where one of the partners is the Victoria & Albert Museum.[44] It is universities, with research as a primary function, that could provide the most sustained and productive use.

Perhaps the most difficult step is to shake off the attitude of control and exclusivity that seems endemic to museums. At the moment museums all too readily assume that the only meaningful research is that which their own staff carry out. Of course the collections must be protected: they are a resource for others, too, now and in the future. The problem is the attitude that only museum staff may confer meaning on the objects; only museum staff may interpret them; only museum staff may have knowledge about them; only museum staff may publish on them. Spalding muses that a good measure of the usefulness of a museum for research would not be publications by staff but instead all the academic research that the museum has facilitated.[45]

Part of the answer lies in exploiting information and communication technologies, particularly to locate relevant material in museums. This discussion will particularly be addressed in Chapter 9: Digitization. Collaboration with research institutions is a fruitful way to promote this use: marketing and outreach to reach individuals is another. It may be that success needs to start with educating the researchers. The chapter which follows, on collections and education, will give some pointers to this.

Notes

[1]Responses to the UK Museums Association's consultation exercise, *Collections for the future*, 2004. Correspondence on the international museum discussion lists, MUSEUM-L, 2004. November, Week 5; December, Week 1. http://home.ease.lsoft.com/archives/museum-l.html. INTERCOM-L (2004). 19 November – 2 December. http://susan.chin.gc.ca/~intercom/

[2]McLaughlin, C. (2003). *Arts of diplomacy: Lewis & Clark's Indian collection.* University of Washington Press.
Lonetree, A. (2005). Arts of diplomacy review. *H-Museum: H-Net Network for Museum Professionals.* Posted Tuesday 1 February. http://h-net.msu.edu/

[3]Sheldon, L. and Costaras, N. (2005). Young woman seated at a virginal – the Rollin 'Vermeer'. *Oud Amsterdam,* in press. I am grateful to Libby Sheldon for details of her research.

[4]Antoine, D. and Hillson, S. (2005). Famine, Black Death and health in fourteenth-century London. *Archaeology International* [8] 2004/5. I am grateful to Daniel Antoine for this description of his research.

[5]Andandé, J. (2000). Benin: textiles in southern Benin. In *Museums & history in West Africa* (C. Ardouin and E. Arinze, eds) pp. 78–86 James Currey.

[6]Brunet, M. *et al.* (2002). A new hominid from the Upper Miocene of Chad, Central Africa. *Nature* **418**(July), 145–151.

[7]Interview: *Natural History Museum.* Curator. 9 July 2004.

[8]Website: *National Library of Australia.* Guides: Australian Family History and Genealogy on the Internet. http://www.nla.gov.au/oz/genelist.html
Website: *Imperial War Museum.* Family history. http://www.iwm.org.uk/server/show/nav.00100a

[9]IWM (2003). *Corporate plan 2004/7.* Imperial War Museum.

[10]NMDC (1999). *A netful of jewels: new museums in the learning age.* National Museum Directors' Conference, p. 7.

[11]Websites: *AMOL.* Australian Museums Online. http://www.amol.org.au/collection/*Artifacts Canada.* Canadian Heritage Information Network. http://www.chin.gc.ca/English/Artifacts_Canada/index.html
Cornucopia. Museums, Libraries and Archives Council. http://www.cornucopia.org.uk

[12]Websites: *National Gallery.* National inventory of European painting, 1200–1900. http://www.nationalgallery.org.uk/collection/inventory.htm
National Biological Information Infrastructure. Museums and collections. http://www.nbii.gov/ datainfo/syscollect/collections.html
Oline Register of Scientific Instruments. http://www.isin.org/

[13]Interview: *Natural History Museum,* 2004. (See note 7)

[14]Website: *National Biological Information Infrastructure.* (See note 12)

[15]For a review of archaeological collections in the UK, with references to other reviews, see Merriman, N. and Swain, H. (1999). Archaeological archives: serving the public interest? *European Journal of Archaeology* **2**(2), 249–267.

[16]Interview and email correspondence: *Deakin University.* I. Schacht, PhD candidate. Project: Making room for the past: determining significance in archaeological collections from historic sites. 21 October 2004.

Website: *Deakin University*: Cultural Heritage Centre: Research and consultancies: Making room for the past: Determining significance in archaeological collections from historic sites.
http://www.deakin.edu.au/arts/centres/CulturalHeritage_Centre/research/making.room.php

[17]Childs, T. (2003). Challenges in conserving archaeological collections: responsibilities of the archaeological profession and its members to the management of archaeological collections. In: *Out of the past, for the future: integrating archaeology and conservation. A conference theme at the Fifth World Archaeological Congress, Washington D.C.* WAC.

[18]Merriman and Swain's article reviews in detail all the reports to that date: Merriman and Swain, 1999. (See note 15)

[19]Website: *LAARC*. Museum of London Archaeological Archive & Research Centre. Catalogues. Links to: home > archaeology > LAARC > catalogues. Museum of London. http://www.museumoflondon.org.uk/

[20]Website: *LAARC*. (See note above)

MoL (1998). *General standards for the preparation of archaeological archives deposited with the Museum of London.* Museum of London.

[21]Paine, C., ed. (1992). *Standards in the museum care of archaeology collections.* London: Museums & Galleries Commission.

[22]Website: *LAARC*. (See note 19)

[23]Bott, V. (2003). *Access to archaeological archives. A study for Resource and the Archaeological Archives Forum.* Resource (now the MLA).

[24]The Science Museum: author's experience with a specialist society.

[25]Interview: *Museum of London.* H. Swain, Head of the Department of Early London History. 1 June 2004.

[26]Bowlt, C. Contribution to a seminar: *The future for collections.* Institute of Archaeology, University College London. March 2002.

[27]Website: *MNHN, Paris*: Musée National d'Histoire Naturelle:
http://www.mnhn.fr/museum/foffice/tous/tous/HistNatMuseum/collections/pqcollections.xsp

[28]Olmi, G. (1985). Science – honour – metaphor: Italian cabinets of the sixteenth and seventeenth centuries. In *The origins of museums: the cabinet of curiosities in sixteenth- and seventeenth-century Europe* (O. Impey and A. MacGregor, eds), Clarendon Press, pp. 5–16.

[29]Exhibition: Canadian Museum of Nature (2004). *Finders Keepers.* Exhibition viewed February 2004.

[30]Website: *Tree of Life.* Tree of Life web project. http://tolweb.org/

[31]Merriman (1991). *Beyond the glass case: the past, the heritage and the public.* Institute of Archaeology, UCL. pp. 80–82.

[32]Fisher, P. (1997). *Art and the future's past.* Harvard University Press. p. 28.

[33]Website: *Surrey Institute of Art & Design.* Crafts study centre.
http://www.surrart.ac.uk/index.cfm?articleid=1607

Website: *Goldstein Museum of Design.* University of Minnesota.
http://goldstein.che.umn.edu/Goldstein-Museum.html.

[34]Interview: *Museum of London.* C. Ross, Head of Department of Later London History. 3 December 2004.

[35]Bennett, J. Seminar: *The uses of collections: science history collections.* Institute of Archaeology, University College London. 20 March 2003.

[36]Interview: *Chippenham Museum & Heritage Centre.* Curatorial Assistant. 14 June 2004.

[37]*Norfolk Museums & Archaeology Service.* Study Centres.
http://www.museums.norfolk.gov.uk/default.asp?Document=210&Submit=go

[38]Website: *Pitt Rivers Museum.* Notes for research visitors.
http://www.prm.ox.ac.uk/researchnotes.html.
Interview: *Pitt Rivers Museum.* 22 October 2004.
Website: *Pitt Rivers Museum.* Museum research. http://www.prm.ox.ac.uk/museumresearch.html.

[39]Department of the Environment & Heritage (2001). *Australia State of the Environment Report 2001: Natural and Cultural Heritage Theme Report.* Australian Government. CSIRO pub. p. 140.

[40]Spalding, J. (2002). *The poetic museum.* Prestel. Chapter 7.

[41]Interview: *UCL Institute of Archaeology.* E. Graham. 16 June.
UCL Institute of Archaeology (2004). B. Sillars. 17 June 2004.

[42]Nieuwhof, A. and Lange, A.G. (2003). Op weg naar een nationale referentiecollectie archeologie (Feasibility study for a national archaeological reference collection). Rijksdienst voor het Oudheidkundig Bodemonderzoek.

[43]Bott (2003). (See note 23)
Thomson, K. (2001). *Collections and Research. Submitted to the Working Party on Renaissance in the Regions, May 15, 2001.* Museums Libraries and Archives Council. URL: http://www.mla.gov.uk/information/policy/collectionrsch.asp.

[44]Website: *AHRB Centre for the Study of the Domestic Interior.*
http://www.rca.ac.uk/csdi/

[45]Spalding (2002). p. 98. (See note 40)

5 Collections for ongoing learning

The educational role of museums is at present, considered very important in the UK as well as in many other countries.[1] It is well recognized that real, three–dimensional objects can engage attention in many ways, and that much can be learnt from them about technologies, design, other cultures, the past and the present, and the natural world. Yet, in museums, emphasis is on educational activities using exhibits and programmes, with little use of the collections themselves.

The chapter will first introduce some models that have been developed to help understand the processes of learning, and examine what the role of objects might theoretically be. Much is written about school education in museums, and so the focus here will be on adult education, and in particular on the uses of collections in university teaching. Second, I want to concentrate on what can be learnt and taught *from* the collections, using objects as the basis for education, rather than learning that just uses the subject of the museum as the peg for general educational activities. An art gallery might offer lectures on art history; a science museum, debates on current controversial issues. Neither of these is about the collections. Learning from the collections and objects in them pushes museum educational activities further into the heart of the museum. Both informal learning, not leading to a recognized qualification, and formal learning, usually in partnership with an educational institution, will be discussed.

About learning

Why do we hear so much about audience participation from museum educationalists? How best to teach people: conversely, how do people learn? The main conceptual stances recall that ancient Chinese saying:

I hear and I forget;

I see and I remember;

I do and I understand.

Many models have been developed on how people learn. A few selected approaches will be discussed here: teacher directed, learner centred, and collaborative[2]. These broadly correspond to behaviourist (focusing on teaching) and constructivist (focusing on learning and the learner) approaches, with collaborative learning being a combination of the two.[3]

Behaviourist learning is the 'empty vessel to be filled' model: as Stephen Weil, astute commentator on American museum affairs, has it, 'the baby bird waiting with its beak open for the careful museum to feed it with pre-digested information'.[4] It assumes that there is a body of accepted knowledge to feed to the learner. The teacher or communicator delivers classes or lectures and leads the process of instilling information and knowledge. Another behaviourist teaching method is stimulus– response, where information is provided and the learner has to respond in some way – by lifting a flap covering the answer or selecting an on-screen button perhaps – after which they receive a response, Yes! or Try again! etc.[5]

The contrasting constructivist, learner-centred model is 'I do and I understand'. The process is under the control of the learning person, who builds on their existing understanding and knowledge by selecting information and inputs from the environment around them. Constructivist learning methods focus on the learner and the processes of learning rather than on teaching: they are active, participatory, hands-on, with no pre-determined outcome to reach.[6]

Both the approaches have their problems. Teaching simply through transmitting information, as in a formal lecture, is often far from effective.[7] On the other hand, learner-centred approaches may 'condemn [such adults] to remaining with existing paradigms of thought and action': what if the learner does not have the basis on which to construct new knowledge and challenge preconceptions?[8] If they are not provided with new information or viewpoints, all they have to learn from is what they know already. In collaborative learning, the teacher and learner collaborate to achieve a common goal. Students actively construct their own interpretation of their experience: learning is an active and continuous process of making personal meanings; both personal and social.

A further option is problem-based learning, a fully realized learner-centred method, in which a problem mirroring real life is constructed for students to address. They are assisted by a tutor to find a solution. A project where students were challenged to create a narrative, drawing from a collection and its documentation, using what they have learnt during the more theoretical parts of their course, would be an example.

Education using objects would offer the benefits of the interactive, constructivist, and collaborative methods but grounded in the physical entity of the object and the hard evidence it comprises. Examine the object in Fig. 5.1: what can be inferred about it from its appearance? The examples

Fig. 5.1   *What can you learn from an object? Function: What was its use, in functional terms? Why is its handle made of wood? Why does the lid lift off? Appearance: What do you feel about the shape? What does the material (silver) say about it? Is it made from this for practical reasons: if not, then why? Can you guess the date? If so, what visual clues would you use? (See p. 69 for some suggestions.)*

of learning from a landscape and of teaching the history of science in the description that follows show how it could work. The students have some knowledge of the context of the object from prior lectures or preparation. The object is a source of evidence that can be discussed. The tutor is present to provide further information that is necessary to prevent the wrong inferences from being drawn.

Of course, different people have different learning styles, and it is often best to combine approaches or to use different ones at different points in a course.

How people think

Understanding the elements of how people think helps to explain why objects could be useful in education. Different types of sensory input are processed in different parts of the brain. Multiple sensory inputs – sight, hearing, touch, and feel – are particularly valuable in learning, and objects can provide these.[9]

The visual qualities of objects are one great potential advantage. Visualization and images play a vital part in learning and in thought. In the West, words, whether spoken or written, are very important. However, successful speeches often use visual metaphors, and in fact many people think primarily in images, not in words. Einstein is often quoted: 'Words or language … do not seem to play any role in my mechanism of thought' … 'my elements of thought are … images'.[10] One can recall numbers, facts and so on better by associating them with images: this was noted by the Greeks in classical times and developed as the concept of the theatre of memory (see Chapter 7: Memory and identity). The history of science students in the example below said that better recall was a particular advantage of that event.

Objects – things – perform an important stabilizing function for us. In spite of what we may think, we control very little of what goes on in our minds, and artefacts help us to objectify and ground ourselves in reality. Individuals use perhaps quite humble objects to create particular frames of mind for themselves, or they may, more ostentatiously, use things to convey a sense of who they are. It is the humble objects that link them to their past that people often especially prize.[11] It is those same humble objects that can provide a window into the lives and thoughts of past or different people, and hence let us understand and learn about them in a vivid way.

Can objects that were meaningful to some people (their previous owners, the curators who acquired them) evoke meaning for others, and so help them to construct new ideas about the world, new knowledge? Objects do not in themselves carry meanings, but if a person has learnt about their context (or can be guided to interpret what they see) the object can provide a vivid impression, a new experience for them as well.[12]

This is the hope of those studying material culture: that by observing, or experiencing objects, people may be able to engage with other cultures in a very direct way, through their senses, without verbal processing. Students might thus share in some way the experience of those who made or used them. From examining an object such as a teapot without the aid of prior knowledge it could be inferred that it held liquid, that the liquid was hot, that it was used to dispense the liquid, and that the liquid contained particles needing to be strained out. As well as this intellectual analysis the teapot, depending on its appearance, might evoke feelings such as substantial, cheerful, motherly, or beautiful, showy, expensive. Teapots are mostly used on social occasions involving chat and conversation so it might have these connotations, too. Its domed, rounded shape might even conjure up feelings, perhaps unconscious, about maternal nurturing! Undertaking such an analysis undoubtedly helps people to learn to look at things and from that to understand something of their function, of the maker's intentions, and of the messages that they evoked in their original use.[13]

In the 1970s a very popular series was shown on BBC television, *Ways of seeing*. This investigated easel paintings and demonstrated how they bore messages about society and the subjects depicted in them. An equally popular book was subsequently published. Between them the book and the series showed in a highly accessible way how these objects help to shape perceptions at the time when they were painted, and equally today.[14]

Object-based learning: some examples

Object-based learning can claim very early origins. In excavations of the Babylonian city of Ur, dating from around 600–539 BC, an assemblage of objects 1600 years earlier than their context was discovered. This has been interpreted as a school collection (even including a ceramic 'label').[15] The didactic power of objects was a primary motivation for establishing public museums in the nineteenth century.[16]

Learning from a landscape[17]

A landscape used as a basis for an undergraduate course is an excellent example of the special learning experience that studying artefacts could provide. Although a landscape is not exactly an object, it is certainly an artefact; it could even be a collection. The undergraduate students have no knowledge or experience of the subject: they come from 'architecture and landscape architecture, mathematics and history, electrical engineering and dairy husbandry; they are, in effect, a random grab from the population of a very large public university. … most students view ordinary landscape simply as a time-consuming obstacle that lies between where they are and where they want to be, to be crossed over as quickly as possible but otherwise ignored'. With the benefit of a little preparatory reading, the hundred or so students are taken on a one-day field trip to a small town in rural Pennsylvania, to demonstrate 'what a finite bit of that world has to teach them.' They study maps and aerial views, they climb to the top of small hills to look down on the town, they walk in the main street and observe architectural styles, construction materials (stone, wood, brick, concrete), they note which shops are closed and which are flourishing, where major buildings are being re-used[18] … an exercise in what can be learned through careful observation that will surely stay with them permanently and provide them with much pleasure in the future. Learning as a way of life.

In this example, the concept of three orders of magnification is used: the context – social, geographical, historical, and economic; views from a distance, through maps, aerial views or hilltop vantage points; and finally the maximum magnification close-up view at street level.[19] This three-layered approach could be used in many imaginative ways with collections and objects.

Learning with music collections[20]

The York Gate collection of the Royal Academy of Music in London is a celebrated example of historic musical instruments used in teaching and research. For instance the stringed instrument collection was formed in the nineteenth century for the express purpose of teaching and performing music:

> *The Academy's outstanding tradition of training string players of the highest calibre is given testimony by the number of alumni pursuing solo careers or who are principal players in orchestras and chamber ensembles throughout the world. Through a specialist programme of solo, chamber music and orchestral performance, the Academy comprehensively prepares students for a professional career. ...*
> *The Academy hosts master classes by members of the teaching staff and regularly welcomes distinguished visiting performers. ...*
>
> *The Academy's collection of over 250 stringed instruments, including 25 Cremonese instruments, is the most significant of its type worldwide. Many instruments are available for student use. The staff of the on-site stringed instrument workshop advise students on maintenance of their own instruments ....[21]*

The instruments are used in music education (many sessions are open to the public), and also studied in courses in physics and the technology of music in University College London. Students investigate, for example, the tuning of an instrument and the physics of sound transmission. The photographic and archive collections are also a teaching resource. Student options include projects to research an aspect of historical music or music making, to produce an organized archive and report on it. An excellent learning exercise for students, this also has the practical benefit of helping to make progress in cataloguing the large archive and photographic collections, something that pleases students and staff alike.[22]

When the policy of actively using the instruments in the collections in this way was announced there was a lively debate in the British press. It was argued that if all instruments were used in this way then we would lose this entire heritage. Others held that if they were not played the instruments would be 'dead'. The latter argument is an appeal to emotions rather than reason, as no material property of an instrument is changed if it is played, except that it deteriorates faster or may break. Arguments against using instruments in the RAM collection are not strong, as most of them have already been extensively repaired and altered in the nineteenth century.[23] But only finite and diminishing numbers of unaltered historic instruments exist, and so the indiscriminate use of them is of serious concern. Playing historic instruments almost always requires them to be modified in some way and causes deterioration.[24] (see Chapter 3: Collections: Using functional objects).

Learning with history of science collections

The Oxford University Museum of the History of Science has collections of scientific instruments, including many very early examples – and among notable later objects, a blackboard with calculations written in chalk by Albert Einstein. A one year Master of Science course is taught entirely through the collections: an experiment in understanding the history of discovery and invention.[25]

Traditionally, the history of science is taught as a process of conceptual change that was brought about through intellectual effort. Yet there are many examples, such as those described in Collin's and Pinch's book, *The golem*, of how what is discovered or concluded is influenced by the actual apparatus and instruments used. Pasteur established that disease spreads through the propagation of microscopic organisms, contrary to the then prevailing belief that they could spontaneously generate from a suitable substrate such as rotting material. He had great difficulty with his experiments and only achieved the 'correct' results with the help of luck. It was very difficult to achieve complete sterilization with the equipment of the day, and the properties of microorganisms were imperfectly understood.[26] In school science, as many of us will remember, our experiments hardly ever gave the 'right' result, even with something as simple as measuring the boiling point of water.

The Oxford course works from the question: how can these material objects illuminate the history of science? They can, of course, in many ways, some similar to those relating to the sewing machine discussed below, and others relating to their purpose and function. By using an astrolabe you can gain a much more real and vivid appreciation of the mathematics of the time than by reading about it. The course has to avoid becoming just a course in connoisseurship.[27]

In one of these classes a group of students spent a couple of hours studying the features of a rule-like brass object. From its maker's name, they could deduce its date. They questioned whether it was authentic or if it could be a reproduction. They spent most of their time working out its use, from lettering on it 'Borde measure', 'Timber measure', from figures and marks, and from the way that it could be unfolded and fixed in different positions. They eventually understood that its function was to measure lengths and approximate volumes of timber. To work this out they had to draw on what they had learnt in previous lectures and ask the tutor very specific questions. The class showed that it is possible to work out from the evidence of objects what they were used for, but only to an extent – knowledge of many aspects of the context and other sorts of evidence was also needed. The object told something about how people at that time went about solving problems in their daily trade and their understanding of mathematical concepts. The students felt that they could remember much better what they were learning by having the object as the focus of the class.[28]

Before we get too carried away by the evidential virtues of objects, however, it should be noted that they do indeed have limitations. For instance they sit in parallel with, not in opposition to, the study of texts. There are examples of what objects do provide as evidence and what they do not: such a realization would be a valuable thing to learn, too. 'Objects can illuminate words; they cannot replace them'.[29] Images and other sensations cannot be used to construct narrative: it is difficult or impossible to reconstruct or explain sequences of events without words.[30]

What do students learn?

Students value encounters with real objects, as we know from their evaluations of courses which include this experience.[31] Objects have a very wide variety of 'meanings' to offer in education.[32] We have seen that using several senses can help in learning. But learn what? More and more, we need people who can make connections across the hard boundaries between conventional disciplines.[33] What could be learnt, for example, from a sewing machine?

Engineering: design and technical problem solution

Art and design: forms, colours, decorative features

History of technology: introduction of sewing machines followed introduction of interchangeable standard parts in gun manufacture

Social history: changing economic status of women

Economic history: move of manufacturing from domestic to factory based

History of costume: changes in costume and fashion due to introduction of mechanical sewing.[34]

Some of these topics could be followed just by knowing that sewing machines existed or by looking at images; for most, much more could be learnt by studying a physical object. In fact, the sewing machine is an apt example. It is often said that sewing machines were invented to utilize the technology of interchangeable parts that had been developed by the Singer Company for making guns. To test this, the Smithsonian Institution assembled four guns and found that the parts were in fact not interchangeable.[35] Maybe some guns had interchangeable parts, but obviously, not all did. (We don't know whether they compared sewing machines, which in my experience require extremely precise engineering if they are to work).

Museums, collections, and education: the potential

Most museums have an educational role. Work with schools is more publicly known and much written about,[36] but many provide for adult learning, too. The Smithsonian Institution runs a Resident Associate Programme offering a huge range of educational programmes many of which centre on the subject matter, if not the actual objects, in the collections. The Victoria & Albert Museum and the National Maritime Museums in London do likewise; there are many other examples.

Collections for education

Some of the early beginnings of museums lie in collections for learning and teaching. Yet, the widespread impression is that at present only small parts at best of museum collections are used in education (there are no hard data on this). Some university collections are an exception. This is partly because of well-founded anxiety that objects will be damaged; partly because of cost – of security if objects are made available in stores; of proper equipment for protecting objects if they are to be closely examined; of staff to identify objects, move them to where they are required, and put them away again. If the bulk of the collections were to be more used this would certainly be more feasible for adult learning than for schools and children (Fig. 5.2). Education departments in museums often use handling collections: objects that are designated as semi-disposable, or at least that have special protection.

Informal and formal learning

Informal learning needs to be distinguished from formal learning. Formal learning has a clear objective: a qualification. For formal learning in museums, experience suggests that partnerships with education establishments are most fruitful, in which the education partner provides the structure and the qualification.

The education for adults that museums provide is almost always informal learning, which does not lead to a recognized qualification. There are plenty of examples, such as training for volunteers or guides; demonstrations and workshops; lectures and symposia; guided tours. Educational studies show that in informal museum education, people look for an

Fig. 5.2 *Collections for learning and research. The varied ethnography and other objects in the Marischal Collection of the University of Aberdeen are stored in plastic crates on racks*

experiential learning process that allows them to construct new knowledge and to learn interests and skills. They look for the involvement not just of the intellect but also of the different senses and emotions, and for stimulating social interaction with others.[37] In spite of these varied requirements, straightforward lectures by museum staff are popular, too. Given proper provision of facilities, space, and effective access to objects, any of these activities could be designed with a greater emphasis on the collections.[38] Facilities would not be much different from those required by researchers (see Chapter 4: Research). Undoubtedly such opportunities would be very attractive: people generally love contact (not necessarily literally) with objects, and the sense of privilege that they would gain from activities focusing on collections. These events are not cheap, however, as explained further here.

Museums' contribution to formal learning – courses that lead to a qualification that is recognized by employers and other education institutions – is most successful when they are in partnership with a university or college. Some examples are the long-standing partnership between the Victoria & Albert Museum and the Royal College of Art, offering MA and MSc qualifications in conservation and the history of art. Museum/ university partnerships are discussed in the next section. Some museums have offered their own qualification but they seldom have the resources to keep this up for any length of time. It is outside their main remit, students cannot call on the normal sources of grants to attend, and the lack of a recognized qualification undermines the appeal of such schemes.[39]

Online education provision involving museums and collections is gradually developing, with organizations like *Fathom* and *AllLearn*[40] offering collections-based courses. *Fathom* has evolved into an archive of free material: it included fourteen universities, museums, and publishing companies. *AllLearn* is an alliance of the Universities of Oxford, Stanford, and Yale; course materials include extensive reliance on museum collections (see also Chapter 9: Digitization).

Universities and museums

Universities can make use of their own collections for teaching, and they could also form partnerships with other museums for that purpose.

There have been a number of studies and surveys of the collections of universities, and their museums. The general finding is that although many of these collections were formed specifically for university teaching and research, times change and the collections are now mostly only residually useful for these functions.[41]

Despite the gloomy trend that affects some university collections, there is reason for hope. In 2004, a survey of the collections of University College London was undertaken. They include the Petrie Museum of Egyptian Archaeology, the college art collections, the Grant Museum of Zoology and Comparative Anatomy, the Geological Sciences Collections, the Institute of Archaeology collections, and other departmental collections from the sciences, medicine, and anthropology. The survey found that, from archaeology to zoology, each of these collections was drawn on for several undergraduate and postgraduate courses (see Fig. 5.3, where archaeological ceramics are being used in teaching). The collections were also used for informal learning at various levels.[42] Clearly, collections can be used successfully in university teaching. There are many other examples.

Also, universities often have departments of continuing education and museums are popular as partners with them, offering as they do a different and interesting sort of experience. [43]

Partnerships between university departments and museums outside the university are quite widespread. In the early 1970s, the US National Endowment for the Arts published a survey which showed that nearly two out of five museums had a relationship with a university level institution. The larger the museum financially, the more likely it was to have such a programme. Internships were frequent (these will nearly always involve working on collections), but nearly half were involved in credit courses as well.[44]

Most of the British national museums, such as the British Museum, the Victoria & Albert Museum, the Natural History museum, and others, have active joint programmes with universities. In Australia there are joint courses with the National Museum of Australia/the Australian National University; in Canada, Museum Victoria, the Royal British Columbia Museum, the First Peoples' Cultural Foundation, and the Cultural Resource Management Program of the University of Victoria. These are just a few examples from a cursory search: there are many other university and museum partnerships worldwide.[45]

Further, the existence of museum collections generates the need for courses in museum studies and curation. All over the world courses such

Fig. 5.3 *Using a collection for learning. Students in the Institute of Archaeology, University College London, learning to use the evidence from ceramics in interpreting archaeological sites*

as these are being offered, and they involve partnerships, whether short term placements and internships or fully shared teaching, with museums.[46]

But do these university/museum partnerships involve the collections, or is the focus on the subjects of the collections – history of art, history of science – or on other museum activities and the ever-dominant exhibitions? If collections objects are used, to what extent is this? The various reports on university museums and collections cited earlier found that museum collections were too little used in teaching. Also, we have no data on the use of collections in museums other than university ones – a gap in our knowledge that could usefully be filled.

In a useful development in the UK, the funding bodies for university funding and for research have recognized museum collections as the valuable resource that they are, including them in grant programmes aimed at promoting excellence in teaching and learning. The objective is to instigate, extend, and consolidate the use of collections objects. Courses that are benefiting include art and design, art and architecture, facilitating cultural empowerment, and a range of undergraduate research skills using the collections of museums of rural life and zoology. The Arts & Humanities Research Council in the UK intends to extend the reach of its funding to include non-university organizations such as museums and their collections.

Conclusions

Adult learning, both resulting in a formal qualification and informal, for enjoyment and personal information, has been the focus of this chapter. Education theory suggests that learning through or based on objects and collections could be very effective. The examples of teaching music and history of science show some highly innovative ways of teaching. It would only benefit university education if objects were more widely used. Collections constitute a large and potentially valuable resource that should be well employed.

To achieve greater use of collections requires those in universities to consider how objects could be used in teaching, and museums to be active in approaching them. Partnerships between universities and museums can work well but only if the museum properly dedicates staff to this. Fitting this commitment into another job will not work, as the museum's interests must always come first. There are resource implications for both museums and universities, and sustained funding is essential.

For the benefit of both museums and universities, there is a need for serious research into the particular benefits of using objects for learning, and to tackle the practicalities of object-based teaching. In the UK there is a great deal of current research and interest into more imaginative ways of teaching and learning, and it would be good if museums and universities could join in this.[47] Something as simple as an analysis of the potential uses of different collections in the various academic areas would be invaluable.

Informal adult learning in museums is better established, at least in larger museums. Many examples can be found. It does not need the rigorous structure of curriculum and assessment needed in teaching leading to a formal qualification. Museum education staff can organize it without outside intervention. Such programmes are subject to the different but equally ruthless judgment of the market: if they don't attract students they won't survive.

Museums themselves, it is often said, erect barriers around the collections.[48] Curators and conservators guard the collections – the one the intellectual and ownership aspects, the other the physical preservation ones. Only certain staff have the right to access and 'use' collections. Even within the museum, activities and projects proposed by non-collections staff are too often resisted as 'not invented here'.

If museum collections were used as a resource for adult, college and university learning as extensively as they theoretically could be, this would have a major impact on museum resources. A greater use of collections and objects in education could transform collections practice, purpose, and their recognition in society. The museum would need to devote staff to actively contacting and working with outside organizations. Special attention would need to be paid to preventing damage and deterioration of collections. But a useful collection is a well looked after collection. On both sides, one depressingly frequently reads of unrealistic commitments of time and resources that lead to less than successful projects.[49] As with other uses of collections, the main conclusion must be as to what would really make a difference is organizational priority, managerial will, and sufficient, sustained funding.

Notes

[1]See different countries' definitions of a museum. Website: *ICOM*. The definition of the museum. *ICOM News: Thematic files*.
http://www.chin.gc.ca/Applications_URL/icom/definition_museum.htm.
Also for example, this purpose of museums in West Africa is discussed in several of the contributions in Ardouin, C. and Arinze, E., eds (2000). *Museums & history in West Africa*. James Currey.

[2]Sachatello-Sawyer, B. *et al.* (2002). *Adult museum programs: designing meaningful experiences*, AltaMira Press. p.101.

[3]Hein, G. (1998). *Learning in the museum*. Routledge. Chapter 2.

[4]Weil, S. (2002). *Making museums matter*. Smithsonian Books. p. 65.

[5]Hein (1998). p. 15. (See note 3)

[6]Hein (1998). pp. 27–38. (See note 3)
[7]Hein (1998). p. 15. (See note 3)
[8]Sachatello-Sawyer *et al.*(2002). p. 99. (See note 2)
[9]Robertson, I. (2002). *The mind's eye.* Bantam, Chapter 5.
Hein (1998). p. 15. (See note 3)
[10]Robertson (2002), pp. 15, 90. (See note 9)
[11]Csikszantmihalyi, M. (1993). Why we need things. In *History from things,* (S. Lubar and W.D. Kingery, eds) pp. 20–29. Smithsonian Institution. pp. 22, 25.
[12]Kavanagh, G. (2000). *Dream spaces: memory and the museum,* Leicester University Press. p. 22.
[13]Prown, J.D. (1993). The truth of material culture. In (Lubar and Kingery, eds), pp. 1–19.
[14]Berger, J. (1972). *Ways of seeing.* BBC and Penguin.
[15]Lewis, G. (1992). Museums and their precursors: a brief world survey. In *Manual of curatorship: a guide to museum practice,* 2nd ed. (M. Thompson, ed.) pp. 5–21, Butterworth-Heinemann. pp. 5–6.
[16]Bennett, T. (1995). *The birth of the museum: history, theory, politics.* Routledge. pp. 25–32.
[17]Lewis, P. (1993). Common landscapes as historic documents. In (Lubar and Kingery, eds), pp. 115–139: pp. 119–120. (See note 11)
[18]Lewis (1993). (See note 11)
[19]Lewis (1993). p. 119. (See note 11)
[20]Interview: *Royal Academy of Music.* F. Palmer, Curator of Collections. 9 June 2004.
[21]Website: *Royal Academy of Music.* Links to: > departments > strings > bowed instruments.
http://www.ram.ac.uk/departments/index.html
[22]Interview: *Royal Academy of Music.* (See note 20)
[23]Interview: *Royal Academy of Music.* (See note 20)
[24]Arnold-Foster, K. and La Rue, H. (1993). *Museums of music.* Museums & Galleries Commission, pp. 24–25.
[25]Bennett, J. (2003). Seminar: *The uses of collections: science history collections.* Institute of Archaeology, University College London. 20 March 2003.
[26]Collins, H. and Pinch, T. *The Golem: what everyone should know about Science.* CUP. (1993). p. 90.
[27]Bennett, J. (2003). (See note 25)
[28]Seminar in the course, MA in the History of Science. *Museum of the History of Science, Oxford.* Attended 27 October 2004.
[29]Macquet, J. (1993). Objects as instruments and signs. In (Lubar and Kingery, eds), pp. 32–40. (See note 11)
[30]Robertson (2002). p. 37. (See note 9)
[31]UCL, various dates. Course evaluations by students.
[32]Pearce, S. (1992). *Museums objects and collections: a cultural study.* Leicester University Press. Chapters 7 and 8.
[33]Kelly, M. ed. (2001). *Managing university museums.* Organization for Economic Co-operation and Development. p. 11.
[34]Durbin, G., Morris, S., and Wilkinson, S. (1996). *Learning from objects.* English Heritage. pp. 4–5.

[35]Brown, I. (1993). The New England cemetery. In Lubar and Kingery, eds, pp. 140–159. p. 143. (See note 11)

[36]Numerous works including Hein, 1998 (See note 3); reports such as Anderson, D. (1997). *A common wealth: museums and learning in the United Kingdom: a report to the Department of National Heritage.* Department of National Heritage.

[37]Sachatello-Sawyer *et al.* (2002). Chapter 2. (See note 2)

[38]MLA (2004). *Space for Learning: A Handbook for Education Spaces in Museums, Heritage Sites and Discovery Centres.* Museums, Libraries & Archives Council.

[39]The National Maritime Museum, London ran a formal course in the conservation of globes for some years in the 1990s; the Science Museum, one in the conservation of science and industry objects. Both ceased after a very few years due to the reasons explained.

[40]Websites: *AllLearn.* Alliance for Lifelong Learning.http://www.alllearn.org. *Fathom.* Fathom: the source for online learning. Columbia University. http://www.fathom.com.

[41]Kelly (2001). (See note 33)
AVCC (1996, 1998) *Cinderella Collections: University Museums & Collections in Australia* (with update 1998). Australian Vice-Chancellors' Committee, 1998. UMG (2004). *University museums in the United Kingdom.* University Museums Group.

[42]UCL (2004). *Current and prospective uses of UCL Museums and Collections.* Unpublished report, available in UCL library.

[43]UMG, 2004. (See note 41)

[44]In the 1990s a number of university–museum partnerships in the USA were described in detail. Worthy, E., Jr. (1990). The Smithsonian Resident Associate Program. In *Museums and universities: new paths for continuing education.* (J.W. Solinger, ed.) pp. 131–144. American Council on Education/Macmillan Publishing Company.
David, H. (1990). Museum–university partnerships close-up. In (J.W. Solinger, ed.) pp. 117–130. (see above)

[45]Museologia (2002). *Museologia. An international journal of museology.* 3 (1 & 2). Museum of Science of the University of Lisbon. http://www.museu-de-sciencia.ul.pt/museologia/index6.html

[46]As an internet search on 'museum studies courses' demonstrates.

[47]The Higher Education Funding Council for the UK funds research into education, and there are numerous university departments engaged in this, as well.

[48]Responses to the UK Museums Association consultation for its enquiry, *Collections for the future.* Museums Association (2005).

[49]See examples in Gould, H. (2004). *What did we learn this time?* The museums and galleries lifelong learning initiative. Department for Education & Skills.

Flea Market

By John Fuller

Place du Jeu de Balle, Brussels

And there will never be a time
When we will go down in the darkness,
Waiting until the platform clears

To open the stiff doors of the last tram
To Silence, lifting our failing feet
And unwillingly replacing them

Until we reach that square of dispersals,
To see our own lives laid out
On the cobbles for the scavengers.

We will never weep to see our pathetic
Trophies laid out on newspaper,
Turned over by the toe of profit

Or still heaped in their cartons of haulage
Where nothing is thought to be beautiful
That cannot survive its ownership.

The things we liked are like the things
We did, kept by us and remembered,
But imperfect to the judicious eye.

Weaknesses like photographs,
Faces instinctively lifted towards
A supposed immortality.

Wounded plates preserved in the uniform
Of their fortunate brothers, loved music
Cheapened by pencil and blackened corners.
The things that are only what they pretend
To be for as long as one pays them attention:
Paper flowers, magazine parts.

Objects that tease by confusing the appetites:
The mammary jelly-mould, the mannekin
Corkscrew, the can-can casse-noisette.

The trophies from foreign shores and occasions:
The coloured sand, the Exhibition
Mug, the aluminium amulet.

What has always been said is also
True: you can't take it with you.
So let us establish a useful countdown

Like eating the contents of the fridge
Before departure, to the last undated
Egg, saved rice and dwindled caper.

Such were a satisfying meal,
Though frugal, and appropriate
To the condemned prisoners we are.

All these objects that we believe
Define us: they ache already with
Our love, and their forgottenness.

6 Collections, memory, and identity

In the popular mind, museums are overwhelmingly about the past. This is often thought to be a disadvantage that needs to be overcome. Yet people greatly value both preservation of the past and representations of it as long as it is presented in a relevant way.[1]

Remembrances may be on several levels. At the personal and family levels, an object or objects may signify a person's past life or loss. At the level of the place, the collections of local museums may help to construct a sense of continuity and of place.[2] In collective or cultural memory, memory shared with others is a vital component of cultural identity.[3] At the level of the nation-state, objects may represent political power and hegemony (or its loss), commemorate events of cataclysmic significance such as the Holocaust, wars, and military adventures or may be trophies from a more influential and powerful, perhaps colonial, rule in the world.[4]

People's sense of identity, whether cultural or social, depends on a remembrance and record of their background, culture, and roots. Sometimes the essence of this is intangible, traditions passed on verbally or through enactments (which often involve objects, as in religious ceremonies or music). Often, objects of one sort or another are used to represent or memorialize the past. People who have been subject to a diaspora may particularly value finding things that help to foster a sense of their cultural roots. 'I would say a mixture ... we can't call [our homeland] our home now and we can't call this home but a mixture of both ... we belong to both of them ...'.[5] When the Horniman Museum was built in the nineteenth century it was in a middle class commuter suburb, Forest Hill, London – unlike its social environment now. 'The Horniman collected the world – and then the world came to Forest Hill', as a sometime director of that museum said.

'In a way, all collecting can be seen as an ongoing attempt to cope with the fact that time goes by.'[6] Since the past begins at this moment, all the objects in collections represent the past in some way. Precisely because they are held to represent past events, they may at the same time play a vivid role in the present. In Western culture, old master paintings refer to the past, when they were made, and which many of them depict, but they also send messages about the present, since it is the wealthy and powerful (individuals or indeed countries) that possess them.[7] Objects representing past military or political events may invoke the current political standpoint on them. There is the notorious example of the exhibition in the American Air & Space Museum of the Enola Gay, the aeroplane from which the atomic bomb was dropped on Hiroshima in 1945. The theme of American and Japanese acts of war being shown side by side and as equally tragic and regrettable was furiously disputed by the US army veterans' organizations. They opposed any suggestion that America was other than totally justified and blame-free. The incident eventually led to the resignation of the director of the museum.[8] In other contexts, artefacts from the cultures of indigenous peoples are sometimes seen as standing for the colonial past. There may be demands for their return to present day cultural descendants. This may be felt to symbolize a degree of reparation for unhappy times.[9]

Concepts of memory and identity

The theory of memory is a rich field of enquiry in both arts and science.[10] One approach, which is useful in considering museum collections, contrasts scientific memory and romantic memory. Scientific memory is identified with systems of classification beginning in the ancient world with Aristotle and continuing into the Renaissance. Romantic memory is the aspect of intuitive, instinctual, emotional 'landscapes of the mind'. It deals with the individual rather than the cosmos.[11] The museum collection could be seen as embodying scientific memory, and people's encounters with objects as expressions of romantic memory.

These viewpoints are from work in the West, but objects – things – are widely known for their ability to summon emotional memories. In 1689, the Japanese poet Matsuo Basho on his journey along the narrow road to the deep North came across a stone by the roadside commemorating battles of old: 'Here before my eyes was a monument … through which I could see into the hearts of the men of old … I wept for joy'.[12]

Objects play a wide variety of roles in memory. They may provide visual prompts such as aids to navigation made and used by Pacific islanders. Portraits may act as remembrances of people. Items specifically made for burial of the dead are common. Religious relics are venerated by the faithful. John Mack's book, *The museum of the mind*, brings in Helen of Troy, Sir John Sloane, Sigmund Freud, the *bulaam* of the Kuba in Central Africa, the Maya and mariners in the Marshall Islands in the Pacific together with many other people and examples to provide a vivid illustration of just what a range of objects is specifically created and used throughout the world in various exercises of memory, and of their prevalence in everyday life and in collections.[13]

Memory systems and metaphors

In societies where knowledge is not primarily communicated in writing, aids to memory or memorizing are important. The concept of the theatre of memory or memory palace arose with the classical Greeks and has seized the imagination ever since. In the Renaissance it played a part in the birth of the museum.[14] In *Hannibal*, Robert Harris depicts his monstrous anti-hero, Hannibal Lector, visiting his labyrinthine memory palace to recall Clarice Starlings' address:

> ...*The third alcove from the door on the right is dominated by a painting of St. Francis feeding a moth to a starling. On the floor before the painting is this tableau, life-sized in painted marble:*
>
> *A parade in Arlington National Cemetery led by Jesus, thirty-three, driving a '27 Model-T Ford truck, a 'tin lizzie', with J.Edgar Hoover standing in the truck bed wearing a tutu and waving to an unseen crowd. Marching behind him is Clarice Starling carrying a .308 Enfield rifle at shoulder arms.*

Clarice Starling's address is, of course, 3327 Tindal, Arlington, VA 22308.[15]

Many people have seen parallels between memory theatres and museum collections, ordered and classified.[16]

Memory: personal and social

The memories of a person are major components of their identity and personality. As we all know, particular objects, places, smells, or sounds may summon up the very essence of a past experience (even though we may in fact, as time goes by, be remembering a memory). At a functional level, people need to remember the times of trains, how to navigate in the Pacific,[17] or to learn to recount narratives (proverb ropes used in Lega villages in Kivu, the Congo).[18] Group memories include those of the family, which often have the home as their focus, especially furniture and possessions:

> Human beings and objects are indeed bound together in a collusion in which the objects take on a certain density, an emotional value – what might be called a 'presence'. ... In their anthropomorphism the objects that furnish [the traditional space] become household gods, spatial incarnations of the emotional bonds and the permanence of the family group. These gods enjoyed a gentle immortality until the advent of a modern generation that has cast them aside, dispersed them ...[19]

Collective memory operates in a broader social context too. It is a powerful cohesive force for groups such as supporters of football teams or members of particular social classes.[20] Individual memory and collective memory are iterative and mutually reinforcing. 'The individual remembers by placing himself in the perspective of the group, but the group realizes and manifests itself in individual memories'.[21]

Histories are usually thought of as being constructed through accounts of the past that can be examined and debated: memories only have this property if they are made explicit, perhaps in an exhibit.[22] Histories may be written and published; in some cultures there are ceremonies in which narratives are recounted for public debate and examination. Among First Nations living on the Pacific coast of Canada and northwestern America it is the custom to confirm the boundaries and ownership of their territories by public recitals of detailed narratives of their occupation. Territorial claims can be challenged by others present. It has been suggested that these narratives go back to the period of deglaciation over 10 000 years ago.[23]

Histories are by no means universally agreed or recognized versions of the past as demonstrated in the example of the exhibition of the Enola Gay cited earlier. Even if published in written form, history, it is argued, is not embedded as a memory at an individual level: it has to be brought to life through commemorative events and so on, or, indeed, through museum exhibits. Thus, history might be designated the memory of the nation-state, even though there is no such thing as a universally accepted history (Fig. 6.1).

Contingent memory

Whether individual, collective, or even written history, memory is not a fixed, passive storage system: it is dynamic, changing according to different circumstances. The unconscious is always at play, rearranging conscious memories in time and space, juxtaposing some and splitting or reshaping others, suppressing or recalling.[24] Memory has been likened to stones from antiquity that are re-used to make different, later buildings.[25]

Museums and memory

Discussions of museums and memory can be confusing because they do not deal with the schizoid nature of the museum as an institution. Museums have two personae, the exhibit and the store: communication and collection: as it were, voice and memory. Both play a vital role.

The store of memory

Museums, in their storehouse aspect, that is their collections, are seen to be strongly related to memory. Collections since the sixteenth century

Photo: Science Museum

Fig. 6.1 *Memory of science, technology, and industry on a grand scale: the Science Museum. Industry collections summon up the disappearance of whole ways of life. Neatly racked on pallets so that they can be moved, this collection can also be visited during open days several times a year, at the Science Museum Wroughton, UK*

have been created to record, exemplify, and order the wondrous variety of the world, nature, and artifice. For instance, a zoological and botanical garden with complementary cabinet and alchemist's laboratory were specified in 1594 by Francis Bacon.[26] Objects in museums are grouped into collections, often physically; documented, catalogued, and stored. Figure, 6.2 shows a museum collection shrouded to protect it from pests and light: a form of museum unconscious. Or perhaps objects slip into the unconsciousness of the museum when they lose their identity – their unique number that links them to their documentation? (Fig. 6.2).

Classification and meaning

The system of visual classification used for natural history embodies the Western reductionist scientific perspective. It has been developed for a specific purpose: to understand the natural world, the way it has been formed, and how it can be exploited, and to communicate that understanding.[27] The power of sight and the classification of the visible serves words – in the West we value words. Things that can be seen can be precisely described and classified and observations can be shared with others and agreed to be accurate.

Photo: S. Keene

Fig. 6.2 *Shrouded memories. Racked ethnography collections protected from light, pests and dust by Tyvek breathable non-woven covers. The museum's unconscious?*

Classification systems express functional, scientific memory. But in museums, this same system of visual classification has been applied in areas to which it is not so well fitted, such as material culture and social history. Here, there are many ways of classifying – by period, function, form and so on – but dividing things up in any of these ways can undermine the very reason for collecting them. For example, a complete table setting from *The Pharmacy*, a fashionable London restaurant, was collected by the Museum of London. The objects are looked after in several different collections (textiles, metals, printed ephemera, photographs of the restaurant and so on). Theoretically they could be reassembled from their acquisition numbers but this is unexpectedly difficult.[28] It is easier to re-use stones from antiquity in later buildings than it is to re-assemble them as the original building.[29]

The classificatory approach is taken to its logical conclusion in the inclusion of anthropology and ethnography displays in museums of natural history. The Pitt Rivers Museum in Oxford shares its building with the museum of natural history; the Royal Museum for Central Africa near Brussels and the Smithsonian National Museum of Natural History both display people's cultures in the same spaces as natural history. Yet, most of the culture of Americans of European descent is represented in the Museum of American History (and now, of course, American Indian cultures are represented also in a full scale designated museum and collections store). In museums, my ethnography is your history.

The museum as scientific memory is at odds with the romantic, instinctual, and emotional memory that constitutes social meaning. Categorization is seen to be at the expense of the individual wishing to illuminate their own narrative. Any attempt to fix museum collections within a classification system is bound to fail, as all such systems are subject to the preconceptions of time.[30] Objects have no intrinsic meaning: they can take on whatever persona the viewer or owner projects on them.[31] Curators do indeed find that it is difficult to use objects collected within one collection in the activities of a different one – archaeology and city history, for example.[32] Different contextual information is collected according to the purpose of acquisition and each kind of 'story' requires a different assemblage of objects.

On the other hand, collections are valued precisely for their ability to fix memory. Natural history collections are the very framework of the understanding of the natural world. In them are kept the type specimens – the name bearers – the exact example from which a new species is identified. They can be purposely developed to record the history of largely non-literate societies where the written record alone would be seriously incomplete, as in South Africa where collections in the Nathal Museum play a valuable part in recording the history of apartheid and the struggle against it.[33]

The voice of memory

Exhibitions, communication, and interpretation are concerned with memory, too. If the collection is the museum's memory it might be said that, like all memories, it is undetectable by any except the owner, unless communicated in some way. (Even the owner may not be conscious of the memory – like objects present in museum stores but misplaced and therefore invisible to the museum). Through exhibits museums actually affect and construct memory, by representing some peoples' memories rather than others, and by creating or modifying the memories of those who visit the exhibit.[34]

American local museums (like many other local museums) provide good examples of this. For the visitor, the past can in no other way be so vividly experienced. Summoning up the American West are the actual jeans worn by the outlaw, with the bullet hole where he was shot: here, even, is the dim but very visible sepia photograph of the rustler being hanged, watched by the community who have come by horse and cart to see justice done.[35]

An exhibit speaks only for the person or people that construct its story: if objects that relate to the memories of others are used in it (as in the Enola Gay) this may be seen as the theft of memory and hence cultural identity.[36] Better is to invite groups external to the museum to put on exhibits and hence to construct relevant social memories. In London, in 2003, local museums were invited to identify a 'Local Hero' (they included a film star, a footballer, people who had contributed to community support, a dancer and others). The Heroes donated objects special to them to the collections (the collective memory) and an exhibit (the voice of memory) was constructed in each museum. Other examples are described in Chapter 8: Enjoyment.

Working with memories

Museums quite often develop programmes of work on memory using collections objects with the elderly and others. Many people very much enjoy and benefit from these sessions. But, as ever, each person is an individual: some emphatically do not wish to revisit their memories. It is common experience that people who went through the world wars mostly do not particularly want to revisit these experiences. Associations can range from 'value, treasure, pleasure', to 'the present is fine, the past pointless and irrelevant', to 'integrating – coming to terms with life and death, belief', 'pain, depression, bereavement', 'trouble, regret, sorrow (or even despair)' – a taxonomy of reminiscence has been developed. An integrative experience might include a life review; a transmissive one would pass on tradition or memory, 'gifting' it to someone; a narrative one would use storytelling; an instrumental approach would draw on the past to help with current problems. Escapism is fantasy – the past was a golden age; an obsessive experience would mean brooding on the problems of the past. These concepts help those running such projects to understand the need for intelligence and sensitivity, and to be aware that people's reactions may be far from straightforward.[37]

Identities

We turn now to examine identity and its relationship with collections. Identity and memory are inseparable, and objects – things – are very significant in building and maintaining both. Objects play key roles in both individual and social identity.[38] Captain Cook's voyages of discovery are key components in the cultural memories of both the west and those who were 'discovered' (Figs 6.3 and 6.4).

Collecting objects means conferring value and institutional memory on them (and by inference the context that they represent); (See Figs 6.3 and 6.4, for example) not collecting them implies disregard for those memories and their context.[39] But in conferring permanence museums also take control of the meaning and associations of the objects, since museum collections (in concept if not always in reality!) are also seen as the epitome of organizational principle. The museum further expresses power by controlling access to them and use of them.

The representation of identities in museums is fraught with difficulty. Caught between the rocks and shoals of non-representation, inappropriate representation, illicit ownership, and disputed rights, it seems that museums are damned if they do and damned if they do not. If there are no or too few representative objects in the collections then some people will feel overlooked. But then if there are objects, they may represent pasts that will offend others. A practising artist or maker may inadvertently be categorized as non-mainstream if their works are acquired as part of a positive programme.[40] The person acquiring an object may have been mistaken about its significance, or a person from the originating culture may feel patronized by token collecting by someone from a different culture. Then again, no one person or thing can claim the right to represent a whole culture.

However, people understand these complex issues, and they can be pleased to find things relating to them on display. In London, 'We live locally, we have Black people around and Asians and White people so I mean we could have things from each culture. That would be interesting'. In setting up the Manhiyia Palace Museum in Kumasi, Ghana, the senior members of the Asante people understood very well the role that museums can play, and of what would be required for theirs to achieve their specific objectives of communicating their culture.[41]

Where there is relevant legislation, it seems it is working well. In America the Native American Graves Protection and Repatriation Act (NAGPRA) has been in force since 1990 and institutions there are fully implementing it. Aboriginal remains, at least in South Australia, are addressed in the Aboriginal Heritage Act (SA) 1988 as well as other Australian legislation, considered to be more or less effective.[42] Claims for return of such remains from museums and universities are quite frequent and, at least in the UK, government policy encourages compliance.[43]

Even if strongly held, views are often modified in discussion. Some indigenous Australian claimants, after consideration, have left items in the museum.[44] Sometimes return is more difficult because of conflicting claims such as those over Mungo National Park where there was no residential core of Aboriginal custodians.[45] The park is now controlled under an Aboriginal co-management arrangement. Legislation sometimes only provides the framework for dispute: under the NAGPRA legislation there

Fig. 6.3 *Captain Cook's second voyage, to Otaheite. The flagship of the Otaheite fleet, 26 April 1774. 'The vessels were decorated with flags, streamers &c. so that the whole made a grand and noble appearance such as we had never seen before in this sea'. (Cook, J. and Forster, F., 1821. The three voyages of Captain James Cook: Vol. III. Longman, Hurst, Rees, Orme and Brown: p. 319.)*

has been a detailed investigation to determine the ancestry of Kennewick Man, an ancient skeleton found in Washington State, US, for example.[46] Negotiations can have the positive effect of creating continuing good relationships with the indigenous people to whom the items are connected. Rather than rush to repatriate objects, better to at least explore the many examples of serious engagement between museums and the people whose cultures are represented in collections, on the initiative of either and to mutual benefit.[47]

In the UK, such views exist as well. Our culture is represented in museums to the point of satiation, but we can still feel ambivalent about the ownership of our history. Many people demonstrated passionately against English Heritage's excavation of Seahenge[48] and others have fought for and won the right to celebrate the solstice in the circle of Stonehenge. I was born in North Wiltshire – I am sad that the contents of all the barrows on the North Wiltshire downs are now in museum showcases or boxes and bags in store. People long ago had wanted to leave the dead in those prominent places together with their equipment: who can seriously believe that their things will now last another three or four thousand years? (I admit that it was not until I saw a museum display about them that I realized what a dramatic concept they represented!) It is too

Photo: P. Narracott

Fig. 6.4 *A Tahitian mourning dress from Cook's second voyage, in the Pitt Rivers Museum, Oxford (Acq: 1886). 'The ... upper parts Mother-of-pearl shells, with an edging of feathers from the tails of Tropick-birds. The apron, of small bits of Mother of pearl curiously put together, & ornamented with European beads, and opercula of shells; the Tassels of pigeons feathers'. (Accession numbers 1886.1.1637.2.1; 1886.1.1637.2.2; 1886.1.1637.3.1)*

late for the objects in these examples – the things could not meaningfully be returned to the barrows and we cannot reconstruct Seahenge – but it does demonstrate that the (allegedly) scientific construction of history through archaeology is not always welcomed.

Memory in the case of military museums

The National Park Service certainly never thought of starting a collection when it entered into an agreement with the Vietnam Veterans Memorial Fund, who were going to build a memorial to those who had served in Vietnam and those who made the ultimate sacrifice. At that time, we were concerned only with receiving a memorial that was to heal the wounds, suffered during the Vietnam era, of the Nation and its individuals whether they were pro-war or anti-war.

But as we know, this is exactly what happened. The public began leaving 'things' at the Memorial which later became known as memorabilia. (Text from Vietnam Veterans Memorial Website).[49]

The US National Parks Service now manages a vast and growing collection of items left by visitors at the foot of the Vietnam Veterans Memorial. Others, less convinced of the righteousness of the American cause, have donated their medals to the War Remnants Museum in Ho Chi Minh City (previously Saigon) (see Chapter 3: Collections, and Fig. 2.4).

Common assumptions are that the principal purpose of military museums is to glorify or commemorate war – to represent the history of the nation-state. Some military museums still do act in this way. Most support commemorative events by lending objects or providing a venue. But they also provide for memorialization at a much more intimate and personal level.

The Tank Museum, in Bovington, UK, provides a good case study. It holds the most comprehensive and significant collection in the world of tanks and related items. There is a supporting library and archive including a large photographic collection, housed in a purpose-built research facility. There are about 125 000 visitors a year to its displays and exhibitions, and 2000–3000 visits and enquiries to its library and archive, of which about 200–300 are actual visits.[50]

The museum of course plays a part in national memorialization. Early tanks are sometimes lent to appear in commemorative ceremonies in London and there are ceremonial visits to the museum. It is close to the main military training base for armoured vehicles and warfare, the Armour Centre, whose important visitors are often taken to the museum, and it maintains very close links with the Royal Tank Regiment.[51]

However, like the Vietnam Veterans' Memorial, a more important contribution to memory by the museum is at the level of the individual and the group. There need to be places where people can commemorate their membership of a group or a community, and the personal sacrifice that this may entail. Military service creates a vivid life experience, with intensive training for each person in their responsibility to the other members of their group. Service in tanks particularly enhances this. Soldiers live together, they fight together, and they know that in the end, they may die together.

A growing number of people visit to discover and see objects associated with their relatives. These occasions are emotional and touching; tears are often shed. Several generations of family members may be present. Veterans, too, may visit to find memories of past comrades, and to leave remembrance crosses and wreaths.

The Tank Museum staff take this very seriously. Memorial books have been set up in a Remembrance Room with the name of everyone who died while on service. Significant objects offered for the collection are usually accepted, even if only one or two representative items. The Museum is now collecting people's own memories as well, through a programme, *Calling all tank men*, and via a personal history project of the BBC, *The people's war*. Sometimes people send written memoirs, sometimes verbal accounts are taped, and transcribed by volunteers.

Like those from the London docks who wanted to donate things to the Docklands Museum (described below), those offering memories to the Tank Museum often feel that their part was too insignificant to be of general interest. But it is felt in the museum that they were part of a larger whole and that their individual testimony is very valuable. Published history, especially of wars and warfare, is constantly revised and re-interpreted. Personal testimonies and objects provide a grounding in real evidence.[52]

Discussion: implications

Objects themselves (if one knows what they are) can carry an enormous emotional charge for the viewer. The visit of representatives of Yup'ik elders from Alaska to see their ancient cultural treasures is described as an exciting, even joyful, occasion (see Chapter 8, Enjoyment). The formal evidence of national events can provide this thrill: the piece of reinforced concrete that caused the collapse of the Ronan Point tower block flats in London in 1968, and led to the abandonment of a whole system of public building; the piece of the Comet airliner that in 1954 crashed into the sea off Sicily, and which led to the understanding of the phenomenon of metal fatigue (both objects in the stored collections of the Science Museum). In the National Museum of Ireland are displayed the touchingly home-made looking uniforms of people who fought in the Easter Rising in Dublin; around the walls are portraits of those who were executed, with their ages and dates of execution.

Collecting memory

History museums (broadly defined) have to grapple with people's expectations that they will collect memories. When the Museum of London's

Museum in Docklands first opened, it found that local people visited to tell the curators about photographs or other records of the past that they had. The visitors wanted to talk to a curator, who they saw as an authoritative figure who could provide a wider and perhaps validated context for their memories of working and living in the London docklands.[53] This is a common experience for curators of local or history museums.

The problem is that although an object may hold intense emotional and memory significance for one person, it does not belong in a museum collection unless it also serves collective memory. This is the traditional Western view, at any rate. But even here we see that military collections are a special case, perhaps on the grounds that if people have served the national purpose in this way they deserve special recognition. To construct a wider significance for an object, the experience of a person might be recorded orally or otherwise, or perhaps their belongings may be a good representation of a moment in the history of material culture. Or, as in the example of the *Local heroes* project (mentioned earlier) an object that was obviously familiar or significant to a famous person (national or local) might embody a flavour of their personality in the collective memory.

The significance of objects does not reside in them, but in the mind of the viewer. In archives, the objects constitute the meaning: with museum objects, the viewer (or the contextual material) does. John Fuller's poem, *Flea market*, expresses the sadness of seeing the dissipation of things that had born memories for someone (p. 82). Even among ethnic groups there will be wide disagreement between individuals about what is significant.[54] The most fruitful approach may be that developed in the SAMDOK programme in Sweden, in which thematic collecting groups decide on collecting strategies and coordinate efforts among museums.[55] In another approach, the Museum of London has adopted a series of themes, which are revised at intervals.[56]

Of course, benefits are not all one way: from the museum to its public. Many objects or even collections are poorly documented, and people can identify them or provide information about them, or contribute memories or knowledge to enrich the context for them. There are many ways in which museums can (and some do) facilitate and enable people to contribute to the richness of the collections: collaborative exhibition development; consultation and collaboration over new buildings and museum developments; witness seminars, in which those who have been involved in an event discuss or make presentations about their perception of it; positive projects such as *Local heroes*, described earlier. Many people like to contribute to a common pool of experience and memory.

This has implications for the processes of the museum. The act of collecting, of acquiring an object for the collection, traditionally the second role-defining moment for a curator (the first – the opening of their exhibit), is now much more clearly only the tip of the iceberg. May the days never return when a curator would object to the amount of information required: 'but it'll take so long we might miss acquiring another object'.[57]

As part of the process of widening the ownership of museums' collective memories, they need to adopt more of a brokering role than their previous didactic one. This is not an easy new approach to construct when museums are expected at the same time to maintain their long tradition as authoritative and trusted information providers. It seems that museums will have to learn the art of cultural arbitrage.

Conclusions

The museum plays two roles. As memory storehouse, the collections represent classification and preservation of memory and knowledge. As memory voice, the exhibits play an active role in constructing memories and identities for audiences. Memory acts at various levels: individual and family, social, and nation-state. Memory is not fixed: far from it, at every level memory is shifting, continually revised and reconstructed according to personal, social, and political context. Views of the past change dramatically over time, and written and recorded history is by no means immune to this. Museum collections serve the function of grounding histories and memories in physical objects, but paradoxically, the meaning of the object lies in the changing perception of the viewer.

Museums can play a powerful role in society and in building memory and identity.[58] They can be major providers of the social glue that constructs personal, social, and national identities, maintains the social order and builds the social capital that enables us to collectively and individually succeed (see Chapter 10: Values).

From a Utopian perspective, museums deliver cultural benefits that serve and develop people's aspirations. They can enable each of us to create memories that share a little of those of people from other cultures and hence, to construct more inclusive and broader collective memories.[59] Their collections in particular can be seen as having the potential to legitimize the whole range of cultures in society.

The darker converse is that in representing some identities and not others, museums can exclude. People respond by neither visiting museums nor using their services[60]. Museums can also serve a social engineering function. Behind every benign political utterance about social inclusion and opportunity lies the same nineteenth century *realpolitik* that if the 'socially excluded' visit museums they may acquire more desirable social habits and be more economically valuable[61] (see Chapter 10: Values).

Hence, museums are some of the most powerful history institutions (more so than libraries and archives, which do not interpret and communicate in the same way). Some of the quite dramatic changes in museums during the late 1990s and the early 2000s are due to the revision of the histories they represent, for instance shedding the colonialist perspective. As Coser wrote, 'the past is a social construction, mainly, if not wholly, shaped by the concerns of the present'. He cautioned: '… the present generation may re-write history, but it does not do so on a blank page'.[62] Coser wrote in the recent recollection of the fall of Stalinism. He described the way in which citizens of the Soviet Union had had to expunge their earlier views (memories) of politicians as wicked and re-invent them as heroic individuals. Perspectives on communism are again under revision. The Museum of Communism in Prague is welcomed in a 2002 *Newsweek* report as '*A tribute to barren shops*'.[63] Its advertising flyer is illustrated by the face of Stalin, directions to it are, ironically, '*above McDonald's, next to Casino*', its strap line, '*Dream, reality, nightmare*'. Collections offer a grounding in real, physical things even though the objects in them may be given new meanings.

Do we need collections for memory and identity, or will exhibits and participatory programmes do instead? Do we need so much stuff? Toffler expressed as 'future shock' our urgent need to maintain continuity with our past as a means of coping with the *tsunami* of new experiences and goods.[64] Social history collections are those that it is most often argued could be reduced through disposal. We have seen that they are some of those that particularly constitute memories, both individual and collective (see also Chapter 5: Ongoing learning). Collections and memories are intensely personal: we have found that people are not infrequently moved to tears by encounters with objects. At the same time, collections build collective memories and public histories. At a time when the concept of the nation-state is challenged by the forces of globalization and the emergent communication technologies, perhaps this is not the moment to start a wholesale jettisoning of the basic memory cells – the objects in the collections – however imperfect the assemblage and however redundant some of them may seem to present revisionists.

Notes

[1]Trevelyan, V. (ed.) (1991). *Dingy places with different kinds of bits: an attitudes survey of London museums among non-visitors*. London Museums Service.

Bott, V. (2003). *Reflections: mapping cultural diversity in London's local authority museum collections*. London Museums Agency.

[2]DCMS (2001). *The historic environment: a force for our future*. Department of Culture, Media & Sport, pp. 7–8.

Interview: *Chippenham Museum & Heritage Centre.* Beverley Hoff, Assistant Curator. 14 June 2004.

[3]Coser, L. (1992). Introduction. In *On collective memory* (M. Halbwachs) pp. 1–34. University of Chicago Press. pp. 20–22.

[4]Thwaites, P. (1996). *Presenting arms: museum representation of British military history, 1600 – 1900.* Leicester University Press. p. 1.

Coombes, A. (1998). Museums and the formation of national and cultural identities. *In Museum studies: an anthology of contexts* (B.M. Carbonell, ed., 2004) pp. 231–46.

[5]Interviewee quoted in Trevelyan, ed. (1991) p. 49.

[6]Winzen, M. (1998). Collecting – so normal, so paradoxical. In *Deep Storage: collecting, storing and archiving in art* (I. Schaffner and M. Winzen, eds) pp. 22–32, Prestel-Verlag. p. 22.

[7]Berger, J. (1972). *Ways of seeing.* BBC and Penguin. Ch. 5.

[8]Harwit, M. (1996). *An exhibit denied: lobbying the history of Enola Gay.* Copernicus. p. 423.

[9]Human Remains Report *(2003). Report of the Working Group on Human Remains.* Department of Culture, Media & Sport.

Website: *National NAGPRA Online Databases.* National Park Service, National Centre for Cultural Resources. US Department of the Interior. http://web.cast.uark.edu/other/nps/nagpra/

[10]Sutton, J. (1998). *Philosophy and memory traces: Descartes to connectionism.* Cambridge University Press. Chapter. 1.

[11]Samuel, R. (1994). *Theatres of memory.* p. vii. Verso.

[12]Downer, L. (1990). *On the narrow road into the deep north.* Sceptre. p. 50.

[13]Mack, J. (2003). *The museum of the mind.* British Museum Press.

[14]Samuel (1994). pp. x-ix. (See note 11)

[15]Harris, T. (2000). *Hannibal.* pp. 286–289 Dell Publishing Company.

[16]For example, Mack (2003). Chapter 1. (See note 13)

[17]Mack (2003). (See note 13)

[18]Exhibit: Royal Museum for Central Africa, near Brussels. *Congo: nature and culture.* 2004-5.

[19]Baudrillard, J. (1968). *The system of objects* (trans. J. Benedict from La Système des objects, Editions Galliard, 1968). p. 16. Verso, 1996.

[20]Coser (1992). p. 21. (See note 3)

[21]Halbwachs, 1992: p. 40. (See note 3)

[22]Coser, 1992: 22. (See note 3)

Crane, S. (2000). Introduction: of museums and memory. In *Museums and memory* (S. Crane, ed.) pp. 1–16, Stanford University Press, p. 6.

[23]Harris, H. (2000). Remembering 12 000 Years of History in Canada: The Oral History of Northwestern North America. Paper delivered in: *CIDOC 2000. Collaboration, content, convergence: sharing heritage knowledge for the new millennium. August 22–24, Ottawa, Canada.* ICOM: CIDOC.
http://www.chin.gc.ca/Resources/Cidoc/English/index.html

[24]Samuel (1994). p. x. (See note 11)

[25]Halbwachs (1992). p. 47. (See note 3)

[26]Hooper-Greenhill, E. (1992). *Museums and the shaping of knowledge.* Routledge. p. 78.

[27]Checkland, P. (1981). *Systems thinking, systems practice.* John Wiley & Sons. Chapters 2 and 3.

[28]Interview: *Museum of London.* C. Ross, Head of Department of Later London History. 3 December 2004.

[29]Halbwachs (1992). p. 47. (See note 3)

[30]Hooper-Greenhill (1992). p. 9. (See note 26)

[31]For example, see Hooper-Greenhill (2000). *Museums and the shaping of visual culture.* Routledge. p. 162.

[32]Interview: *Museum of London.* F. Grew, Curator, Department of Early London History. 11 June 2004.

[33]Dominy, G. (2000). South Africa: Collecting the material culture of apartheid and resistance: the Natal Museum's Amandla Project, 1992–94. In *Museums & history in West Africa* (C. Ardouin and E. Arinze, eds) pp. 5–17, James Currey.

[34]Crane (2000). p. 2. (See note 22)

[35]Exhibit in the Jake Jackson Museum & History Centre, Weaverville, California.

[36]Wilson, D. Drake (2000). Realizing memory: transforming history. In Crane, pp. 115–136. (See note 22)

Brodie, N. *et al.* (2000). *Stealing history: the illicit trade in cultural material.* Commissioned by ICOM UK and The Museums Association. McDonald Institute for Archaeological Research.

[37]Memory sessions are thoroughly reviewed in Kavanagh, G. (2000). *Dream spaces: memory and the museum.* Leicester University Press. Chapter 8.

[38]Csikszantmihalyi, M. (1993). Why we need things. In *History from things* (S. Lubar and W.D. Kingery, eds) pp. 20–29. Smithsonian Institution.

[39]Crane, (2000), p. 2. (See note 22)

[40]Poovaya, N. (1998). Keys to the magic kingdom. In *Colonialism and the object: empire, material culture and the museum* (T.Barringer and T.Flynn, eds) pp. 111–125. Routledge. p. 115.

[41]McLeod, M. (2004). Museums without collections: museum philosophy in West Africa. In: *Museums and the future of collecting* (S. Knell, ed.), pp. 52–61. Ashgate. p. 56.

[42]Gostin, O. (1993). *Accessing the Dreaming: heritage, conservation and tourism at Mungo National Park.* Aboriginal Research Institute Publications. p. 32.

[43]Human Remains Report (2003). (See note 9)

[44]Interview: *UCL Institute of Archaeology.* P. Ucko, Director. 15 June 2004.

[45]Gostin (1993). (See note 42)

[46]Website: *Kennewick Man.* National Park Service, Archaeology and Ethnography Program. US Department of the Interior. http://www.cr.nps.gov/aad/kennewick/index.htm

[47]See number of examples in the papers in: Peers, L. and Brown, A. (2003). *Museums and source communities.* Routledge.

[48]Website: *Seahenge,* Flag Fen Bronze Age Centre. http://www.eastmidlands.info/flagfen/seahenge.htm

[49]Website: *Vietnam Veterans Memorial.* National Park Service, Archaeology and Ethnography Program. US Department of the Interior. http://www.nps.gov/mrc/indexvvm.htm

[50]Interviews: *The Tank Museum.* John Woodward, Director. 11 June 2004. David Willey, Head of Collections. 27 June 2004.

[51]Thwaites, P. (1996). *Presenting arms: museum representation of British military history, 160 – 1900.* Leicester University Press. pp. 16–17.

Interview: The Tank Museum, John Woodward. (See note 50)

[52]I am particularly grateful to David Willey for an extended interview. Interview: *The Tank Museum,* David Willey. (See note 50)

[53]Interview: *Museum of London.* F. Grew. (See note 32)

[54]Witcomb, A. (1997). On the side of the object: an alternative approach to debates about ideas, objects and museums. *Museum management and curatorship,* **16**, 4, 384–399.

[55]Steen, A. (1999). Samdok: tools to make the world visible. In *Museums and the future of collecting* (S. Knell, ed.), pp. 196–203. Ashgate.

[56]Reynolds, R. (2000). *Collecting 2000.* Museum of London.

[57]Personal experience in 2000.

[58]Anderson, B. (1995). *Imagined communities: reflections on the origin and spread of nationalism.* Verso. p.62.

[59]Trevelyan, ed. (1991). p. 47. (See note 1)

[60]Tissier, D. and Singh Nathoo, S. (2004). *Black and ethnic minority engagement with London's museums: telling it like it is.* ALM London.

[61]Henry Cole is often quoted in this context, for instance in Bennett, T. (1995). *The birth of the museum.* Routledge. p. 21.

[62]Coser (1992). p.25. (See note 3)

[63]Krosnar, K. (2002). A tribute to barren shops. *Newsweek, Atlantic Edition,* 11 February.

[64]Toffler, Alvin. *Future shock.* Bantam, 1971. Chapter 1.

7 Collections and creativity

This chapter explores the inspirational qualities of museum collections. They elicit a response through many forms of art – art itself, architecture, design, music and sound, literature. Many artists use museums and collections as the media for works they create. Creativity is not restricted to art, of course: technical design and invention are creative processes, too.

The idea of plucking objects out of their useful contexts and allocating them to tidy academic categories is quite odd. Once in the museum collection, it is obvious that the familiar object no longer has its same role in the world: if it is a chair like one at home, it is not to be sat on. The objects in museums have undergone a 'violent resocialization'.[1] The familiar and recognizable are juxtaposed with the unfamiliar and strange. To play with these ideas is a very creative process – to put together an odd assortment of objects, choosing them for reasons unrelated to their museum-assigned category – their shape or their colour, perhaps; to make collections of non-museum objects in order to explore the idea of the museum collection, and so on. The rigid classification system of the museum is an invitation to artists to disrupt it.

It is not only artistic creativity that is inspired by collections. Technical invention and creativity are central to the world today. Designers and engineers visit museum collections to discover how problems have been approached in the past or in order to draw on earlier designs.[2]

Theories of creativity

Creativity depends not only on a person's imagination and persistence at a point in time, but on being able to build on the results of previous creative endeavours. Richard Dawkins has put forward the idea of the meme, a unit of cultural inheritance that allows ideas to be passed down through generations, just as genes transmit physical characteristics.[3] To create cultures based on ideas and symbols, ideas must be crystallized, pinned down, and transmitted.[4] We are used to thinking of text- and word-based media as the main way of doing this. But we see first, and make the words to describe later.[5]

Things embody far more information than can be put into words. In the previous chapter the relationship of objects to memory and identity, both individual and collective, was discussed. Natural history specimens to this day are sent around the world on loan to enable new species to be identified. As collections and museums developed in seventeenth century Europe, objects were used as a means of understanding and codifying what was known about the world. In a sense it was the collection, not the component objects, that was the cultural message. But things that have been fabricated are an important means of cultural transmission. They carry information about the processes of their manufacture, about their use, and about what they symbolize.

Symbolic marks on decorative artefacts as well as artefacts have been interpreted by some as offering the earliest evidence of 'the moment in which images and concepts became more stable than neurons and synapses'.[6] Archaeological sites in many countries – in Africa, the Near East, and Europe – have produced pigments, bone fragments engraved with patterns and personal ornaments, from both Neanderthal cultures and those associated with the remains of anatomically modern humans. The earliest such artefacts are dated to around 37 000 years ago, from the Lower, Middle, and Upper Paleolithic.[7] 'The conscious use of material culture to store information is a fundamental feature of any specialized … intelligence'.[8] Objects, then, have a long history as transmitters and recorders of cultural information.

Examples

Early artefacts that have survived from between 20 000 and 35 000 years BP include musical instruments: two assemblages of bird bone pipes from Geissenklösterle, Germany, and Isturitz, France. They have chamfered finger holes that are offset for musical fingering, and may have had reed mouthpieces as do the modern clarinet or oboe. At least two of the pipes have these features in common even though they are separated in time by hundreds or even thousands of years. It is suggested that these artefacts demonstrate the transmission of technical invention.[9]

Things have long been consciously used in this way. Religious objects have been used since the earliest of times to transmit ideas about what should be venerated and about how religions should be observed. Natural history specimens underpin knowledge and under-standing of the natural world. Objects have been used to demonstrate technology, design, and invention, too. The use of models is a sign of the primacy of tangible, visual representations. For example in the US and in the UK, an application for a patent had to be accompanied by a model until towards the end of the nineteenth century when it was finally deemed impractical.[10]

The art of the collection

The infinitely many different meanings of the museum collection are above all explored and uncovered by artists.[11] Artists are intrigued by the idea and concept of the museum, by its processes (categorizing, cataloguing, storing, transporting), and by the idea of interfering with the carefully controlled official story and flow of existing exhibitions. They understand very well the function of the museum in expressing social power and dominance, and hence the impact of disrupting this in some way.[12] The art work, *The sculpture of the Grant Museum* (an example is shown in Fig. 7.1) used a sound guide commentary to describe some of the displayed zoological specimens as though they were art works.

Photo: S. Keene

Fig. 7.1 *The sculpture of the Grant Museum. Brittle stars and starfish. Exhibit 3 in the sound artwork, by Ann Byrne and Dan Smith.*
'These massless bodies have been made visible through the effective exploitation of their inherent flatness. The thin, pentagonal shapes are held in place between the fibrous background and glass foreground, composed with both harmony and sobriety. The flatness is suggestive of a picture plane that is neither too casual or overly laboured, but is instead one that has been arranged with skilful consideration. The positioning of the constitutent pieces suggests a set of swirling movements, and the subtle use of colour avoids garish polychromy in favour of a sensitive opposition, and it is this contrast that defines the finest details along the thin, wispy tentacles'

Startling at first, because the visitor is expecting a scientific discourse, this suggested that there were completely different ways of enjoying the collection.[13] Many of these explorations use the concepts encountered in Chapter 6: Memory and identity.

From Yves Klein's *Le vide,* a completely empty white-painted space, to Arman's *Le plein,* a room in the same gallery stuffed completely full of detritus collected from the streets of Paris in the 1950s, to Thom Barth's toppled glass gallery-within-a-gallery in Vienna, artists have explored the perception of the museum space. There are many examples of artworks constructed within or as exhibitions, either as installations or as trails where the visitor is guided through an unexpected series of objects. So far these experiences have been situated in museums or galleries – they could be an exciting way to explore stored collections.

Some artists use the concept of the formally categorized scientific collection. Allan McCollum, exploring taxonomic systems, contrasted plaster casts of classical sculptures on display with a huge assemblage of casts of dinosaur bones in the Carnegie Museum of Art, Pittsburg (*Lost objects,* 1991). Mark Dion's work, *Tate Thames dig* (1999–2000), consists of a vaguely museum-style cabinet containing finds from an exercise in which assistants collected finds from the Thames foreshore and sorted them into categories. Other artists' collections are similar to those that would be assembled by a history curator. For example, Nikolaus Lang's exploration of the grouping and classification of artefacts: *For Mrs. G. Legacy – food and religious hoard* (1981–82) is a vast collection of material found in an old lady's house. Others are Jeffrey Vallance's *The Nixon museum* and *The traveling Nixon museum* (1991), collections of memorabilia and trivia. Ironically, these artworks depend on fixed and frozen assemblages of objects, although this characteristic is one of the most tempting targets of attack for artists.

Artists are also interested in the stored collections and the hidden processes of the museum. Andy Warhol exploited the idea of collections stored away (kept on ice?) – *Raid the icebox* (1970). He insisted on using whole portions of the collection – all the shoes, crammed into their storage racks, and all the chairs, for instance. (Rather like the precautionary clean underwear one is meant to wear in case one is run down by a bus, we had better make sure our stores look neat in case some passing artist takes a creative fancy to them. Or should we, rather, aim for creative chaos and imaginative juxtapositions?). A large multi-site exhibition in the late 1990s, *Deep Storage,* explored the artistic theme of collecting and archiving from the 1960s onwards.[14] Marcel Duchamp's *Boîtes-en-valises,* made in the 1940s, are assemblages of objects within unfolding cases that are meant to recall museum packing cases.

Even the less celebrated internal workings of museums can be captured as art – *Incident at the museum, or water music* (1992), an installation by Ilya

Kabakov, uses buckets and sheets of polyethylene draped over objects. Dario Lanzardo took the opportunity to capture the poetic character of objects in store in wonderful (published) photographic studies of the move and temporary storage of collections of the Natural History Museum, Turin.[15]

New media

Museums and collections are important to the growing digital media arts sector. Museums have been enthusiastic about the web, and many now have websites and are clients of new media designers. New media exhibits are commonplace in displays. The Design Museum, London, the Cooper-Hewitt, Washington, and others worldwide are already adding new media and digital items to their collections. Museums are doubly important because they are about the only chance for the long-term survival of these completely virtual works, which are, in essence, new components of the intangible heritage.

Digital media have an enormous potential, not yet exploited at all seriously, for enlivening, explaining, and enhancing access to collections. Technologies that can be used to link people and collections in real places, that get away from keyboards and screens, could be revelationary. Another challenge for designers in digital media will be that posed by online collections. As the internet evolves, the pressure will grow on museums to list their collections online. One argument often used against this is that collections are too boring to interest people: here is where new media designers and artists could come to the rescue.

Collections, design, and technology

Collections of decorative art objects are extensively drawn on by designers. Indeed this is at the very heart of the Victoria & Albert Museum's mission. Designers are encouraged to learn from and draw on its collections through exhibitions like *Designing in the digital age* (2000) and *Radical fashion* (2001), and through partnerships with universities and colleges (see Chapter 5). The V & A operates the National Library and the National Archive of Art and Design. As a contrasting local example, the Adivart State Museum of Tribal and Folk Art in Khajuraho, India, aims to present examples of the vibrant tribal and indigenous arts and crafts of the region and act as a design development centre, to build links between urban and rural people, to provide a new market for craftspeople, and to also be a source of new techniques that they can use.[16]

The Cooper-Hewitt Museum, the US National Design Museum, 'believes that design shapes our objects, environments, and communications, making them more desirable, functional, and accessible'.[17]

Museums have a valuable role in promoting cross-disciplinary partner-ships between design and technology: for example, a symposium was organized by the Cooper-Hewitt in 2005, *Extreme textiles*, dealing with new textile technologies.

It is not only the decorative arts that serve creativity. Among visitors to study the collections of the Tank Museum are technologists and engineers who want to investigate past solutions to particular design and engineer-ing problems.[18]

Stories from collections

Collections and authors

The idea of treasure – a particular type of collection – is a recurring theme in literature from the earliest times. Treasure, guarded by a fierce, terrify-ing dragon, is a theme in the Saxon poem, Beowulf, possibly written in the eighth century AD (see poem, page 119). Centuries before that, perhaps around the eighth century BC (the date is debated), Homer depicted the treasure of Troy. Many other early writers described treasure.

Henry James was an early adherent of museum exhibitions. The Grand Gallerie in the Louvre, which he visited when he was young, made a deep impression on him: for some reason he had a vivid nightmare about it 55 years later. Museums feature in many of his novels. Although exhi-bitions provide him with creative material James makes only passing references to private collections and does not exploit this concept.[19] The same is true of James Joyce – possibly for less elevated reasons. Museums, in particular the museum in Kildare Street, Dublin, now the National Museum of Ireland, get a number of mentions in Ulysses, largely on account of the sparsely clothed female statues to be admired there. In connection with Leopold Bloom's schemes for social regeneration,

> The keeper of the Kildare Street Museum appears, dragging a lorry on which are the shaking statues of several naked goddesses, Venus Callipyge, Venus Pandemos, Venus Metempsychosis, and plaster figures, also naked, representing the new nine muses, Commerce, Operatic Music, Amor Publicity, Manufacture, Liberty of Speech, Plural Voting, Gastronomy, Private Hygiene, Seaside Concert Entertainments, Painless Obstetrics and Astronomy for the People.[20]

A few extra inspirational muses there, then, which would raise eyebrows if they appeared in the museum's corporate plan.

Writers continue to be intrigued by the idea of collections. The *Phantom Museum* is a collection of short stories by various authors all inspired by the Wellcome Collection, now in the care of the Science Museum, London, and it is the actual stored collections and the store itself that are the subject.[21] The Wellcome collection is an extraordinary phenomenon: it was amassed by Sir Henry Wellcome up to his death in 1936. Sir Henry sent out agents worldwide, instructing them to collect objects to do with medicine, of whatever date or kind. The consequence is that the main part of the Wellcome Collection, in the Science Museum, includes everything from prehistoric stone and ceramic objects through classical and ethnographic collections to more traditional types of objects such as medicine chests, surgical instruments, and dental equipment – an enormous assemblage that is in itself wonderfully artistic. (The dental furniture collection retains the characteristic smell of dentists' rooms long gone, upsetting if you are nervous about visits to the dentist. Another collection that has an historic smell is the railway carriages in the National Railway Museum – tobacco smoke and old cooking.)

Other works include detective stories. For instance in Colin Dexter's book *The daughters of Cain*, Inspector Morse solves a murder carried out using a knife from a display in the Pitt Rivers Museum, Oxford.[22] Poetry, too, is inspired by collections, and a few notable examples are published in this book.

Collections and films

Museums and museum objects have been popular with film-makers from 1920, and no doubt earlier. About 266 films involving museums have been tracked down in other research.[23] A search of the many thousands of films listed on the *Internet Movie Database* reveals 198 films with plot summaries containing the word 'museum'.[24] The earliest film that I found is *My lady's garter* (1920): '*A thief known as The Hawk has stolen the treasured Garter from the British Museum. One of the men pursuing the thief is mistakenly thought to be The Hawk himself, and so must seek his quarry while himself being hunted*'. This is typical of two common themes, theft from a museum and the British Museum. *Topkapi* (1964) is another well-known example of the theft genre – raiders target the Topkapi Museum in Istanbul.

Another frequent theme is an ancient object that comes to life or turns out to house some sort of malign spirit. The 1932 animation, *Betty Boop*, has Betty locked in a museum overnight and made to sing at the skeletons' dance. In *Ghostbusters II* (1989) a sinister painting comes to life while under the hands of the picture restorer. The year 2001 brought trouble with mummies to both the British Museum and the Louvre: *The mummy returns* has the British Museum rashly acquiring the mummy Imhotep which comes to life and walks forth seeking immortality, while scientists in the Louvre inadvertently activate the spirit Belphégor (*Belphégor – le fantôme du Louvre*) by using a laser scanner on a sarcophagus.

Other well-known films featuring museums include comedies such as the incomparable *Bringing up baby* (1938), with Cary Grant and Katherine Hepburn embroiled in a dinosaur bone for a museum collection, a baby leopard and each other, and thrillers such as *The Thomas Crowne affair*, where the challenge is to steal a Monet painting from an art museum. In science fiction we have *Star Trek, Superman,* and a Popeye film, *Rocket to Mars* (1946), with possibly the most inventive storyline yet. Popeye and Olive Oyle are visiting a science museum, when Olive Oyle accidentally launches one of the objects – a rocket ship – to Mars, with Popeye aboard. On reaching Mars, Popeye discovers a plot to destroy the earth. He manages to frustrate this plan, aided by ingesting a can of spinach in the usual way.

The celebrated film-maker Peter Greenaway deals with museums in a different manner, more like the artists discussed earlier. He has curated exhibitions, and admires 'the potency of real objects' at the expense of the 'phoniness, fakery, and pretence' of film. In an exhibition of objects to do with measurement he speaks of 'objects exhibited as [film] properties, but not invented – with a history and provenance' and 'organizing principles – that's what civilization is all about … ordering the chaos'.[25] Greenaway sees his films as strongly related to museums; for example, a 1992 television programme, *Darwin*, consists of eighteen dense tableaux representing Charles Darwin's Down House, or possibly a representative nineteenth century scholarly writing place. The room setting display/film set is enlivened through lighting schemes, important to Greenaway. There are also a parade of animals and a variety of displays for instance, of paleontology.[26]

It might be imagined that museum collections would be a source for researching props and scenery for movies, but authenticity is not a high priority for today's myth makers. 'It's the illusion of authenticity that people like. They want things to feel authentic, but they really don't care about the details'. Ridley Scott, the director of the successful film *Gladiator*, when told that ancient Romans probably never had pavement cafés, is said to have declared that he would therefore be filming 'the first coffee bar in Roman history'.[27] Television features such as *Pompeii* (2003) or *Rome* (2005), or the many TV versions of novels such as those of Jane Austen, do use museum collections to research costume, for example. It can work the other way round, though; when *Gladiator* was released a complementary exhibition was displayed in the British Museum (and other countries) featuring collections objects to do with gladiators. On the whole, the exhibition made the film seem quite convincing.

Films featuring museums are on the whole, not serious ones. They are mostly comedies, mild thrillers, romances, and horror movies, with a few disaster movies and detective films. Nevertheless, they speak clearly to the popular perception of the museum: a place apart from normal, everyday life; dusty, dark, mysterious, with arcane processes being carried out by strange obsessive curators and näive restorers and scientists. Neither exhibitions nor collections in store are the focus: 'the museum' is a sort of composite of both, and its psychological depiction is of a place where surprising and extraordinary things can happen – a place with hidden depths and many secrets.

Collections, music, and sound

Collections of musical instruments are inspirational in a number of ways. Instruments kept unrestored enable new replicas to be created that are faithful to past designs and techniques. In this way they underpin the early music movement. Collections can inspire performances and even compositions that use the particular historic nature of the instruments.[28] Literally using collections objects is controversial, however, unless the object has already been altered so much that it is more or less a replica – an issue that is further discussed in Chapter 3: Collections and Chapter 5: Ongoing learning.

As an example of a collection that is principally for use, the Royal Academy of Music lends selected instruments such as its Stradivari violins to prominent musicians to use in performances, and it also offers a lively programme of performances, workshops, and seminars for students, staff, and public.[29] Many other collections also allow their instruments to be used in performances. On the other hand, the Horniman Museum does not allow its instruments to be played. Instead it illustrates its collections in its Music Gallery through a new media interactive exhibit that allows an example of any selected instrument to be heard as being played in its own country by indigenous musicians (illustrated in Fig. 9.1). Musicians from abroad now visit the Horniman collections to see examples of instruments that are rare in their countries. In the Musical Instrument Museum in Brussels, instruments can be heard through headphones as one walks around the showcases. These are good examples of the intangible heritage (the recorded performances) enriching the tangible, using digital technologies.

Sound installations in galleries are sometimes part of art installations. Kabakov's *Incident at the museum, or water music* (as mentioned earlier) has an accompanying sound composition of the appropriate kind (drips). In the Grant Museum of Zoology, the sound guide comments not on the scientific attributes of skeletons, shells, and mammoth hair, but as though they were art works (see Fig. 7.1).[30] Some people find this entrancing: others are baffled and annoyed. These examples are within exhibitions – the potential of using electronic sound guides with collections in stores has not been exploited at all.

Collections as places

Each collection has a characteristic appearance and landscape, depending on the type of collection, its size, the museum that owns it, and the way in which it is accessed and used. Three of the London national museums share a building – a large converted Victorian office structure – for storing their collections. Each section of the building has a very different feel, according to which museum collection it houses. A collection can be experienced as a place.

Museum buildings

One of the world's outstanding buildings was inspired by collections: Alfred Waterhouse's Natural History Museum in London, completed in 1880 after ten years of planning. The Victorian German Romanesque style chosen by Waterhouse permitted the rich decoration of every surface with natural forms, exploiting the characteristics of the terracotta facing material. An evocation of Fingal's Cave in west Scotland greets the visitor in the entrance portal. The bare iron and glass over the central hall displays the building materials themselves. All sorts of animals, birds, and plants twine and climb around the columns and over every surface. At each level, one finds new examples of natural forms and material: the sills between the high level arches are each made from a different kind of rock; ceilings are covered in tiles illustrating British flora. The whole building expresses the natural world and the collections (seventy million specimens) as such a rich and bountiful resource that one could never hope to fully appreciate the whole. But we must be wary of these impressions. Victorian celebrations of the diversity of Creation, whether in a building or in a collection, illustrate a common moral to do not only with the essential goodness of nature, but also its availability to us for exploitation.[31]

The absence of objects can be as eloquent as their presence. In Berlin, Libeskind's Holocaust Museum was at first empty of exhibits. The absence of objects stood for the absence of people. In the holocaust exhibition in the Imperial War Museum, London, worn shoes cast into a pile said to the visitor that their owners were gone.

Contemporary art and art museums, and the art to be displayed in them have a reciprocal influence. The art works created, often in response to public exhibition spaces, take advantage of the scale and dynamics of the building. Buildings in turn respond to the nature of the art.[32] One of the best examples must be Tate Modern where works of enormous size are required to make any impact in the generator hall of the ex-power station.

The architecture of collections

The tradition of designing stores for treasured collections goes back at least to the Shôsô-in in Nara, Japan (see Fig. 1.1). The Shôsô-in was built in the eighth century to house the imperial Japanese treasures, particularly from China, then seen as the source of high culture, but also from other countries with which Japan had contact – Persia, India, and Greece. The building is constructed of cedar baulks, with joints designed to close in humid conditions and open in the dry to ensure a clement climate for its precious contents. (The same principle is followed today for personal kimono chests.) Although the Shôsô-in is still there, its contents have, sadly, despite more than 1200 years of preservation in their original building, been transferred to a nearby concrete building with mechanical climate control.

The design of buildings for museum collections is predictably less flamboyant than that for public museums. In general, it is only quite recently that collections stores have been designed as buildings separate from the museum. As late as the 1960s, the Museum of London was opened with the intention that the whole of the collections should be stored within its building in the City of London. This was impractical from well before the day it opened.

The design challenges offered by collections can inspire an interesting architectural response. Sometimes only a straightforward warehouse type store is required, as at the UK Science Museum's site at Wroughton in Wiltshire, but often the store is constructed as part of a new museum development. Notable buildings are to be found all over the world.

The two curving buildings of the Canadian Museum of Civilization, opened in 1989, stand side by side overseeing the Ottawa River. One of the buildings houses the museum exhibition galleries; the other, the collections and offices. The beautiful and imaginative architectural design is based on the topography of the land at the time, over 15 000 years ago, when the Ice Age glaciers were melting and people first came to Canada. But it is highly functional, too: above all, the building had to meet the preservation needs of the collections – a stable climate in extreme outdoor temperature fluctuations, protection from theft, fire, and other dangers, and functional collections management. In the collections building the offices are constructed around the outside so as to buffer the climate for the collections housed in the central space [33] (see Fig. 11.2).

The Collections Resource Centre of the Smithsonian Institution's Museum of the American Indian, in Washington, D.C., is designed to preserve and also for use. It allows for collections objects to be used for viewing or for ceremonies. It includes an indoor ceremonial room and an outdoor ceremonial area. In Australia, another building including the storage of collections from indigenous cultures, Bunjilaka, part of the

Melbourne Museum, was similarly designed in collaboration with Aboriginal peoples.[34]

In London, the Natural History Museum Darwin Centre and in Paris, the Réserves of the Musée des Arts et Métiers in St Denis are both new buildings for collections (see Figs 11.1 and 1.2). The Darwin Centre is an addition to the Waterhouse building, with a supplementary function to allow a degree of public access to the collection through facilities for public lectures and guided tours. The Musée des Arts et Métiers Réserves is functional but imaginative. Enclosed in its aerofoil shapes are the French national collections of the history of science and technology, conservation workshops, and facilities for those wishing to research the collections.

At the Weald & Downland Open Air Museum near Chichester, UK, the Gridshell building is constructed using a framework of green oak lathes. Housing the collections, a conservation workshop, and space for education activities, it perfectly complements the technology of the historic buildings on site and has won a number of architectural awards (see Fig. 1.3).

The architecture of collection stores

A building for a museum is an opportunity for client and architect alike to make a strong cultural statement. Responding to the nature of the collection itself can be the source of the most creative architecture, when the museum has the vision to recognize its collections as a wonderful, creative, and inspirational resource.

Inspiration for the public

Clearly, collections are inspirational in many ways and to many people. The focus of this chapter has been on the use of museum collections by professional artists and designers. But it should not be forgotten that museums offer a plethora of outreach and visitor activities, and events so that the public, you, and I, can do creative and artistic things related to the collections (Figs. 7.2 and 7.3). Our children may be even better provided for than we are, but still there are arts events for all like *The Big draw*, a British national drawing events month, or community arts programmes like *Parallel journey* at Tate directed at people of any age and especially popular with senior citizens, or *Inspiration base: Antarctic fun* at Te Papa Tongarewa, the National Museum of New Zealand.

Discussion

Collections are drawn on in many creative ways. How can museums increase these uses? It is more and more common practice for museums

Photo: S. Keene

Fig. 7.2 *Mrs. Janet Knell, drawing, in the Grant Museum of Zoology, University College London. Mrs. Knell has been drawing natural history collections for a long while in the Natural History Museum, London, and now, in the Grant Museum*

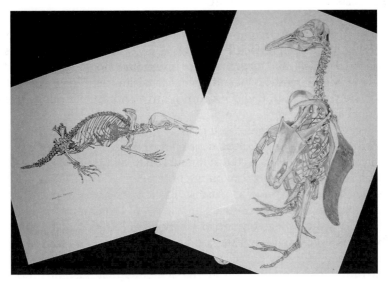

Fig. 7.3 *Drawings by Mrs. Janet Knell*

of every kind to set up artist in residence or writer in residence projects to promote and facilitate this use of collections. Straightforwardly, more artistic programmes such as these could be set up to specifically focus on stored collections.

Museums could be more positive about marketing their collections as a resource available to work with. All sorts of conventional museum events – new displays, galleries, conferences – could include a creative dimension. Creativity could assist the use of collections for the other purposes discussed in this book – research, education, enjoyment, memory, and identity – through making the existence of the collections better known and through devising imaginative ways of providing access. Other possible creative uses of collections are explored in Chapter 8: Enjoyment.

Funding and resources are a constraint. Artists have to have money to live: artistic projects have to be funded, and proper resources are needed if the collections are to be more accessible. But which is more likely to gain more resources: collections inaccessible in stores, little accessed and little known, or collections used as a live resource? There are many things that museums could do that do not require extra funding. Simply encouraging (and providing training) for all the staff in the museum to include the collections in their programmes and activities could achieve a lot.

Creative partnerships also need to be developed with relevant institutions and education courses. Naturally, the collections need to be managed so as to facilitate access to them in ways that will not cause them to deteriorate.

Conclusions

I agree with the artist, Mark Dion, of course: 'The museum needs to be turned inside out – the back rooms put on exhibition and the displays put into storage.'[35] Dion, hero to archaeologists because of the cultural glamour he has bestowed on their material, turns out to play that role for museum collections more generally.

Collections are more than just a classification system and a record: they are a medium, too. They play an important part in shaping people's imagination and ideas. It is well recognized that they have been used to construct and perpetuate social hierarchies and power structures. At present, they largely continue to express the societies of the past. But we depend on the evolution of ideas and ways of looking at the world as much as we do on the evolution of technology. In fact it is essential that our ideas develop so that we do not destroy ourselves through the application of science unmoderated by any human consideration. Cultural conservation, the organization of the activities that sustain traditional community life, is beginning to be seen as equally as necessary as environmental conservation for human survival.[36] Museum collections could be used towards this end.

Therefore, it is very important that artists take the museum's expressed received wisdom and turn it inside out, upside down, and juxtapose seemingly unrelated things. They should do more of this so as to shake us out of our accustomed ways of thinking and inspire creative ideas. And not only artists – we could all benefit from a more creative and playful relationship with the ideas we can find in collections.

Notes

[1]Preziosi, D. (2004). Brain of the earth's body: museums and the framing of modernity. In *Museum studies: an anthology of contexts* (B. Carbonell, ed.) pp. 71–84, Blackwell. p. 77.

Fisher, P. (1997). *Art and the future's past.* Harvard University Press. pp. 10–11.

[2]For example, those interviewed about the uses of collections at the Tank Museum, the Museum of London and the Royal Academy of Music all mentioned that people accessed the collections for these reasons.

Interviews: *The Tank Museum.* D. Willey, Head of Collections. 27 June 2004. *Royal Academy of Music.* F. Palmer, Curator of Collections. 9 June 2004. *Museum of London.* C. Ross, Head of Department of Later London History. 3 December 2004.

[3]Dawkins, R. (1989). *The selfish gene.* Oxford University Press. pp. 192–194.

[4]d'Errico, F. *et al.* (2003). Archaeological evidence for the emergence of language, symbolism, and music-an alternative multidisciplinary perspective. *Journal of World Prehistory*, **17**, No. 1, March 2003, 1–70.

[5]Robertson, I. (2003). *The mind's eye.* Bantam Books. Chapter 1.

[6]Changeux, 1983 cited in d'Errico *et al.* (2003). p. 32.

[7]d'Errico *et al.* (2003). pp. 3–6. (See note 4)

[8]Mithen 1996, cited in d'Errico *et al.* (2003). pp. 1–70. (See note 4)

[9]d'Errico *et al.* (2003). pp. 39–48. (See note 4)

[10]Website: *Rothschild Petersen Patent Model Museum.* http://www.patentmodel.org/History.aspx

[11]Putnam, J. (2001). *Art and artifact: the museum as medium.* Thames & Hudson, pp. 8–31. This book is a comprehensive survey of the subject. Examples below are drawn from it unless otherwise referenced.

[12]McShine, K. (1999). *The museum as muse: artists reflect.* Museum of Modern Art, New York, pp. 11–23.

[13]Chatterjee, H. and Wallace, M. (2003). *The sculpture of the Grant Museum: a wunderkammer project by Ann Byrne and Dan Smith.* UCL Art Collections.

[14]Schaffner, I. and Winzen, M. (1998). *Deep storage: collecting, storing, and archiving in art.* Prestel.

[15]Lanzardo, D. (1998). *Arca Naturae: le collezioni 'Invisibili' del Museo Regionale di Scienze Naturali di Torino.* Mondadori.

[16]Interview: M. Thomson and F. Keene, July 2004, and museum brochure.

[17]Website: *Smithsonian, Cooper-Hewitt, National Design Museum.* http://ndm.si.edu/INFORMATION/index.html

[18]Interview: *The Tank Museum,* David Willey. (See note 2)

[19]Titner, A.R. (1986). *The museum world of Henry James.* pp. 6–7, UMI Research Press.

[20]Joyce, J. (1922). *Ulysses.* Shakespeare. Episode 15, Circe.

[21]Hawkins, H. and Olsen, D., eds (2003). *The Phantom Museum and Henry Wellcome's collection of medical curiosities.* Profile.

[22]Dexter, C. (1995). *The daughters of Cain.* Crown Publishing.

[23]Hall, M. (2000). In the popular gaze: museums in the movies. In *Researching material culture* (S. Pearce, ed.) pp. 87–115. Material Culture Research Group, Occasional papers, No. 1. University of Leicester: School of Archaeological Studies, pp. 113–115.

[24]All examples from plot synopses on the website: *Internet movie database.* http://www.imdb.com/

[25]Pascoe, D. (1997). *Peter Greenaway: museums and moving images.* Reaktion, pp. 197, 208.

[26]Website: *Greenaway: Darwin.* http://petergreenaway.co.uk/darwin.htm

[27]Quotations from Winner, D. (2005). A blow to the temples. *The Financial Times, FTmagazine.* Issue no. 90, 29 January, p. 34.

[28]Interview: *Royal Academy of Music.* F. Palmer. (See note 2)

Arnold Foster, K. and La Rue, H. (1993). *Museums of music.* Museums & Galleries Commission.

[29]Interview: *Royal Academy of Music.* F. Palmer. (See note 2)

Notable musical instrument collections and their policies on playing their instruments are listed on: Website: CIMCIM. *ICOM International Committee of Musical Instrument Museums and Collections.* http://www.music.ed.ac.uk/euchmi/cimcim/

[30]Chatterjee, H. and Wallace, M. (2003). *The sculpture of the Grant Museum: a wunderkammer project by Ann Byrne and Dan Smith.* UCL Art Collections.

[31]Yanni, C. (1999). *Nature's museums : Victorian science and the architecture of display.* Johns Hopkins University Press.

[32]Putnam (2001). p. 184. (See note 11)

[33]Website: *Canadian Museum of Civilization.* Written in the stone: an architectural tour of the Canadian Museum of Civilization. http://www.civilization.ca/cmc/architecture/tour12e.html, and /tour15e.html.

[34]Fookes, R. (2003). Museum design for Aboriginal collections. *ICOM News,* no. 3, p. 4.

[35]Corrin, L.G. *et al.* (1997). *Mark Dion.* p.17, Phaidon.

[36]Kreps, F.C. (2003). *Liberating culture.* p. 13, Routledge.

Beowulf: the treasure and the dragon

Extracts from the translation by Howard D. Chickering, Jr.

Lines 2752–2775
Wiglaf son of Weohstan has killed the dragon that guarded the treasure in the barrow, but Beowulf has been mortally wounded in the fight. Wiglaf enters the barrow to see the treasure.

Then, as I have heard,   Weohstan's son,
hearing the words   of his wounded ruler,
quickly obeyed him,   took his link-shirt,
ringed battle-webbing,   under the barrow's roof.
Once past the seat,   the victorious thane
—brave young kinsman—   saw red gold, jewels,
glittering treasure   lying on the ground,
wondrous wall-hangings;   in the den of the serpent,
the old dawn-flier,   stood golden beakers,
an ancient service,   untended, unpolished,
its garnets broken.   Helmets lay heaped,
old and rusted,   and scores of arm-rings
skillfully twisted.   How easily jewels,
gold in the earth,   can overcome anyone,
hide it who will—   heed it who can!
There he also saw   a golden standard
hanging over the hoard,   intricate weaving
of wondrous skill;   a light came from it
by which he could see   the whole treasure-floor,
gaze on the jewels.   There was no more sign
of the dragon, now dead.   Then, as I've heard,
alone in the barrow,   he rifled the hoard,
old work of giants,   loaded an armful
of gold cups and dishes,   chose as he pleased,
took the standard too,   the brightest emblem.

Lines 3030–3055

The warriors go to see the results of the great battle with the dragon. Beowulf and the dragon lie on the with the treasure beside them, with death's chill over all.

The company rose,   went down unhappily
under Eagles' Cliff   to look with tears
at the awesome sight.   On the sand they found,
at his hard rest,   with life-soul gone,
the man who had given them   their rings many times.
The terrible armor   of the shining dragon
was scorched by his flames.   In length he measured
fifty foot-paces.   Once he controlled
the air in joys,   had ridden on the wind
throughout the night,   then flew back down
to seek his den.   Now he lay there,
stiff in death,   found no more caves.
Beside him were piled   pitchers and flagons,
dishes in heaps,   and well-wrought swords
eaten by rust,   just as they had lain
in the deeps of the earth   for a thousand years.

8 Collections for enjoyment

It would be possible to lose sight of the fact that collections can simply be highly enjoyable: they can be great fun. The mixture of objects, the bizarre juxtapositions, things one never knew were needed or existed, all combine to make a richer picture of the world, or vivid connections to the past. This was the basis for the *Wunderkammer:* the Cabinet of Curiosities. Objects from a Wunderkammer collection, natural and artificial 'wonders' donated by Marquis Ferdinando Cospi in 1675, including a unicorn horn (in fact a narwhal tusk), are still displayed in the Museo Civico Medievale, Bologna, now to be marvelled at as a glimpse of past ways of seeing things. There are various ways in which people can enjoy the collections other than through exhibits. Stores tours, visitable storage, visible storage, events using collections objects, activities where people or groups can use collections directly are some of them. This chapter will explore the question of how more people could enjoy more of the collections.

Michael Ames in 1985 wrote an eloquent plea for wider and more open access to the collections.[1] He argued that this was the way to counter the widely recognized elitist nature of museums. Access, he wrote, is otherwise highly structured, predetermined, and controlled by museum professionals so as to be 'correct', 'safe', 'understandable', and 'educational', criticizing: 'the arrogance to assume that we serve our visitors by offering intellectual access to less, not more, and the less to be of our expert choosing'.[2] Finding ways of making the collections more openly available is key to being able to show that they are useful.

Most people have no idea that collections exist at all, other than what is on display. A number of studies indicate this, in the US, Australia, and recently the UK.[3] From the US study it was also concluded that there was little curiosity about them. In contrast, the Australian work found that people were interested in finding out about particular objects in more depth, although results are not reported for interest in the collections as a whole. In the UK study, three-quarters of visitors to the visitable store had not known about it beforehand. However, after visiting, 86 per cent said they would like to return.[4]

How and what we enjoy

The term *enjoyment* has connotations of relaxation, but of engagement too. An enjoyable encounter with collections would not be a daunting experience but it would be interesting and engaging, not dull and boring. So what makes an experience enjoyable? Or, conversely, unenjoyable? How can the objects be made interesting? And what do people like or dislike about their experiences of museums?

What people do and do not like about visiting museums is well understood. Whether you visit museums frequently, occasionally, or never depends, of course, on who you are and what you are: your social, educational, and economic circumstances. It also depends on whether you are seeking a quiet, contemplative experience – essentially solitary – or a lively outing with family and friends.

Social theorists have analysed the role of the museum in expressing and controlling social relationships. Bourdieu and Darbel in the 1960s established that a visit to an art museum gave some people a sense of cultural ownership and belonging, while others felt inferior and excluded.[5] The architecture and space syntax of many museums and the behaviour that is expected of visitors combine to make them feel like places outside normal everyday experience. Other museums, more ordinary and less daunting, fail on other grounds: in a typical response to an enquiry into London museum visiting, they were condemned as 'dingy places with different kinds of bits'.[6]

These research findings are confirmed by other empirical work. A survey in the USA in 1983 identified three population segments: frequent visitors, occasional visitors, and those who never visit museums at all. Another one in the UK in 2001 used the same three categories.[7] In both cases, decisions to visit or not to visit depended on people's perceptions and expectations of the museum.

Figure 8.1 depicts the results of a psychological survey of people's perceptions. No wonder many are reluctant to visit a museum if the best that can be said of it is that it has, physically, exhibits, rooms, and staff. Interestingly, the psychological perception of the museum as watchful, dark, static, is the way that 'the museum' is portrayed in films (see Chapter 7: Creativity).

Factors other than perceptions of the museum also come into play. A museum visit is a decision on how to use leisure time. Six major factors that occur in most surveys are:[8]

- being with people – social interaction
- doing something worthwhile
- feeling comfortable and at ease with one's surroundings
- a challenging new experience

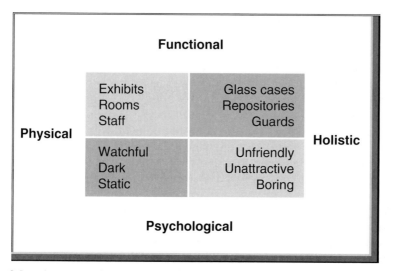

Fig. 8.1   *Aspects of the concept of 'a museum'. The diagram is divided vertically according to whether the perception is of the functional aspects of 'a museum' or its psychological feel; horizontally, according to its physical aspects or the more holistic experience. (Reproduced from Vaughan, R. (2001) Images of a museum. Museum Management and Curatorship, 19(3), 255.)*

- an opportunity to learn
- active participation.

According to these studies, people who frequently visit museums want something worthwhile to do, a challenging new experience, and the opportunity to learn. Those who rarely or never visit want to socialize with people, to feel at ease, and to actively participate. Learning and challenging experiences are for them reasons not to visit. They seek a less controlled and inhibiting experience, some of them favouring outdoor activities. A later study identified the most decisive factors in deciding to visit as *being with people* (attractive to those who seldom visited, but not to frequent visitors) and *having an opportunity to learn* (the converse).[9]

It should be noted that while frequent visitors are more likely to have been 'socialized' into visiting museums when they were children,[10] a number of reported interview remarks show that a school visit can put the person off visiting museums for life.[11]

Broadly speaking, more specific studies reinforce these findings. They include a survey for London museums, a focus group study of six museums in the USA for the Getty Trust, and a detailed survey of the Blist's Hill multi-site open air museum in the UK.[12] The Getty study added the factor of people being anxious about not knowing enough to understand the objects or art: a problem that resulted in 'not feeling at ease', 'people like me don't go to this sort of thing'. In the concept of cultural capital, an individual requires a certain level of education and cultural experience before they can appreciate a cultural activity (discussed further here, Chapter 10: Values). The conclusions on visitor likes and dislikes may be summed up as: the modern museum's core product is the experience it provides.[13] This means that people take into account not just the exhibits or the exhibition, but the ambience, clear signage, the café, the shop and opportunities to interact socially and to actively participate – or, on the other hand, to have a peaceful contemplative visit undisturbed by chatter and noisy socializing.[14]

The challenge for museums is that while the factors that influence whether people visit museums or not seem fairly clear, those who visit frequently have, or had at the time of the reported studies, very different preferences to those who visited rarely or not at all. What pleased some, others hated. This is at the root of the lively debate in the early 2000s in the UK on whether or not museums, by appealing to more people, were 'dumbing down' what they offered to their adherents.[15]

Of course, commercial products, services, and venues have no problem with segmentation like this. Each is positioned to appeal to one segment of the market or another. Publicly funded organizations like museums do not on the whole have that option. Social pressure means that it is no longer acceptable for them to design their experience purely for those who frequently visit; economic pressure demands a return on the public funding that goes into even independent museums; political pressure demands that they promote social cohesion by encouraging those who seldom or rarely visit to do so (see Chapter 10: Values).[16] But museums cannot afford simply to give up on their well-educated, well-off frequent visitors either. The US study found that 45 per cent of all visits were by these people.

So, what can be learnt to inform the provision of encounters with collections? There is no one size that fits all. It depends on whether the aim is to attract the maximum number of people, or to give a few people the maximum benefit from the collections. Those who seldom visit museums will seek an experience that is sociable, informal, fun, and interactive. Such a visit would also appeal to those with families or visitors to entertain. To please museum *aficionados* the experience would be more informative and thoughtful, perhaps challenging. For everyone, the visit would need to provide for the other components of a nice outing: it is the overall *experience* that counts. Ideally it will include some sort of surprise: 'imbue the visitor with a sense of discovery and create an element of wonder'.[17] Opportunities for just such a variety of experience can be offered by using museum collections.

Enjoying stored collections

Variations on public storage are visible storage, in which objects can be seen through glass or as part of a gallery, and visitable storage where there is no structural division and visitors can either walk around freely or join staffed tours.

Various forms of public storage are common in museums, as the usual internet search for variations on 'museum collections store tours visits' will quickly establish. In the UK alone there are at least 24 examples. They include the Darwin Centre of the Natural History Museum, London, which is as glamorous as any multi-million pound gallery (see Fig. 11.1). More such facilities are opening as parts of new museum developments, especially those funded by the UK national lottery, which demands a level of collections access in projects to which it contributes. Open-air museums such as agricultural or rural life museums could also be considered a type of open storage, since they do not usually have large collections in store, but they offer a rather different type of experience, although studies of them may help to understand what works in public storage.

Visits to collections

Science collections are some of the most difficult collections when it comes to attracting the public. Not only are science, technology, and industry of interest to fewer people than, say, decorative art collections, but many of the objects can be hard to understand: scientific instruments, groundbreaking in their time, in appearance grey boxes with dials; oily looking machines; dental chairs and surgical instruments. Undaunted, for many years the Science Museum, London, offered tours of its stores to members of donating commercial companies – and they were very popular with a wide range of employees.[18]

In 2004, the museum began to offer bookable tours to the general public. The marketing department put out the message: there were interviews on radio, television, and the national press. The result was that the museum received over 1500 enquiries within a day of going public. The tour programme, from October 2004 to May 2005, offered 700 places on 46 tours. All tours were fully booked, with a waiting list of 200 people.[19] This programme, although staff intensive, shows that collections can be popular attractions given senior management support and enthusiastic marketing (Fig. 8.2).

The National Railway Museum, York

The Warehouse, which opened in 1998, is the museum's main store for medium-sized to small objects related to the railways. The objects include

Fig. 8.2   *John Liffen, curator, explaining an aeroplane model to a tour of the Science Museum's stores*

for instance models, signalling equipment, and signs. Funding was provided for it partly because it promised public access to the collections. Objects are stored on simple racks with plastic sheet fixed over them for a degree of security. People can walk around unaccompanied. The objects have minimal labels: catalogue sheets offer more information. In 2003, a visitor survey found that a very large proportion of visitors were very satisfied with their experience, and indeed 86 per cent would make a return visit.[20] Positive aspects were a sense of history, that it brought back memories, an exciting adventure, the attraction of behind the scenes, the density of objects. 'I'd rather see all this than a quarter displayed properly'. Visitors enjoyed the non-conformity, the informal layout, and many specific objects. Dislikes (only 18 per cent of responses) included insufficient information, difficulty of seeing objects, the warehouse atmosphere, and lack of interactive activities. The most popular improvement suggested was more information about the objects, a need that could be met through digital provision. The report recommended that little needed to be changed: '*Market the mystery*'.

Decorative arts in Ireland

The decorative arts collections of the National Museum of Ireland provide examples of both visible and visitable public storage. These collections are housed in an eighteenth and nineteenth century barracks complex: they have been gradually moved in since 1994. This has provided an opportunity to bring the collections together from various dispersed and unsatisfactory stores, and to house them so as to provide much greater access for the public:

What's In Store

There are now 10 000 extra reasons [in fact there are 17 000!] to visit the National Museum of Ireland – Decorative Arts & History at Collins Barracks. For the first time in the history of the organization the entire national reserve collections of silver, glass, and oriental collections, as well as a fraction of the Museum's Ceramics collection are on view in this new visible storage facility. 'What's In Store?' is a behind the scenes Museum experience rather than an exhibition. Special tours of this visible storage facility are available.[21]

Inside the museum building much of the display space is used for normal exhibits, but the objects are always the dominant element in the display. In a visible storage gallery a two-storey backdrop of objects behind tall glass walls gives an idea of the range and diversity of the collection. There is now also a 'what's in store' gallery with 17 000 objects from the decorative arts collection fully visible to the public. In the long term, it is planned to create a storage facility for all the museum's collections, which will have public access designed in from the beginning. Other areas are primarily stores, but also accommodate public conducted tours (Collins Barracks is shown in Fig. 10.2).[22]

Public storage: discussion

In his 1985 article Ames questioned, does open storage help to make the museum more relevant or useful to the community?[23] He cited examples (and there have been many more since, besides those described earlier) to show that such facilities were popular. Making the store a public facility can, in some circumstances, be a successful way of making the collections accessible to people. We do not yet have the information to enable us to understand why it does or does not succeed.

However, public storage – perhaps especially visible storage, behind glass – is not without its problems. Glenbow Museum, Alberta, set up visible storage in one gallery as a prototype, but it was not found successful, so other approaches are now used.[24] The area looked as though it was meant to be a display, but was not sufficiently attractive; the storage furniture was not robust enough to withstand popular use; it was expensive and heavy and did not hold many objects. The intention has not been lost, however. The museum has a very large and interdisciplinary collection, which would be extremely difficult to showcase in a complete visible storage system. Instead, collections on display are made as dense as possible – through drawer units in exhibits, dioramas, and resource areas in exhibits. Some smaller educational exhibits bridge visible storage and a traditional display, with a great density of artefacts for comparative purposes but also some, for interpretation. There are behind the scenes tours of collections areas.[25] The Wallace Collection, London, is similarly finding it difficult to maintain its visible storage facility, partly due to sheer lack of space to accommodate changing needs, and partly due to staff costs.

In a detailed review of visible storage in 1990, the arguments for and against a proposed system in a small museum in Manitoba, US, were assessed. This was to be storage behind glass as in a very dense gallery, freely open to the public. A number of small local museums with similar arrangements were visited and staff interviewed. It was found that while there were considerable benefits, there were issues to be addressed as well.[26]

Some major issues identified are: physical damage to objects from a generally less stable and protected environment; increased security risks; the public think it is a conventional exhibit with insufficient information; equipment suffers wear and tear; curators find it difficult to retrieve objects for study; staff are embarrassed about duplicates or trivial objects; more enquiries are generated; having to work in semi public area; and finally, the cost.

All these issues have solutions, although they need to be taken seriously in the design, operation, and resourcing of public storage facilities. It does seem to be visible storage, with collections behind glass, that particularly gives rise to problems: it is more expensive than simply adapting standard storage to be visitable, and perhaps the storage equipment is more cumbersome because of security requirements. The Horniman Museum, London has circumvented these problems for its musical instrument collection by including a large proportion of the objects on dense display in its music gallery. About 1500 instruments are mounted in giant vertical cases and in pull-out drawers beneath them. To complement the display, a robust and extremely well-designed digital system enables visitors to see information and to listen to recordings of many of the instruments being played in their indigenous settings. This arrangement, illustrated in Fig. 9.1, is very successful with visitors of all ages.

The whole question of why public storage of various sorts succeeds or doesn't succeed needs much more investigation, as it is potentially the most effective way to make the collections more accessible.

Personal visits

Some people have very specific reasons for wanting to visit collections. There are family visits to see objects in military collections that have belonged to a relative, described in Chapter 6: Memory and identity (see Fig. 8.3). A three-week visit of Yup'ik elders, members of a First Nation in Alaska, to see collections from their culture in the Museum für Volkerkünde, Berlin, was an exciting and moving event.[27] The visit was organized and facilitated by an anthropologist who worked in Alaska. The elders spent three weeks with the collection, identifying objects and their uses, recalling what they meant in their culture, telling stories, singing, laughing, arguing, and sometimes crying. They did not seek the return of the objects: rather, they wanted to recover their meanings, so as to tell their children and young people and thus help keep their culture alive. (Attitudes to repatriation vary: some indigenous people do feel strongly that young people need to be able to touch and handle things to understand the full significance, while others for various reasons do not wish the return of objects.[28]) The group was able to work in the store without supervision or control by the museum professionals: without this, it would have been far less successful, or even a failure.

With freedom to access the collection, it was an occasion for intense enjoyment. The Yup'ik elders expressed deep gratitude both to the collectors and to the museum, for keeping the objects safe. In contrast, visits where objects have instead been produced one at a time by museum staff, to be inspected under close supervision, have been painful occasions, productive for no one.[29]

People using collections

Public storage allows many people to enjoy the collections visually, but there are other arrangements whereby they can engage with them

Fig. 8.3   *A volunteer ex-member of the Tank Regiment talking to visitors about some objects from the collection of the Tank Museum*

actively and directly, in museum-like ways or for cultural activities. Accounts suggest that these measures are very enjoyable for people, some of which have been described in the previous chapters.

The growing movement in the US, Canada, New Zealand, and Australia towards transferring objects to cultural centres closer to the people to whose cultures they belong has been noted. In Canada, as described, there is often still a degree of control over physical access to objects although there may be arrangements whereby they can be borrowed and taken out of the centre for cultural ceremonies.[30] In Australia, quinquennial State of the Environment reports review cultural heritage issues. Museums are now very conscious of their social role. Following a policy produced in 1993 by the Council of Australian Museums Associations, the move to repatriate objects from museums to people from indigenous cultures continues to strengthen, with nineteen agreements on the return of material between 1995 and 2000, of which almost half were from 1999–2000. Objects pass on to the care and control of the indigenous people. They are often housed in cultural centres or keeping places, now quite numerous (25 were funded in 1999–2000). Return of objects and materials is not always straightforward, though. Sometimes, communities do not want to take material, for various reasons; sometimes just one or a few people are driving the initiative, so that it is vulnerable if they give up; there are examples where returned objects have subsequently been stolen.[31]

The Collections Resource Centre of the National Museum of the American Indian, like a number of museums in North America, has been specifically designed to allow for objects to be fed with offerings, for some to be stored out of casual sight, and for ceremonies to be performed there using them.[32] The Resource Centre is near Washington, D.C., so members of source communities have to travel there. In the growing movement to establish cultural centres (for instance, in Canada, New Zealand, Australia, the US), objects from museum collections are kept far more under the control of people from those cultures. There may be arrangements for objects to be taken out of the centre to be used in ceremonies.[33] Other examples are described from Indonesia, where in a museum in East Kalimantan, clothing that belonged to the royal family is worn periodically in ceremonies and official gatherings. Other Indonesian museums similarly house objects that may continue to be used by the previous owners or by the local community.[34] People may also leave offerings with objects in the museum. The professional staff of the museum do not necessarily see this as 'proper' museum behaviour, but they accept it as local practice. People in Indonesia are becoming more 'museum-minded', it is reported, accepting museums as safe repositories for valued things that might otherwise be stolen or sold on the international art markets.[35]

In addition to the moral rights of the situation, repatriation of objects is a recognition that it is highly desirable for objects of all types – from incoming Australian communities as well as indigenous ones – to be preserved in their context: *in situ*, close to the cultural community. 'The ideal way for Indigenous communities to maintain control over their heritage is to have ownership of their lands'.[36] If this is not possible, then acquisition requires to be with full documentation: oral history, video, and perhaps sound recordings, photographs and so on. Otherwise, heritage objects are seen as something separate from the environment and the cultural context to which they relate and may become curiosities or art objects.[37]

Local museums in America and Australia are often wonderful expressions of local interest and involve enthusiastic volunteers in their operation. The role of the Community Curator in New South Wales is described as one of developing skills and raising awareness of the local heritage.[38] This is a good way of maintaining people's interest and engagement and addressing Ames' concern that even if a local community helps to develop an accessible collection, it might not provide lasting interest.[39] It has been found that public storage is popular for small local museums, where people can relate the collections to their own experiences and localities.[40] This is interesting, because these are exactly the sorts of collections that are most often seen as difficult to justify.

In this vein, it is not the people from indigenous cultures alone who can be helped to reconnect with their heritage through work with museum collections. In the UK, there is a great deal of concern from the government that those variously defined as belonging to the lower socioeconomic sectors or 'socially excluded' should benefit from museums. Many studies have identified them as having little interest in the cultural heritage at least as defined by the better off and more powerful.[41] Yet it has also been found that people from these sectors identify very strongly with material objects. A comparison has been drawn with Richard Hoggart's work in *The uses of literacy*: 'the core of working class attitudes ... is a sense of the personal, the concrete, the local ...'.[42]

Addressing these issues, the Open Museum initiative in Glasgow, begun in the early 1990s, was a project where the City Museum provided staff and facilities for local people and groups: people who would not otherwise visit museums.[43] Facilities were provided so that people could use collections in the same way as museum staff: selecting objects for local exhibits, making reminiscence kits, using them in art classes, and in local activities. Several moving personal experiences are set out, such as that of going into a museum store to select objects, just as the Yup'ik elders did in the Berlin museum (aforementioned). Working with real museum objects had a particular impact. Individuals are quoted as saying that the experience had helped to change their lives for the better. The cost was modest: £23 000 a year is cited, presumably in addition to staff salaries.[44] One may feel some cynicism about individual redemptive stories that provide good publicity material, but by 2000 the Open Museum had produced 884 exhibitions and handling kits, and provided enjoyable experiences for 375 000 people, targeting those who would never otherwise have benefited from the museum experience at all.[45] It continues in a slightly different form, with a new Resource Centre and local facilities.

Collections can be taken to people, too. Such projects are often temporary, but then why not try something for a while from time to time? The India Museum, Kolkata, operates a popular outreach programme, a museum on wheels that serves West Bengal, Orissa, and Bihar, and belongs to those states. This museum bus is intended to give rural populations an idea of what a museum collection is and how it may be used. The mobile Guide Lecturer will organize or feature the collection in cultural programmes as well as provide this service for schools.[46]

People using collections: discussion

As with any powerful form of interaction and expression, there can be problems in placing too much emphasis on 'the community'. A community includes some but excludes others. People do not have a uniform set of identities. Stressing difference may not be helpful: and there may neither be sufficient attention to differences within communities nor to

Photo: S. Keene

Fig. 8.4 *A visitor exploring the collection in an exhibit in the Canadian Museum of Nature, Finders keepers. The exhibition explained the reasons for the collections and what was involved in documenting, conserving, and researching them. More exhibitions like this would help to raise public awareness*

similarities between groups. Of the many roles for objects, the most valuable might be to represent not the differences but the commonality of the experiences that we all share in our lives.[47]

The extent to which museum staff should assist and control such projects is a debated topic. It is easy to lean so far towards political correctness that they stand aside entirely, and to assume that the only authentic representation is that produced by community groups themselves.[48] This ignores the fact that there are many histories, many differences in perception between members of community groups. Museum professionals should have knowledge and a wider viewpoint that individuals do not: it is one of their responsibilities to add the value of this to what is done. Moreover, their professional skills are valued: learning such skills is found to be an important part of the enjoyment of working on a museum project.[49]

Thus, the Western Australian Museum has a policy to connect people with collections by providing local spaces and the support to enable members of self-defined communities or groups to put on exhibitions. A lesson drawn from one such project was that it is naïve and irresponsible to imagine that the museum can stand aside and leave the process entirely to the group: this denies the usefulness of the public space of the museum whose role is precisely to translate between different groups. From a different continent, a Canadian First Nations individual is quoted: 'the Museum ... is a place that can provide a more "neutral" ground. It can be a place where non-Native people can explore and increase their understanding of our cultural traditions, our histories, and get a sense of the diversity among First Nations. Meanwhile, this exploration can happen outside of our own communities, in a place where non-Native people are comfortable and where we don't need to feel our privacy infringed upon'.[50]

Conclusions

The chapter has addressed the question: how can more people enjoy more of the collections? Two perspectives have been discussed: public storage of various types and ways of enabling people to use the collections (Fig. 8.4). These are different sorts of experience. Both can be successful, both have some problems, but there are plenty of examples where these have been overcome.

On public storage, the inference (yet to be tested) is that this is most successful where arrangements are informal. This is only realistic where the collections do not have great monetary value (items may still be very desirable to collectors, however). There may well be a virtue in comparative lack of funding. At the Science Museum, Wroughton, and the National Railway Museum people visit, basically, a well-organized collection store with little adaptation for a public role. The Horniman

Museum music gallery succeeds because it is clearly an exhibit, although a very dense one. It is where visible storage has been constructed, at considerable cost, that visitors have been confused as to whether it is an exhibit or not, and the benefit is perhaps lost from informality, and a sense of discovery and serendipity.

Not all collections can be made available in this way. Some are too valuable, some too vulnerable, some are definitely a resource for specialist research. But some of those that are found most difficult to justify – history collections – certainly could be.

In facilitating more active use and engagement with collections, the experiences described suggest that deep enjoyment and benefit comes when the museum professionals play an enabling role and not a controlling one. People love undertaking actual museum processes, working to curate an exhibition or prepare a reminiscence box for instance, and when they are accorded the same powers, privileges, and responsibilities as museum staff. It is not argued that museums and their staff should abrogate their responsibilities. Far from it: staff should be concerned to use their skills to support people's enjoyment of collections, and to transfer them more widely.[51] The Museum of London Conservation Department runs a very popular programme for a wide range of volunteers, young and old, to work on the archaeological collections.

A parallel has been drawn with the ubiquity of self-service shopping.[52] Would retail businesses serving the wide public contemplate returning to the model where customers have to go through an assistant who filters their wishes? Museums seem to be stuck in this moderated and filtered past way of doing things. It has been suggested that the visitor experience of accessible collections may be so qualitatively valuable that all of the museum's traditional approaches should be re-assessed.[53] This may not be comfortable for museum professionals, but especially for those hard-to-justify local history collections, museums should give the public a chance. If museums really want to engage with the full spectrum of their audiences, then they must provide more varied ways of doing so – ways that reach deep into the collections, the centre of the museum professional fortress.

Notes

[1]Ames, M. (1985). Deschooling the museum: a proposal to increase public access to museums and their resources. *Museum*, **37**(1), 25–31.

[2]Quoting Duncan: Ames (1985). pp. 25–26. (See note above)

[3]Kelly, L. (1999). Developing access to collections through assessing user needs. In *Fringe Benefits: Community, Culture, Communication, Museums Australia Conference, Albury*. Museums Australia.

Gyllenhaal, E., Perry, D. and Forland, E. (1996). Visitor understandings about research, collections and behind-the-scenes at the Field Museum. *Current Trends in Audience Research and Evaluation*, **10**, 22–32.

[4]Holdsworth, R. and Bryan, R. (2003). *National Railway Museum: Warehouse display report*. Questions Answered: unpublished report. p. 7.

[5]Duncan, C. (1995). Civilizing rituals: inside public art museums, Routledge. p. 5. Merriman (1991, repr. 2000). Beyond the glass case: the past, the heritage and the public. Institute of Archaeology, UCL. p. 78.

[6]Trevelyan, V. (ed.) (1991). *Dingy places with different kinds of bits. An attitudes survey of London museums among non-visitors*. London Museums Service. p. 36.

[7]Hood, M. (1983). Staying away : why people choose not to visit museums. *Museum News* **61**(April): 50–57.

Vaughan, R. (2001). Images of a museum. *Museum Management & Curatorship*, **19** (3), 253–268.

[8]Hood (1983). p. 51. (See note 7)

[9]Hood (1983). p. 55. (See note 7)

Vaughan (2001). Table 2. (See note 7)

[10]Hood (1983). p. 54. (See note 7)

[11]For instance, quoted in Trevelyan, ed. (1991). p. 35. (See note 6)

[12]Trevelyan, ed. (1991). (See note 6)

Walsh, A. (ed.) (1991). *Insights : museum visitor attitudes and expectations: a focus group experiment*. J.Paul Getty Trust.

Beeho, A.J. and Prentice, R.C. (1995). Evaluating the experiences and benefits gained by tourists visiting a socio-industrial heritage museum. *Museum management and curatorship*, **14**, No.3, pp. 229–251.

[13]Beeho and Prentice (1995). p. 230. (See note above)

[14]For example Walsh, ed. (1991). pp. 13, 29. (See note 12)

[15]Appleton, J. (2001). *Museums for the people: conversations in print*. Academy of Ideas.

[16]Stephen Weil discusses the public subsidy received by independent museums in the US: Weil, S. (2002). *Making museums matter*. Smithsonian Books. pp. 75–80. The UK Department of Culture has made support for wider audiences a priority since the mid-1990s: most recently in DCMS Cultural Property Division (2005). *Understanding the future: museums and 21st century life: the value of museums*. Department of Culture Media & Sport. p. 14.

The government of the Netherlands makes similar demands: Ministrie van OCenW (1999). *Culture as confrontation. Principles on cultural policy in 2001–2004*. Ministerie van Onderwijs, Cultuur en Wetenschap, Netherlands.

[17]Beeho and Prentice (1995). pp. 230–231. (See note 12)

[18]Author's experience in managing the Science Museum's small objects store, 1992–2000.

[19]Interview: *Science Museum*. X. Mazda, Curator. 19 August 2004.

[20]Holdsworth, R. and Bryan, R. (2003). *National Railway Museum: Warehouse display report*. NRM: unpublished report.

[21]Marketing statement on Website: *National Museum of Ireland*. http://www.museum.ie/. 5 February 2005.

[22]Interviews: *National Museum of Ireland*. R. Ó Floinn, Head of Collections. 6 April 2004. P. Mullarkey, conservator. 7 April 2004.

[23] Ames (1985). pp. 25–26. (See note 1)

[24] Slater, D. (1995). Visible storage: the Glenbow experiment. *Museum International*, No.188, **47** (4), pp. 13–17.

[25] Email communication (2004). B. Carter, Ethnology Curator, Glenbow Museum. 12 August.

[26] Thistle, P. (1990). Visible storage for the small museum. *Curator*, **33**(1), pp. 49–62, pp. 52–54.

[27] Fienup-Riordan, A. (2003). Yup'ik elders in museums: fieldwork turned on its head. In: *Museums and source communities* (L. Peers, and A. Brown, eds) Routledge. pp. 28–41.

[28] A member of the Kwakiutl people is quoted as believing that young people needed to see objects in: Clavir, M. (2002). *Preserving what is valued: museums, conservation and First Nations.* UBC Press. p. 78. Others (Maoris, Indigenous Australians) are reported as not wishing for the return of cultural material: Kreps, F.C. (2003). *Liberating culture.* Routledge. p. 73; Department of the Environment & Heritage (2001). *Australia State of the Environment Report 2001: Natural and Cultural Heritage Theme Report.* Australian Government. p. 118.

[29] Fienup-Riordan (2003). pp. 39–40. (See note 27)

[30] Clavir (2002). pp. 160–163. (See note 28)

[31] Department of the Environment & Heritage (2001). p. 118. (See note 27)

[32] Email communication: *Smithsonian Institution* (2004). P. Nietfeld, Collections Manager, National Museum of the American Indian, Collections Resource Centre. 30 June. For other examples see Kreps, F.C. (2003). *Liberating culture.* Routledge. Chapter 4.

[33] Department of the Environment & Heritage (2001). pp. 118–121. (See note 28)

[34] Kreps (2003). pp. 30, 40. (See note 28)

[35] Kreps (2003). pp. 57–58. (See note 28)

[36] Department of the Environment & Heritage (2001). p. 120. (See note 28)

[37] State of the Environment Advisory Council (1996). *Australia State of the Environment 1996. An Independent Report Presented to the Commonwealth Minister for the Environment by the State of the Environment Advisory Council.* CSIRO pub. pp. 9–45.

[38] Sear, M. (2004). Use your scone: Hay's Community Curator programme and rural museum development. In: *Food for thought, Museums Australia Conference, Melbourne.* http://www.museumsaustralia.org.au/conference/postconference/finalpapers.htm

[39] Ames (1985). p. 27. (See note 1)

[40] Thistle (1990). p. 61. (See note 26)

[41] Notably Bourdieu, quoted: 'museums betray in the tinest of details of their morphology and organization their true function, which is to reinforce for some the feeling of belonging and for others the feeling of being excluded': Kreps (2003). p. 159. (See note 28)

[42] Witcomb, A. (1997). On the side of the object: an alternative approach to debates about ideas, objects and museums. *Museum management and curatorship* **16** (4) pp. 383–399. pp. 393–395.

[43] RCMG (2002). *A catalyst for change: the social impact of the Open Museum. A report for the Heritage Lottery Fund.* Research Centre for Museums & Galleries.

[44] RCMG (2002). p. 13. (See note above)

[45]RCMG (2002). p. 14. (See note above)

[46]Interview: M. Thomson/staff of the India Museum, Kolkata, December 2004.

[47]Witcomb (1997). p. 389. (See note 42)

See poem: *South Coast Midden*, R.F. Brissenden. In Department of the Environment & Heritage, 2001. p. 110. (See note 28)

[48]For instance, recounted in Barnard, M. (2002). Kist and tell: the Greater Pollock Kist. *Museums journal* February, pp. 36–37.

[49]Clavir (2002). pp. 200, 209. (See note 28)

Witcomb (1997). p. 397. (See note 42)

[50]Clavir (2002). pp. 200, 209. (See note 28)

Witcomb (1997). p. 397. (See note 42)

[51]Clavir (2002). pp. 200, 209. (See note 28)

RCMG (2002). Chapter 3. (See note 43)

[52]Ames (1985). p. 31. (See note 1)

[53]Thistle (1990). p. 61. (See note 26)

9 Collections and digitization

The developing information and communication technologies permeate our daily lives, in defiance of the enormous hype about their effects and significance. Even people who do not personally connect with the internet are not immune – global commerce, military, and even cultural uses are bringing about changes that reach practically everywhere. There is an engaging website about the technologies of the Burarra people, who occupy a small, remote, and little developed territory in Arnhem Land, Northern Australia, developed with their full cooperation and editorial control.[1] The community has said that it is happy with the website and with the feedback they have received from around the world. The effects of this global publicity have not been studied, although increased enthusiasm among the Burarra for using computers is perhaps the minimum that might be expected.[2] An exhibition on the same subject in Canberra, it is true, preceded the website, but the web has longer persistence and global reach.

People usually considered to be remote from the reach of technology can also use it in unexpected ways. In Brazil, a team of cartographers and agency people worked with indigenous Amazonian tribes to map their territory using GPS (global positioning systems) technology. The results can be used by the Amazonians to defend their territory against exploitation for logging and gold mining, and their representatives are quoted as saying that this is also a valuable means of transmitting their culture and knowledge to new generations.[3]

However, we should be wary. The emerging realities of the internet are pointing up its inherent ambiguities and paradoxes. Utopian visions of the internet connecting people and providing a truly free and democratic information space are countered by the nightmare dystopia that lies in the ability for surveillance and control on a previously impossible scale.[4] The reality lies in the tension between these – but the foundations of the internet in military technology are still highly significant. Even the term 'cyber' is derived from the Greek term for control and governance.

'Cyberspace' was what William Gibson called the frightening world of surveillance and pursuit that he created in his celebrated novel of the future, *Neuromancer*.

Cyberspace attenuates time and geography, yet it is not placeless.[5] New York and London have enormous flows of financial and commercial data and the infrastructures to support them: they are also great centres of cultural data. In fact, the presence of cultural institutions – the national museums, the national archives and the British Library in London, and the Metropolitan Museum, the Guggenheim, and all the other major cultural centres in New York – actually confer a sense of place on cyberspace. Visiting the website of the National Gallery or the Science Museum immediately summons up a mental sense of London. Visiting the website of the Burarra people whose territory is in Arnhem Land, Northern Australia gives a vivid impression of that place.[6]

The conceptualization and sociology of museums and the internet have not been well explored. Attention has focused on the technologies – how to do virtual stuff and how to do it well – rather than on the why and the wider societal effects.[7]

This chapter will explore the opportunities for collections offered by the technologies of the information age. It is not an exercise in futurology – those are for others[8] – rather, it is an exploration of possibilities. Museums play an important and influential role in politics and society; why shouldn't they have a similar position in cyberspace? Economic policies of investment in electronic cultural resources, for instance in Europe, depict culture as a vital element in European competitiveness and identity. These technologies will also help to shape the future of museums. In particular, there may be profound consequences for the way that museum collections are used and on the value placed on them as collections not only of objects but also of knowledge.

Museum futures

Museums have been diagnosed as being in transition from their mid-nineteenth century European public establishment as 'modern', structured, organizations to becoming 'post-modern' organizations where the visitor or user determines meaning. The essence of the 'modern' museum is a building. The museum in the future will be more a process or an experience – moving out into the spaces of the communities that it serves.[9] As the previous chapters have shown, objects and collections can be important and significant to people. Yet the way that most museums use digital technologies, only allowing access to collections information through interpretative frameworks provided by them, shows that earlier attitudes persist in the digital age.

As digital technologies evolve they will drive the following changes required of museums:

From about things	*to* for people
From one classification system	*to* many meanings brought by the beholder[s]
From objects selected in exhibitions	*to* the collections directly for people
From place-based organizations	*to* ideas and knowledge-based organizations
From central	*to* distributed
From professional control of collections	*to* democratization: the museum makes assets available for others to use creatively.

Digital futures

Just as museums in the actual world must be aware of the wider context for their role and respond to its imperatives, so must they understand the context of cyberspace within which they also are players.

Museums should be aware of the influences of technological determinism: technology drives social development rather than the converse.[10] Technological determinism is a broad concept at the level of society in general, for example the rapid transformational changes brought about by the ownership of cars. This in turn is the product of the invention of the internal combustion engine and mechanized steel working. In the Western world, digital technologies have already evolved from mere tools into the context within which we conduct our lives. The key issues then become not the capabilities of the technologies, but the politics, cultural effects, and moralities of how we use them. To achieve any control over these we have to understand the directions in which technology is driving us.[11] Negotiation with technologies then takes us in directions we had not previously envisaged.

The next few pages will chart some of the ever-growing array of the digital and communications technologies that I believe will have the greatest implications for collections in museums:

- *Content:* classifying versus searching; digitized images; virtual reality; personification; multiple media: audio, video, touch.
- *Infrastructure:* wireless, locative technologies; content delivered dynamically from distributed data; grid computing; standards the foundation for technological evolution.
- *Delivery:* design separate from content; multiple simultaneous publication of content; personalization; user pull, not provider push; get

away from keyboards and screens; portable, handheld; senses other than visual.

- *Rapidity of change:* almost instantaneous promulgation of new ideas; rapid evolution and take-up of technologies; viral marketing by online word-of-mouth.

Content

The quantity of material available on the internet continues to grow. It also becomes more accessible, since the technologies of making content identifiable, and of searching and finding what is relevant are becoming more sophisticated by the day.

Search versus classify

Some argue that the enormous scope of information offered on the web is rendering classification systems redundant, as it is simply no longer possible to locate and classify everything that could be useful.[12] If you wanted to find information on some subject, would you rely solely on someone else's selection via a portal (a site giving links to selected web resources) or similar, or would you want to see everything that was on offer, maybe in addition to the selected information?

Material that was held in web-accessed databases used to be inaccessible. This is not the case now: provided that the databased information (or image) has a proper metadata description (e.g. for a photograph, the main subjects, the format, the photographer, among other data) automated search engines can retrieve it too. A good example is from Museum of Finland. A search on any one of *Artefact type, Materials, Manufacturers, Place of usage*, etc. sends a user request to a variety of collections databases in several Finnish museums.[13] The result will show not only the objects in that category from all the different museums but also all the other categories in which such objects occur, and suggest other things of interest as well. This example is in Finnish but there is an English demonstration facility that shows clearly how it works. Another example is Picture Australia, where images in a number of collections can be searched as one collection.[14]

Each record (in the Finnish museum databases the object records; in the newsfeed – see below – the news item) has been tagged with metadata, and the newsfeed site or the collections search engine searches for the appropriate tags.[15]

Taking the mindset of the information provider further, the UK *24 Hour Museum* website now includes a newsfeed facility (with a useful explanation of how newsfeeds work).[16] If you have a relevant website you can include a piece of html code that will display on the user's screen the headline stories from the newsfeed. Syndication takes this further. If you post something on your website you can add a piece of code that tells newfeeds that it is there and what the subject is. The newsfeed's automated software picks it up and displays it in the newsfeed along with similarly tagged pieces of information from other websites. This technology is not confined to news: it could be collections information that is tagged, and a syndicated collections website could be harvesting interesting items from diverse sources.

Thus we have to move from analysing information in order to fit it into a predetermined structure towards thinking how best to make content findable: the onus is on the provider to ensure that content and the descriptors of it comply with standards and with recognized terminology.[17] This will benefit the provider too, because content will be flexibly reusable in many different applications, and less expensive to preserve for the long term.

An example of this change of emphasis is the Fine Arts Museums of San Francisco's *Thinker* search facility. This facility uses keywords assigned to pictures by non-specialist volunteers (termed the *Word Soup*), as well as those used by conventional art historian curators. It is based on the principle that many of the people searching for a picture will use search terms like the ones used by the non-specialist volunteers rather than formal academic art historical ones.[18]

Technologies for searching sets of digitized images based on the characteristics of the images themselves are also emerging, though more slowly than was envisioned ten years ago.[19]

Digitized images

Art museums have been among the first to fully exploit the internet and are still in the lead in making their whole collections available online. These websites attract huge numbers of users (in 2003, 2.6 million individual sessions to the Tate website: however, 3.6 million to that of the Natural History Museum).[20] Why is this? Images are just more attractive to look at than are bald text catalogue entries – and works of art are created expressly to be visually interesting and rewarding. Images also deliver more information much more quickly. The providers are encouraged by the commercial market for images – a website is an excellent advertisement for a picture library service (for selling the use of images). There is a discussion to be had on copyright, control, and commercialization of publicly owned and created resources.

Virtual reality, augmented reality, and personification

There are several varieties of virtual reality (VR) and three-dimensional representation (3D).[21]

- Virtual reality (VR) – a representation using digital technologies of something that looks as though it exists in the real world, but which is actually a visual construct by the viewer.

- 3D representations – simply images in 3D of something, imaginary or actual displayed on a screen.
- Augmented reality – a real thing can be perceived but is supplemented by some other material produced electronically, often while the user is walking about. This is usually visual, for example information relating to an object can be viewed in headsets. Sound guides could certainly be said to augment reality.
- Personification: more than one electronic or electronically programmed guide does exist (Tourbot) and we are beginning to see digital avatars (personifications of people).[22]

Remote sensing of one sort or another engages other senses. Using touch, it is possible to put on gloves that enable one to 'feel' the actual surface, weight, size, and so on of an object that is perhaps thousands of miles away. *The museum of pure form* is a European project that is demonstrating the viability of this.[23]

Infrastructure

By infrastructure, I mean the underlying technologies of delivery and access to electronic materials.

Wireless technologies

A lot is said about wireless technologies – wireless hotspots in particular generate a lot of excitement. These technologies enable one to use a network without being physically connected to it. Complementary to wireless networks and devices is RFID technology (radio frequency identification device). RFIDs are tiny devices that send electronic signals to identify themselves in response to an electronic query. For example, wearing an audio device, one could walk past a painting, and simply pause in front of it to activate an RFID in the painting label which would tell the audio device to deliver the correct sound guide text.[24] The talk could be generated from a database updated centrally to suit a particular exhibition. Personalisation would identify what the visitor had already heard, so that the narrative seemed as though there was an intelligent guide building on what one knew already.

Locative technologies

These are allied to wireless technologies. This term embraces the clutch of technologies needed to map information onto geographical places, locate the user, and furnish them with information relevant to the place. Geographic information systems (GIS) hold information relating to a geographical area. Global positioning systems (GPS) sense the user's position in the same area. Other technologies sort out what information is required and deliver it in the appropriate manner. There are examples of experimental systems developed for heritage applications – for Pompeii, for example, where virtual reality figures and reconstructions appear to visitors on the site who are wearing the requisite equipment, and for Olympia, where reconstructions of buildings can be seen superimposed on the ruins. At a more pervasive level, mobile telephones increasingly include the option to display locally relevant information.[25]

Web services and grid computing

As material delivered electronically becomes more complex and user requirements more sophisticated, software applications known as web services are being developed, which connect otherwise separate applications on demand. For example, SCRAN (the Scottish Cultural Resources Network) is funded by subscription. If you try to access its content you will be asked for your SCRAN identity, or else to enter via Athens. Athens is an authentication service provided for the UK academic community. If you choose the Athens identification, the service will check your library membership and whether your library subscribes to SCRAN. It will then send the appropriate information to the SCRAN website. SCRAN will then allow you access, or not, as the case may be. The Athens web service has worked between your browser and SCRAN.[26]

Grid computing is computing on an even more enormous scale than we have become used to. It means that both data and processing are distributed among different computers with very high capacity connections. The primary focus at present is on science and engineering (and military uses, of course) but it is being explored for humanities applications, too. If we get to the point of searching across many collections databases as one, then grid computing may be employed.

Delivery

The means of delivering electronic information are evolving as well. 'The computer is everywhere' read the European Commission hype around its 2003 digitization strategy. Indeed, it is everywhere, in our washing machines, mobile phones, CD players and even, on a tiny scale, our credit cards.

Data separate from design

More and more content is distinguished from the frame within which it is presented. This enables an attractive and perhaps personalized design framework to automatically select and display content from a central repository, such as a database or an electronic set of electronic images. This technology is commonplace now in museum websites. For example, if you search the online collection of the National Portrait Gallery, London, the results will appear in a standard format. The design of the surrounding page could be changed at any time and the same information would appear in it. The information is drawn automatically from a separate database and can be corrected or updated independent of the website design.[27]

Personalization

Museums and their websites have large and diverse audiences. Electronic devices can be programmed to 'learn' what individuals are interested in and then to automatically select what information is offered. For example, users can be shown a random set of images, and clicking on the ones that are nearest their requirement brings up a new selection of images that are more relevant to their interest automatically selected from the whole set. For instance you might want to find paintings showing snow scenes from the collection of the Tate gallery. Starting with a set of random images, you might select a landscape, and then be shown increasingly wintery sets from which to select.[28] Other forms of personalization range from 'welcome' pages that reflect the individual's previous interest (as does the website of Amazon, the online bookshop) to handheld electronic labels that deliver information edited to take account of what the user has already read. For instance, in a decorative art exhibition they might only be told once about the art nouveau movement.[29]

Get away from keyboards and screens: different senses

For the moment, we will leave aside devices such as clothing that acts as a computer. Many varied devices are being delivered that will deliver sound, vision, or other experiences.[30] Small handheld screens are commonplace of course and can be combined with wireless computing and RFID technology to deliver specifically tailored information. Some can combine sound, images, and text. Sound guides likewise are found everywhere, although the level of sophistication varies. Technology can now be used that will cause almost any surface to act as a speaker, activated by motion detectors so that the user only has to wave their hand to hear the sound. Could one in this way 'listen' to musical instruments as though they were being played? In the music gallery of the Horniman Museum, London, one can find comfortable benches to sit at, with images of the musical instruments on display projected onto them. Using them as a touchscreen one can select any instrument, see more about it, and hear it played (see Fig. 9.1). Of the senses, sound and vision are easy. Touch can be provided but it is costly, and access is restricted since special apparatus must be worn. Smell is possible though little used: it is not a major sense for humans. (However, some collections do have distinctive smells: see Chapter 7: Creativity: Stories from collections).

Photo: S. Keene

Fig. 9.1 *The Horniman Museum's music gallery (London). Young and old can understand instantly how to use the digital museum bench, which allows them to select information and recordings of the instruments on display*

Using digital technologies, using collections

How can these technologies facilitate the various uses of collections that have been explored?

Research

The availability of information via the internet is transforming research. Literally: not only does it make it much more easier to find out about almost anything, to obtain publications electronically, and to search library catalogues, it also affects the sort of research that is conducted. It seems to me that the debate over whether or not to put basic collections lists online is over – this is the future for the internet – to provide information in a way that is findable. Uses then emerge beyond those envisaged by the providers.[31] If museum collections were listed then at least researchers would be able to know where to find objects of interest to them. There are a number of large scale listing projects, including the Cornucopia project in the UK, which is a collection level listing of UK museum holdings.[32]

Being able to combine records from several databases at once would also facilitate collections-based research. While researching a place, it would be useful to be able to see all sorts of local information in the same window, such as species diversity records, geological survey records, past ordnance survey maps, sites and monuments records, and of course objects in museum collections with a relevant provenance. This can be achieved if the providers of the multiple sources of information comply with the requisite standards, especially for metadata. Standards are at the very heart of the internet and the web, because they ensure that stuff will work with and be combinable with other stuff and be interoperable with it now and in the future.

The development in the research use of museum collections and information, along with other similar cultural materials, was greatly facilitated by the work of the Getty Information Institute, which is now discontinued.[33] The GII brought some of the immense resources of the USA to the service of cultural digitization, providing essential knowledge infrastructure components such as standards, terminology tools like thesauri, and many others. (We should appreciate the irony that the DLib journal in which Fink's article, referenced earlier, is published, is funded by DARPA, the US Defense Advanced Research Projects Agency. DARPA was the prime agent in the very beginning of the internet in the 1960s. We catch the crumbs that fall from these rich tables.)

Objects scanned and reproduced in 3D and virtual reality could be useful for research. There are a number of commercial vendors of the technology, and the price is coming down. Perhaps it is not too far-fetched to imagine a researcher getting project funding for 3D scanning objects rather than travelling to visit them. It is true that scanning cannot reproduce the entire physicality of the object, but on the other hand the scanned images can be manipulated in ways that enhance visual examination – increasing or decreasing the contrast, magnification, and direction of lighting for instance. For valuable and vulnerable objects, it may be the only way to examine an object freely as though one was holding it in one's hands.[34] Then the scanned 3D images could be permanently available for remote study (provided that provision is made, in turn, for their permanent curation and preservation).

Some museums see themselves as major players in online research. The National Maritime Museum, London, for example, has made research and information in general a strategic priority for a number of years. Online provision is a natural progression for it. It publishes the fully refereed online *Journal of Maritime Research* and has an ongoing project, *Collections Online,* to make its collections digitally available.[35] Research in almost any other subject area would benefit from digital access to museum collections information so that objects from different countries in collections all over the world could be accessed from the researcher's desk. It is not only research and museums that would benefit: it would raise the profile and appreciation of other cultures.

Education

Further and adult education is the focus in this book. A growing number of digitized collections are being made available to academic institutions, usually on subscription, for educational and research purposes. They include AMICO, the Art Museums Image Consortium; SCRAN, the Scottish Cultural Resources Network; the Visual Arts Data Service for the UK, and many others including film and television archives.[36] Possibly the crucial advantage of these is uniform licensing agreements and the control of use and access to the digital resources. This benefits not only the museums, which receive some revenue income, but more importantly, users of these resources. While users have to pay, they do gain the advantage of convenience and a more comprehensive collection.

Many projects using digitization begin as research projects but have created educational resources. Just one example is the exploitation of digital images of ancient Greek comedy masks, where small original model masks in a museum collection are digitized in 3D and a life-size version can automatically be sculpted.[37] This enables students of Greek drama to see for themselves the extraordinary ways that these masks functioned. It demonstrates that once collections become accessible and usable, they can be inventively used in entirely different disciplines.

Creativity

Digital art is thriving. More could be done to encourage artists to use the collections themselves, whether with installations in stores or else drawing on them to create different electronic works. As the AHDS Visual Arts database shows, museum collections are seen as a very important resource.[38] There are many examples of installations in a different medium complementing exhibits. In *Shh...* in the Victoria & Albert Museum, London, sounds and commentaries were delivered wirelessly to handheld devices at marked points in the exhibition. *The sculpture of the Grant Museum* at the Grant Museum of Zoology has been described – a sound guide treats zoological specimens as though they were works of art (see Fig. 7.1 for one exhibit).[39]

The web is an appealing and accessible medium, and it is very easy to learn to publish material on it. People would surely love to use museum online collections and objects creatively in their own way if they were permitted to. Some websites enable people to form their own collections within them,[40] but it would be more exciting to assemble objects from across different museum collections (see the Canadian example below).

Memory and identity

Canada and Australia support the cultural and museum use of the internet in order to foster a sense of identity. Much of the impetus to digitize Australian collections arises from the wish to support an Australian identity. 'By providing access to this heritage through a single website entry point, AMOL (Australian Museums Network) preserves and promotes Australia's cultural identity within Australia and in the international arena'. In Canada, the government website generally introducing Canada, links to an interesting government initiative, *Canada's digital collections*. This was a grant programme aimed at providing young people with skills, alleviating unemployment, creating wider internet-based access to Canadian material of public interest and demonstrating productivity enhancement as a result of digitization. 'More than 600 collections are available, celebrating Canada's history, geography, science, technology and culture'.[41] This Digital Collections website is linked to from Sino.net, a comprehensive website for the Chinese diaspora. SCRAN, the Scottish Cultural Resource Network, was funded for similar reasons.

For individuals, digitized collections are an important resource in the search for their past, sometimes their family or personal history but often for the history of their origins as well. Family history research is already an extremely popular interest and undoubtedly the use of online materials for research into people's history will increase. *Moving here* is a website created jointly by a number of UK museums, about migration to England. The project makes collections accessible in a number of ways: objects were identified, properly catalogued with their provenance, and conserved before being digitized, so that they are accessible physically as well as digitally.[42]

Enjoyment

Paintings are the most obvious example of collections (rather than online exhibitions) where enjoyment could be served by digital media. It truly is a pleasure to be able to view images of these great collections wherever and whenever one pleases. One can immediately search for further information about the artist, the subject, the school, or anything else that one is curious about. Art books do not offer the same convenience, and of course few people could afford the expense and the space for a comparable library. Other image collections such as photographs can similarly be enjoyed. Here is another example where an information-rich image could be the link to other collections information – anything, whether local history, technology, politics, or other subjects. It would not matter to the user where the other collection was, either in cyberspace or in real space.

The key idea here is *served by*. The subject matter is not mediated by the museum – the user determines it – to serve the user, the museum must design their online collection to be lexibly searchable. The internet and the web are media that can at the same time broadcast and narrow-cast. They can provide content for as many people as possible through interpreted web productions, but by allowing also for individual retrieval they can at the same time provide for individuals with very specific interests.

An example (long may it persist!) of a completely different sort of collection that can be enjoyed digitally is that of the Canadian Museum of Civilization. Here, the collections are displayed on virtual racks as though one were literally seeing them in store. This is such a pleasant visual metaphor, which clearly puts across the idea that they are the stored collections. Another visual concept is on the website of the Australian Museum, where one can open the drawers of gleaming wooden natural history specimen cabinets. These elegant websites graphically show that collections can be enjoyable (see Figs 9.2 and 9.3).[43]

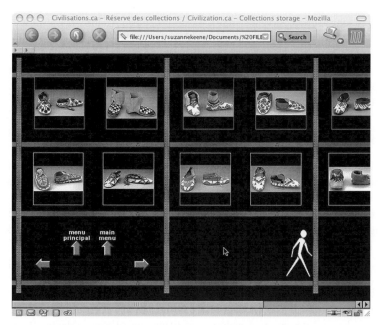

Fig. 9.2 *Plains Indians moccasins in a virtual store. The website of the Canadian Museum of Civilization has objects arranged on storage racks. Click on an object to see information about it*

Fig. 9.3   *An elegant metaphor for exploring museum collections. The collection of the Australia Museum can be explored online by clicking on a drawer in this elegant virtual cabinet*

Discussion

Knowledge sharing

It is often said, but little acted upon, that museums should acknowledge that there are others with complementary roles in building the knowledge that the collections represent. Museums already know that there are many people who have far deeper knowledge of objects in their collections than do their own staff. Very few have enlisted the help of their audiences. The San Francisco Arts Museums' *Word Soup* project of enlisting public help with data improvement and providing search terms is described earlier here. The Spurlock Museum at the University of Illinois found that they were able to greatly improve their collections catalogue with the help of its online users, who contributed corrections and improved information. Once they realized the value of this distributed expertise, the museum set up the means to invite and utilize contributions.[44] These are just two examples of collaborative attitude.[45]

Multiple viewpoints

Pressures on museums to move away from their previous role in controlling the meaning and messages of collections are increased

by digitization. Digital collections serve multiple perspectives and interpretations.

Blurring of roles

Many existing roles will be blurred as digital technologies become
more embedded. It will be obvious (it is already of course) that knowledge about the collections is not the sole preserve of the museum expert.
An online search on a subject of interest will deliver results from museums and other sources alike. Information held by the museum need
not be generated exclusively internally. The museum's knowledge will
be communicated not just inside the museum space but everywhere; and
not just mediated and controlled through exhibitions but openly available
to all.

Authority and trust

The capabilities of digital technologies create a powerful impetus for
museums to move away from being knowledge producers into being
repositories, knowledge brokers, and maintainers of meanings. Many
publicly funded web productions invite contributions from the public.
But what happens to the vaunted authority of museums if they acknowledge that the information they publish could be improved, and like the
Spurlock and San Francisco Arts Museums, seek help from their audience? Museums still have an important role: they are among the most
trusted of organizations, and they must make sure that information and
knowledge is reliable.

Community space

Digital technologies offer the ability for people with common interests
to develop virtual communal spaces – whether based on an interest in
a subject, or on culture or ethnicity. A comprehensive report from
DigiCULT, the European technology watch group, points out that
some online communities – particularly those concerned with gaming –
are huge.[46] There are examples of museums making provision for
outside communities, such as *Moving here*,[47] and even better, *Canada's
digital collections*,[48] but the real measure of success must be whether
outside communities find museum online resources useful enough to
use them in their own pursuits '... for most cultural heritage institutions,
the challenge will first be to embrace the idea of cooperating
with a (non-professional) online community, and then to nurture an
evolving and thriving community that crosses the virtual as well as physical space'.[49]

Cartwright Hall, in the UK, took a step in the right direction. In order to attract teenagers, who normally stayed away from their exhibitions in the proverbial droves, they invited the *Unreal Tournament* gaming community (around 20 000 players online around the world at any one time) to create a game map, for a prize. Digital images of areas of the Hall were provided for contestants to use. There was a successful response, with the winner being flown over from Canada to collect the prize.[50]

Should not the digitized collections of museums be seen as a communal resource? One barrier is museums' obsession with copyright, sometimes to generate income and sometimes to safeguard their digital property. It has to be admitted that this is not without justification. The Reading Museum commissioned a digital version of the Bayeux Tapestry only to find it unexpectedly appear on a website originating in New Zealand – it was used as though it was the website owner's own. Also there may be serious copyright problems if material to which the museum does not hold the copyright is used by others. It may be less problematic to invite the public into the digital space. But if the will is there to enable others to make use of public collections, the technology could be available.

Collecting cultures

As the importance of the meaning of objects, of their different pasts, grows, so the need to collect cultures more holistically becomes more apparent. This means all the accompanying ephemera such as advertising material (which shows so vividly what the object was thought to stand for at the time it was first current) and it also means collecting the intangible heritage – oral history, performances, music, speech, soundscapes, social behaviour, and cooking and meals. Digital technologies are practically the only way to capture and store the intangible heritage since by definition it cannot be physically kept. This ambition brings the risk of a new phase of museum colonialism. But without the virtual texture of life, collections are but fragments of the world.

Digitize and collaborate

Collaborative collections digitization is more and more important. Large scale collaborative collection digitization initiatives include Collections Australia Network, SCRAN for museums in Scotland, Artifacts Canada, run by the long-established Canadian Heritage Information Network, and Cornucopia, a developing database of UK museum collections.[51] Other online listing projects are discussed in Chapter 4, Research. They include the Online Register of Scientific Instruments and the National inventory of European painting. There are many valuable initiatives by smaller museums as well, but there are still objections from curators and others that the information is not ready for public consumption. But then it never is ready. Why not invite the help of the public to improve it?

Conclusions

One thing is very clear from our growing experience of the effects of the internet: once information, of whatever sort – stuff – is available on it neither its uses nor the effects of these uses can be predicted. I long shared the view that it was pointless simply putting collections catalogues on the web: objects had to be selected and framed in a narrative or virtual exhibition. Now, I believe we have moved beyond this. Museums should list their collections online and see what happens.

Pressure on museums to make their collections inventory accessible on the web will increase. Once the extent of their collections can be seen, then among other things museum staff themselves will be able to see what other museums hold. Museums that have implemented unified collections management systems often report that it makes a difference when staff can see what is in each other's collections. A broader view will influence what is collected, and a public view will leverage pressure to make use of those collections.

Attitudes persist: 'we' must interpret the collections for 'them'. This is from the Director of the Neanderthal Museum, the Netherlands: 'Many curators do not understand themselves to be part of a cultural service for the public'.[52] It is countries such as Canada and Australia where there has been a large public investment in infrastructure and communications use for every aspect of life that a service mind set has been promoted. So, as with actual collections, museums need to find ways of stimulating a perception of their digital provision as a resource for others to use.

Digitization is a democratizing force for museums, a force for change. In the comparatively early days of the internet Don Tapscott made some insightful predictions about the effects of digital technologies.[53] Among them was 'disintermediation', meaning cutting out intermediaries: the vanishing travel agent. The consequences of telling people – allowing people to see – exactly what is in the collections might be indifference. On the other hand the world is full of people who enjoy doing out-of-the way things and investigating esoteric subjects. Once the museum professionals have relinquished the controlling lens of exhibitions and themes chosen by them, the collections may assume a central place again. If those who work in museums don't know how to make use of them, why not invite their actual owners, in most cases the public, to bring their own ideas? They might want to use the collections for research, education, memory and identity, creativity, and who knows, for enjoyment.

Notes

[1]Website: *Burarra Gathering*. http://burarra.questacon.edu.au/home.html

[2]Information from Questacon: email communication 10 January 2005.

[3]Amazon Conservation Team (2003). New map helps protect ten million acres of rainforest. *ACT in the news*. January 2003.http://www.amazonteam.org/news/news_0103_article01.html

[4]Lyon, D. (2002). Cyberspace: beyond the information society? In *Living with cyberspace: technology and society in the 21st century*. (J. Armitage and J. Roberts, eds) pp. 21–33, Continuum. pp. 24–29.

[5]Lyon, (2002). p. 25. (See note above)

Castells, M. (2001). *The internet galaxy: reflections on the internet, business and society*. p. 207 ff. Oxford University Press.

[6]Website: *Burarra Gathering*. (See note 1)

[7]For example, the DigiCULT thematic report: Geser, G. and Pereira, J., eds (2004). The future digital heritage space: an expedition report. Thematic Issue 7. DigiCULT.

[8]Geser, G. and Pereira, J., eds (2004). *The future digital heritage space: an expedition report*. Thematic Issue 7. DigiCULT.

Detz, S. *et al.* (2004). *Virtual Museum of Canada: The Next Generation*. Canadian Heritage Information Network (CHIN).
http://www.chin.gc.ca/English/Pdf/Members/Next_Generation/vm_tng.pdf

[9]A summary of these changing perceptions and requirements of museums is to be found in Hooper-Greenhill, E. (2000). *Museums and the interpretation of visual culture*. Routledge. pp. 151–3.

[10]Lyon, (2002). p. 22. (See note 4)

de Miranda, A. and Kristiansen, M. (2000). Technological determinism and ideology: the European Union and the Information Society, Paper to *Policy Agendas for Sustainable Technological Innovation*, 3rd POSTI International Conference, London, United Kingdom, 1-3 December, 2000.
http://www.esst.uio.no/posti/workshops/ miranda.html

[11]Lyon, (2002). p. 32. (See note 4)

[12]Lesk, M. (2003). Size matters: web and book archiving. In *EVA 2003 London, conference proceedings* (J. Hemsley, ed.) pp. 2.1–10, EVA Conferences International.

[13]Hyvönen, E. *et al.* (2004). Finnish Museums on the Semantic Web: The user's Perspective on MuseumFinland. In *Museums and the web 2004: selected papers from an international conference* (D. Bearman and R. Trant, eds) Archives & Museum Informatics.

[14]Website: *Picture Australia*. National Library of Australia.
http://www.pictureaustralia.org
There is a clear detailed description of how *Picture Australia* works:
http://www.pictureaustralia.org/join.html

[15]Cole, T. *et al.* (2002). Now that we've found the 'hidden web', what can we do with it? In *Museums and the web 2002: selected papers from an international conference* (D. Bearman and R. Trant, eds) pp. 63–72, Archives & Museum Informatics.

[16]Website: *24 Hour Museum.* Information about our newsfeed service.
http://www.24hourmuseum.org.uk/etc/formuseums/TXT18198_gfx_en.html
Newsfeed page: www.24hourmuseum.org.uk/home.rss

[17]Geser and Pereira, eds (2004). p. 66. (See note 8)

[18]Website: *The Thinker.* Fine Arts Museums of San Francisco: Advanced Search.
http://www.thinker.org/fam/about/imagebase/
4th Dimension (undated). *4th Dimension success story: The Thinker.*
http://www.4d.com/solutions/thinker.html

[19]For example Website, *Ideé Inc.* Revolutionary visual search technologies.
Espion™. http://www.ideeinc.com/products/espion.html

[20]24 Hour Museum (2004). *24 HM web survey – museum sector web statistics 2003.*

[21]Geser and Pereira, eds (2004). pp. 48–52. (See note 8)

[22]Keene, S. (2002). In your dreams: digital media bring to life real collections.
In *Scanning the Horizon: Proceedings of the **mda** conference, Norwich.* **mda**
Information, **6**(1), pp. 113–116. Website: *The King's kunstkammer.* National
Museum of Denmark. www.kunstkammer.dk.

[23]Website: *Museum of Pure Form.* http://www.pureform.org/

[24]Geser and Pereira, eds (2004). pp. 41–43. (See note 8)

[25]Keene, S. (2004). City histories revealed. *Literary and Linguistic Computing,* **19**, 3,
351–371.
Website: *Lifeplus.* Lifeplus project web page. http://www.miralab.unige.ch/
subpages/lifeplus/
Website: *Archeoguide.* Augmented reality cultural heritage on-site guide.
http://archeoguide.intranet.gr/

[26]Website: *Athens.* Eduserve athens for education. http://www.athens.ac.uk
Website: *SCRAN.* Multimedia resources on history and culture. http://www.
scran.ac.uk

[27]Website: *National Portrait Gallery.* http://www.npg.org.uk

[28]Tateson, R. (2004). Serendipitous interactive browsing of online catalogues.
In *EVA 2004 London, conference proceedings* (J. Hemsley, ed.) pp. 22.1–22.8, EVA
Conferences International.

[29]Bowen, J.P. and Filippini-Fantoni, S. (2004). Personalization and the web from a
museum perspective. In D. Bearman and R. Trant, eds, pp. 63–78. (See note 13)

[30]Geser and Pereira, eds (2004). pp. 16–19. (See note 8)

[31]Lyon (2002). pp. 21–33. (See note 4)

[32]Website: *Tap into Bath.* Collection description databases.
http://www.bath.ac.uk/library/tapintobath/cd-databases/
Website: *Cornucopia.* Museums, Libraries and Archives Council.
http://www.cornucopia.org.uk

[33]Fink, E.E. (1999). The Getty Information Institute: A Retrospective. *DLib
Magazine.* **5**, 3.
http://www.dlib.org/dlib/march99/fink/03fink.html.

[34]Geser and Pereira, eds (2004). pp. 50–51. (See note 8)

[35]Website: *National Maritime Museum.* Collections and research.
http://www.nmm.ac.uk/server/show/nav.005002

[36]Website: AMICO. The Art Museum Image consortium. http://www.amico.org/
Website: *SCRAN.* Multimedia resources on history and culture.
http://www.scran.ac.uk

Website: *AHDS Visual Arts*. Arts & Humanities Data Service: Visual Arts Data Service. http://ahds.ac.uk/visualarts/
[37]Williams, R. (2004). Digital resources for practice-based research: The New Comedy Masks Project. *Literary and Linguistic Computing* **19**, 3, 415–426.
[38]Website: *AHDS Visual Arts*. Arts & Humanities Data Service: Visual Arts Data Service. http://ahds.ac.uk/visualarts/
[39]Exhibits: *Shhh…* Sounds in spaces. Victoria & Albert Museum. 20 May – 30 August 2004.
The sculpture of the Grant Museum. Audio installation. Grant Museum of Zoology, University College London. 2003 ongoing.
[40]Website: *The King's kunstkammer*. National Museum of Denmark. www.kunstkammer.dk
[41]Website: *CAN*. Collections Australia Network. About CAN. http://www.collectionsaustralia.net/site/301.html
Website: *Canada's digital collections*. http://collections.ic.gc.ca
[42]Website: *Imperial War Museum*. Family history. http://www.iwm.org.uk/server/show/nav.00100a
Website: *Moving here*. Tracing your roots. http://www.movinghere.org.uk/roots/
[43]Website: *Canadian Museum of Civilization collections*. Links to: home > scholars > reources > virtual collections storage. http://www.civilization.ca/collect/csintroe.html
Website: *Australian Museum collections*. Collections: flash tour. http://www.austmus.gov.au/collections/flash_tour/index.htm
[44]Marty, P. and Twidale, M. (2002). Unexpected help with your web-based collections: Encouraging data quality feedback from your online visitors. In D. Bearman and R. Trant, eds. (See note 13)
[45]Marty and Twidale (2002). (See note above)
4th Dimension (undated). *4th Dimension success story: The Thinker*. http://www.4d.com/solutions/thinker.html
[46]Geser and Pereira, eds (2004). pp. 5–6. (See note 8)
[47]Website: *Moving here*. Tracing your roots. (See note 42)
[48]Website: *CAN*. Collections Australia Network. (See note 41)
Website: *Canada's digital collections*. http://collections.ic.gc.ca
[49]Geser and Pereira, eds (2004). pp. 5–6. (See note 8)
[50]Manthorp, S. (2004). Shooting Gallery. In J. Hemsley, ed. pp. 6.1–6.10. (See note 12)
[51]Website: *CAN*. (See note 41)
Website: *Artifacts Canada*. http://www.chin.gc.ca/English/Artefacts_Canada
Website: *Cornucopia*. http://cornucopia.org.uk
Website: *SCRAN*. Multimedia resources on history and culture. http://www.scran.ac.uk
[52]Gerd-Christian Weniger, G-C., cited in Geser and Pereira, eds (2004). p. 65. (See note 8)
[53]Tapscott, D. (1996). *Digital economy: promise and peril in the age of networked intelligence*. pp. 68–71. McGraw Hill.

10 Collections and values

Introduction

The word *value* conjures up a number of feel-good aspects, a concept rather than a definition. In earlier days it was considered self-evident that museum collections were valuable and useful, and in many countries it still is so assumed. Now, the need to justify them is more common, as Chapter 1, Introduction, shows. Especially in the UK and the Netherlands, the current political and management culture requires that the cost of everything be known (and the value of nothing, as the saying goes?). One may regret that everything should be reduced to something that can be counted, but still, it is interesting to chart some of the dimensions of the value of collections. As ever, there is a lot written about the economics of museums and galleries, but far less on the collections.

This chapter addresses some interesting questions about the economic aspects of museum collections. What are the values of museum collections, and how can we understand them? What does this tell us about the uses of collections?

The idea of treasure and the value of precious possessions has caught the imagination since the very earliest of times. Things of value, and the more of them the better, have signified power and permanence. In Beowulf, written around the eighth century AD, treasure and things were greatly prized (see Poem, p. 119). The Shôsô-in in Japan has housed royal and religious treasure ever since that same time (see Fig. 1.1). Cathedrals, temples, and other religious institutions have accumulated treasures, too, largely through the gifts of benefactors.

It may be a basic human instinct to value possessions (or at least, a very prevalent one), but we are fickle creatures and we also get bored with our old things and hanker after new ones. A thing is never so glamorous as when we are in pursuit of it. As Marcel Proust observed long ago, 'Desire makes all things flourish; possession withers them'.[1] Value, like beauty, lies in the eyes of the beholder.

Of course, values do not refer only to monetary or economic aspects: cultural value is recognized to exist as well. The previous chapters have explored some of the ways in which collections can be valuable to people. In this chapter, concepts of value will be explored from an economic perspective. We shall then see how these ideas might apply to collections.

Culture and economics

In Beowulf, the warriors were overwhelmed by the value of the treasure that the dragon guarded, as we might be by the golden Celtic treasure in the National Museum of Ireland. But a large proportion of objects in collections inspires no such emotion. No wonder people in museums often find it difficult to justify the existence of the collections: ancient industrial machinery and racks of identical boxes containing potsherds and animal bones have no obvious intrinsic worth (for example, see Figs. 5.3 and 6.1).

Surprisingly, economists may be able to assist. We are accustomed to think of them as devils that impose hard numerical monetary values and ignore the hard-to-define virtues of museum activities and objects. However, they have found principles that do help to understand why collections are of value, and that even provide a basis for some of the complex decisions that people have to make in running museums.[2]

Many different values have been proposed for cultural assets.[3] Here we will discuss just two: economic value and cultural value.[4] In the case of culture, both are complex. Economic value is fairly easily defined: it is generated by the consumption by individuals or collectively of cultural goods and services. Cultural value is different, with social, aesthetic, spiritual, social, historical, symbolic, and authenticity values.

Economic values

Most of the economic value of museums does not derive from their collections. Straightforward economic value is measured in terms of consumption.[5] The museum goods that can be consumed include experiences (visits), along with purchases from museum shops and picture libraries and a variety of services: object identification, curatorial or conservation services, and the hiring of galleries for events. Other less easily defined cultural goods include an enhanced market for the products of artists and craftspeople and for antiques and artworks, and an increase in cultural tourism that might be specifically due to the museum.

Museums provide other economic goods that benefit the public. These include their contribution to public debates on art and culture; their role in defining cultural identity, and in making connections with other cultures; a stimulus for the production of creative works; the collective community value of educational services; the general value of the existence of museums, of knowing that they are there; and diffuse benefits such as option value – the value of maintaining the possibility of visiting or using services and the sense felt by people of a bequest value for future generations.

For individuals, museums offer further, less obvious, economic benefits. Stakeholders such as trustees gain improved standing socially or in employment and a better understanding of cultural affairs. For museum visitors, there is an increase in their human capital: a combination of social capital (access to and membership of useful social circles) and cultural capital (ability to engage in and understand cultural experiences and materials). The more the cultural goods and services a person consumes, the greater their cultural capital and the more they wish for further cultural experience.

There are other outcomes that are not directly delivered by cultural institutions, but which nevertheless happen or are encouraged by their existence. These may include effects on the economic regeneration of a place, since the museum could generate employment and incomes and raise the value of property nearby,[6] and cultural tourism. Although these external effects are often cited by museums in support of bids for funding, such arguments are vulnerable to the objection that they are not specific to a museum or gallery – they could be generated by a range of other businesses or institutions.[7]

Cultural values

Since the nineteenth century and earlier, economists have acknowledged that people need more than just material welfare. Ruskin believed deeply in the intrinsic value of art objects and argued that it derived from the life-enhancing labour that produced them. Long before that, Jeremy Bentham had defined the intrinsic value of a commodity as that which produced 'benefit, advantage, pleasure, good or happiness' later redefining it as the pleasure associated with the act of consumption of the commodity.[8]

The definition of cultural value is not universally agreed on by economists (or by anyone else!), but that does not detract from its importance.[9]

Here we must distinguish between the (confusing) notions of *capital* and *value*. Capital is a stock of accumulated potential value. Value may, like interest from an account or dividends from stocks or shares, be generated from capital. Cultural capital in the context of museums and collections may be intrinsic to objects; it may be possessed by individuals or even by organizations.[10]

The objects held by a museum can be seen as stores of cultural *capital*: that is a prime reason why the institution conserves and maintains them (Fig. 10.1).[11] Cultural *value* is generated for people from the capital, when they access or appreciate the collections in some way, through exhibitions or other activities. Individuals also possess cultural capital. When a person is

Fig. 10.1 *Valuable collections. Alison Boyle, curator, demonstrates an orrery. The astronomy collections of the Science Museum include early telescopes and many other valuable historic instruments. The whole of the collection could never be on display: there would not be room for it. They are often visited in store*

inspired, enjoys, or learns (in this case from objects) then this increases the cultural capital possessed by them, and further, their capacity to increase it still further.

Museums can increase the cultural capital that their collections represent by adding to what is known about them through research, by documenting them, and by a high standard of collections management and preservation. This maintains various aspects of cultural value and communicates messages that the museum places a high value on its collection – messages that are likely to be accepted because museums are perceived as trust-worthy and authoritative institutions.

Cultural value may derive from the relationship of the works or objects to society and the messages they convey about social organization, power and political structures. Figure 10.2 shows Collins Barracks near Dublin: built in the eighteenth century to enforce British rule, it now houses the decorative arts collections and museum of the National Museum of Ireland: a strong cultural statement about change of power and control.

Aspects of cultural value that are intrinsic to the object are:

- aesthetic value (beauty)
- spiritual value because of religious or other associations
- symbolic value because of something the object stands for
- historical value because of evidence or associations with the past
- authenticity value because the object is incontrovertibly the genuine, historic item.[12]

A different view of the cultural value of an object identifies three axes: scientific (information) value; personal narrative value; impersonal narra-tive value.[13] The scientific and information value of an object is an aspect of the cultural capital it represents. Its personal narrative value refers to its value to individuals: for instance, the objects in the Tank Museum

Photo: S. Keene

Fig. 10.2   *Collins Barracks: the Museum of Decorative Arts & History, National Museum of Ireland*

collections that are visited by families to whom they belonged (described in Chapter 7: Memory and identity). Its impersonal narrative value is its symbolic and historic value, perhaps when it is in a public exhibition.

The museum also generates cultural value in a wider, public sense: it fosters general perceptions of the purpose and significance of art and culture. The museum can decode and articulate the intrinsic values of an object. In doing so, it adds to the value of that object as experienced by the museum user. At the level of society, museums create cultural value from their collections through encouraging shared values and perceptions of equality of opportunity for access to cultural goods.[14]

Generational equity and the use of objects

With financial capital there is always a question of whether to spend it now, and be sure of gaining personal value from it at once, or to keep it in the hope that it will increase and be there to generate value in the future for one's self or one's children. There is something to be said for the notion that jam today is more valuable than jam tomorrow that we may never live to enjoy.

These ideas can be applied to the cultural capital of objects, too. Should we simply do all we can to enable the most people to extract the most enjoyment from the collections now, or should we preserve objects as a store of potential value for the future? Is there some way that we can have our cake and eat it, too? The terms used are *inter*generational equity (fair treatment between generations) and *intra*generational equity (the rights of people now to gain some value from their capital).[15]

As in debates to do with the environment, it is argued that it is wrong for one generation to diminish or damage the stock of cultural capital that it inherited.[16] The challenge is to devise ways of utilizing the cultural stock that do not detract from its future value (a challenge that museum conservators are well used to meeting). If this is not possible, criteria are needed to assist in deciding whether or not to enjoy and perhaps, destroy.[17]

An example is the decision on whether or not to play an historic musical instrument. This is often passionately debated. The approach developed by the ICOM International Committee of Musical Instrument Museums and Collections (CIMCIM) is that the older and rarer the instrument (i.e. the greater the cultural capital it stores), the stronger the case against playing it. If it is played, then as large an audience as practicable must be present and the performance must be recorded and if possible, broadcast as well.[18] This will realize the maximum cultural value. On the other hand, an instrument that is not played will (if properly looked after) maintain higher authenticity, historic, and symbolic values: that is, the intrinsic cultural capital that it represents will be greater.[19]

In another example, the cultural capital intrinsic to an object was preserved and increased through the use of digital technology, when the British Museum found alternatives to destructively unwrapping an Egyptian mummy. A television programme was broadcast, reaching perhaps millions of people, a website was produced, good reviews attracted a large number of people to visit, when they can view a video presentation. The economic value of the technologies that were used was enhanced by the cultural value that was generated by using them on an ancient object. This is important in the UK, where science education is attracting too few students. The digital exhibits and the film, which constitute new cultural capital stock, can be re-used indefinitely and in many different places.[20]

From this perspective, the difficult debates on conservation versus restoration, and about whether or not to operate working objects, are about decisions on whether to realize cultural value for the present rather than to maintain it for the future. If an object is used it will be affected, either through damage and wear or because it has to be modified in some way to make it safe or operable. Modification will decrease the authenticity and historic values of the cultural capital of the object, but use may generate cultural value at the time, enhancing the cultural capital of the people who are able to appreciate it better when they see it operated or used.

The current generation itself has rights to generate value from cultural capital. It also has duties, such as the maintenance and enhancement of cultural diversity.[21] We can all choose to eat at MacDonald's, exclusively use Microsoft™ software, and participate in the global use of English, but we can alternatively frequent regional cafés, use web browsers such as Mozilla, and learn a language other than English. Museum collections and objects are an important means of maintaining cultural diversity, since the objects in them are all unique if not physically then because of their provenance and information with which they are associated – their cultural value.

Changes in value

An object has never existed that is treasured and valued equally in all cultures and throughout time, although there may be some items that are universally not valued. The engaging Rubbish Theory deals with the way that the value of an object is rarely, if ever, fixed and intrinsic to it.[22]

When an object is new it is in a 'transient' phase: it is available to anyone, and its price depends on supply and demand. But 'a thing of beauty is a joy for a fortnight'.[23] Over a much longer phase, it is no longer new but has not acquired the glow of age: it may become rubbish. In due time, the object may once again become desirable and if so its value rises again. Yesterday's designer item is today's jumble sale candidate and tomorrow's auction treasure. Of course, it has gained scarcity value in the meantime.

There is more to the cultural value of objects than changes over time, however. It is a matter of everyday experience that value is socially constructed.[24] Bourdieu refers to 'the consumption of specific cultural forms that mark people as members of specific classes'. It tends to be the case that wealthy, powerful people prefer and accumulate objects that are generally perceived as higher value, and that the high value of such objects persists over years or even centuries.[25] This skews collecting. For instance, the everyday dress of ordinary people is often poorly represented in costume collections, which are instead full of ball dresses and wedding suits.[26]

Poor people on the other hand tend to possess objects that may be highly valued by them but which are considered low value by other sectors of society. Museums have to represent both sectors: this must inevitably contribute to the perception that some of their collections are without value.

When an object at some point in its value curve enters a museum, this confers a certain social worth on it. Coming across an object similar to the one that they own (or owned) in a museum affects the way that people see and feel about themselves. Miriam Clavir quotes a member of a Canadian First Nation tribe: 'He looked around [the museum] and he was in awe, and he said, "I never thought I'd live to see this". He was totally in awe. And he grew up in a time when these things were not treasured. I don't know if you've heard me say this, Alf, but it was very moving'.[27] If people find that museums do not have objects that they see as typically theirs, then of course they will feel slighted. Their culture and roots are by implication not benefiting from the cultural value that the museum can bestow simply by having such objects in its collections. People should feel that their culture is valued: this is a moral and social good in its own right. It also supports the economic argument that culture is valuable because it increases social cohesion, which aids the economy in general.

Measuring cultural value

Cultural value cannot easily be measured. There is no common unit of measurement; it is multidimensional and shifting, and partly unquantifiable. However, it is increasingly acknowledged that the cultural heritage has a value. A number of intergovernmental conferences and articles have recorded this developing view.[28]

One way of measuring cultural value that has been quite widely applied to heritage sites and cultural organizations is known as contingency valuation, using a particular tool, willingness to pay (WTP).[29] In WTP exercises, members of the public are asked to estimate how much they would be prepared to pay per year or donate to a fund to ensure the continuing existence of a cultural asset, such as Stonehenge, or public archives and libraries. They are prompted to take account of existence value, inheritance value, and so on. A global monetary sum can then be calculated that it is claimed expresses the value that the public place on the cultural asset. This approach is intrinsically abhorrent to many people who feel that it is impossible to put a price on cultural things that inspire deep emotions and feelings. An objection raised by economists is that it therefore does not account for some economic aspects. It is also criticized for ignoring comparisons between services that people 'must have' such as transport or hospitals, and cultural services that are more discretionary, and further argued that it is such a hypothetical exercise that lacks credibility. Some economists acknowledge that it is at best an imperfect method, but is found useful, and an alternative has yet to be developed.[30]

What do people actually see as the value of museum collections? Problematically, most of them don't realize the collections exist, but there have been many studies of what people think is important about museums. Collections conservation or preservation is always top of or high on the list.[31]

Museums and values

The economic value of cultural goods and services such as museums provide can, then, fairly easily be identified and measured. Economic value arises principally, though not exclusively, from the museum as an organization and a building, in a location, that delivers various services. It is much more difficult to quantify or even to tightly define cultural value. This does not mean that it is unimportant. Culture helps to articulate the values by which people express their identity and work out how to live together and its value needs to be defined using criteria different from economic ones.[32]

The collections are a store of cultural capital that the museum can use to deliver cultural value. What are the processes and functions that the museum can perform in its stewardship of the collections as cultural capital?

Setting value

Museums have a major influence on the monetary value of cultural objects. Art galleries and museums of the decorative arts, in particular, are important to the commercial art and antiques markets. For example, the art history curator places a work in a sequence of others, in time or technique.

From this its monetary value can be established – museums are not oblivious to this. For contemporary works the museum often plays an active part in making the market. In effect the curator has to 'speculate on the work's future as a "past"'. What will be the place of this work in any future series, how essential will it be?[33] In the example of the Vermeer painting, *Young woman seated at the virginals,* scientific information and scholarly research, underpinned by fully researched paintings in museums, authenticated it as being by Vermeer and thus added millions to its value (as mentioned earlier, Chapter 4: Research).

In an example illustrating the Rubbish Theory, Coventry City Museum was presented with the only surviving pattern book for a type of woven silk picture known as Stevengraphs. This enabled the collectors' market in those to continue its buoyancy firstly because a major collection was taken out of circulation and secondly because acquisition by the museum constituted an increase in the status and therefore, the desirability of these objects.[34] The effect is accepted, but it is argued elsewhere that this is in fact a bad thing because far from making things more publicly accessible, they are stuck away in museum stores where no one can benefit from them (i.e. realize their cultural value); and also that it artificially inflates prices.[35]

Adding value

Adding objects to the collections is one way in which museums can increase the cultural capital that they hold. But if an object is simply physically and legally acquired it is not very valuable in cultural terms.

The cultural capital that an object represents is nearly always relative, derived from the perceptions of the viewer, which in turn depend on what is known about it. We have all heard the story of the picture in the attic that is thought to be worthless until it is recognized to be by a famous artist. As if by magic that same picture becomes potentially very valuable. If the museum does not add to the cultural capital of the collections by acquiring, generating, and increasing knowledge and information relating to the collections, then it is failing in perhaps its most important role.

Maintaining value

Information and knowledge about the object need to be maintained because they constitute its social, spiritual, symbolic, and historical value. The other major components of cultural value are beauty and authenticity. These values are intrinsic to the object: they can only be decreased, through damage and deterioration, not increased.

If objects languish, dusty, broken, and undocumented, in corners and heaps in stores – then all that the museum achieves in acquiring them is to make them 'worldless'. 'In so far as the museum is about the past, it cannot be the objects, still obviously present, that are gone, but their worlds'.[36] The museum, uniquely, also has the chance to capture and preserve some elements of the objects' worlds as well. Other objects related to them, images such as photographs, and the intangible heritage of cooking, recipes, stories, songs, and language which give them their meaning – all these are additional aspects of their cultural value.

Does physical preservation alone increase cultural capital? Yes, because on the whole the older an object is the greater its cultural value: and further, the longer it is *likely* to last, the greater its *potential* cultural value.[37]

The question has been posed: do values in museums go through rubbish phases?[38] Indeed they do, as many a disastrous disposal shows. The most notorious one is the burning of the last complete dodo specimen (all except the head and one foot) by the Ashmolean Museum in 1755.[39] It was the very specimen from Mauritius that was in John Tradescant's original collection, passed to the Ashmolean Museum in 1677. I agree with the UK National Museum Directors' Conference that extreme caution should be exercised when contemplating disposals from museum collections on any significant scale. Many objects that have lost their cultural values have regained them when someone has recognized them and re-united them with their information.[40]

Perspectives on value

What other perceptions are there of the values of culture: politically; by museums themselves; and have perceptions changed over time?

Political values

Different countries have very different approaches to cultural and economic values. Attitudes range from Japan, Germany, and France where culture and social wellbeing are most highly valued for their own sake, to the UK and the USA where economic and measurable benefits are more sought after.[41] At intergovernmental and World Bank conferences cultural values other than economic ones are assuming greater importance.[42] Research colloquia on cultural values have been held for instance in Canada by the Canadian Cultural Research Network and in the UK by Demos.[43]

UNESCO provides overviews of national cultural policies for a number of countries worldwide.[44] The general impression from governmental policies is that culture is broadly considered valuable for its own sake and not just for the economic advantages it can confer. Of course, each country is unique in subtle ways, but the range of policy approaches is demonstrated. For example Germany, a country with a tradition of strong commitment to public funding for culture, has a statement which clearly refers to non-economic cultural capital: 'Our lives cannot be founded solely on supposed efficiency, as it would then be incomplete in terms of substance. We need the contexts of philosophy, the arts, and spiritual values which provide everyday life with an orientation framework within which practical goals can be pursued.'[45] At the other end of the spectrum, New Zealand and Ireland are examples of countries where the economic value of culture is stressed. The Himalaya Mountain Institute Museum, in Darjeeling, displays a sign in Hindi and English quoting the Constitution of India, affirming 'It shall be the duty of every citizen of India to value and preserve the rich heritage of our composite culture' (see Fig. 10.3).

In the UK, economic values have dominated national policy for many decades, but arguments are finally being advanced for cultural values. A 2004 UK government report on the value of museums identified such benefits as increased cultural understanding and respect and tolerance for others, fulfillment, and satisfaction from achievement, positive attitudes to experience, and desire for future experiences.[46] From the UK Secretary of State for Culture Media & Sport: '… engagement with complex culture can offer us more – an understanding of, an engagement with, and the satisfying of the deepest of human needs. Addressing poverty of aspiration is also necessary to build a society of fairness and opportunity.'[47]

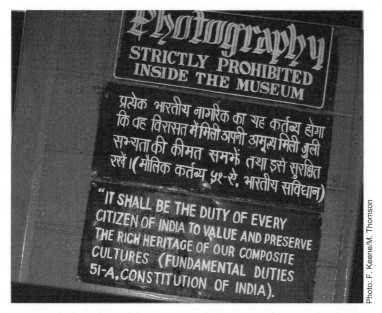

Fig. 10.3 *Notice in the Himalyan Mountaineering Institute, Darjeeling (also a museum) pointing out the duties of citizens towards their cultural heritages*

Changes over time

Attitudes to cultural value in the UK have changed over time.[48] In the post-war period of 1940–1960, as earlier in the nineteenth century, culture was seen as an economic good because of its educational and aspirational value. The 1970s and 1980s were the age of grassroots and social movements, as notions of culture challenged the fabric of social citizenship embedded in, belonging to, and arising from the community.

The mid-1980s saw the dominance of economic values. Culture was important because of the contribution it could make to the regeneration of economies and places, and because it enabled the diversification of local economies away from the previously dominant manufacturing and agricultural industries.[49]

In the early twenty-first century, it is said, we are seeing the 'cultural turn', with culture central to every aspect of government and social policy. In the age of information and the leisure economy, the increasing numbers of well-off individuals exercise a discriminating choice over how and where they spend their money. Companies and even countries need to appeal to sophisticated and culturally aware markets,[50] in places where creative and highly skilled people, essential to the twenty-first economy, want to live. Cultural institutions such as museums not only store and increase cultural capital, they also help people to decode and understand the rapidly changing world by providing a frame of reference from the past and for the present and future. 'Defining cultural knowledge as the key knowledge base of a society recognizes that knowledge is a collective accomplishment, where new knowledge is conditional on what has come before and is rarely if ever generated by an individual in isolation, and is inflected by the cultural, institutional and physical settings within which it is produced'.[51]

Economic arguments and policies have to be based on an understanding of non-economic and commercial values. The value of goods and services is much more dependent on symbolic value than on physical value. The example of the can of Coca-Cola is well known: people pay for the brand and the image since the cost of the actual drink is insignificant.

Perceptions from museums

Museums are much more likely to argue for the various economic benefits of a project than for the enhanced cultural value or cultural capital it offers. Around 2004 a number of strategy reports was produced by the national museums in the UK (in preparation for a government funding round). In discussing both individual museums and museums as a whole, their arguments were disappointingly economics based.[52] Funding bodies, on the other hand, may set requirements based on more purely cultural values. The UK Heritage Lottery Fund rejected the application for funding for the Spiral, a proposed building designed by Daniel Libeskind for the Victoria & Albert Museum. The Fund's director is quoted: 'We thought long and hard about this proposal but finally decided that it would not be able to deliver the major heritage benefits that we expect to see … it did not deliver well against our key requirements of conservation, education, and enjoyment of the UK's heritage.'[53]

In bids for funding, the collections are often mentioned almost in passing as being the component that specifically confers cultural value. Proposals typically refer to the ability to display or to provide access to more of the collections as a valuable outcome. So by implication if not expressly, the collections embody cultural value. But very few bids focus on collections.[54]

Why are museums hesitant in making the case for these values, with the collections at their centre? They seem to have endorsed the triumph of the materialist economic case that forces every bid for improvement to be cast in the form of economic advantage. Voices urging the centrality of cultural values are all too often shrill calls for them to return to the values of high culture for the few.[55] Museums have come to see that services to people are the heart of what they do, but they perhaps need to remember the collections aspect of the UK Museums Association's definition, *'Museums enable people to explore collections for inspiration, learning and enjoyment'*.

Conclusions

The questions addressed in this chapter are: what are the values of museum collections themselves? How can these values be understood? What does this say about the uses of collections? Models and notions of economic and cultural value have been explored and their application to the collections investigated.

Governmental policies and perceptions are the inescapable context for the value of collections. On the whole such policies do accept that culture is essential for its own sake as well as economically. As several commentators have observed, it is in museums that there seems to be something of a crisis of confidence in arguing for cultural values. Museums tend to chase the glittering prize of economic value.[56] They could be more confident in arguing for their fundamental value. Culture has the ability to bring people together and create a stronger sense of community values which are good in their own right. As cultural organizations they have support for this stance from economists and politicians.[57]

When the Science Museum's visitable large objects store at Wroughton was under discussion, those working with the collections assumed that the way to gain financial support from regional and local development agencies was to persuade them of the economic advantages of opening it to the public. It was a marketing colleague who told us that instead we should emphasize its museum-ness: its cultural value.

It would be much easier for museums to promote their collections if they were able to show that they were not just a store of cultural capital for the future, but that value was generated from them for today. The Dutch State Secretary of Cultural Affairs in 2000, in his article *A fortune to display: a consideration of the profits in cultural terms from the Collectie Nederland*, made this very point:

> The shareholders of the Collectie Nederland – and they are the Dutch taxpayers – should be able to assume that the cultural entrepreneurs who curate the public cultural fortune (and this includes museums, archives, libraries and other collection curators) attempt to gain the maximum profits from their input. Not of course for the sake of financial gain. But for the sake of the social and cultural returns that expresses itself for instance through an optimal accessibility and utilisation of the Collectie Nederland for the whole of society.[58]

The preceding chapters in this book have sought to develop ideas about aspects of the cultural value of collections for research, education, memory, creativity, and enjoyment. These all contribute to the cultural values of beauty, spiritual value, symbolic value, historic, and authenticity value. It is hoped that these ideas will encourage museums to deliver more obvious cultural value from the collections. Cultural capital for the future, and the delivery of cultural value now, are complementary, not contradictory. It is important to demonstrate the cultural value of the collections in the present by using them in different ways. A useful collection is a valued collection, a well-looked-after collection, and a preserved collection.

Notes

[1]Proust, M. (1896). *Les Plaisirs et le Jours*. Translated as *Pleasures and regrets*, Louise Varèse (trans.), Dennis Dobson Ltd. (1953).

[2]David Throsby, Professor of Economics in Australia, has studied and written extensively on the economics of culture, and his book is an invaluable source for this subject. Throsby, D. (2001). *The economics of culture.* CUP.

[3]Ashley-Smith, J. (1999). *Risk assessment for object conservation.* Butterworth-Heinemann. p. 84.

[4]Throsby (2001). pp. 23–34. (See note 2)

[5]Throsby (2001). pp. 34–41. (See note 2)

[6]DCMS (2004). *Culture at the heart of regeneration.* Department of Culture Media & Sport. pp. 36–43.

[7]Throsby (2001). p. 38. (See note 2)

Weil, S. (1994). Creampuffs and hardball. *Museum News,* **Sept/Oct,** pp. 42–43, 60, 62.

[8]Throsby (2001). p. 21. (For references to Throsby (2001) see note 2)

[9]Throsby (2001). pp. 30–31.

[10]Throsby (2001). p. 46.

[11]Throsby usefully works through the example of an art museum to illustrate how economic concepts apply to cultural organizations. Throsby (2001). pp. 34–41.

[12]Throsby (2001). pp. 28–29.

[13]Ashley-Smith (1999). pp. 89–91. (See note 3)

[14]Throsby (2001). p. 126.

[15]Throsby (2001). pp. 54–58.

[16]For example, the need to pass on the Australian heritage of landscape, buildings, objects and culture, indigenous and historic, is at the heart of the Australian Government quinquennial state of the environment report and recommendations. Department of the Environment & Heritage (2001). *Australia State of the Environment Report 2001: Natural and Cultural Heritage Theme Report.* Australian Government. CSIRO pub. Section 8: Conclusions.

[17]Mann, P.R. (1989). Working exhibits and the destruction of evidence in the Science Museum. *Museum Management and Curatorship*, **8**, 369–387.

[18]CIMCIM (1985). *Recommendations for regulating the access to musical instruments in public collections: 1985.* CIMCIM: the International Committee for Musical Instrument Collections of the International Council of Museums.

[19]Arnold-Foster, K. and La Rue, H. (1993). *Museums of music.* Museums & Galleries Commission. pp. 24–25.

[20]Exhibition (2004-5, ongoing): *Mummy, the inside story.* British Museum.

[21]Throsby (2001). p. 56.

[22]Thompson, M. (1979). *Rubbish theory: the creation and destruction of value.* OUP.

[23]Thompson (1979). p. 22. (See note above)

[24]Throsby (2001). p. 22.

Thompson (1979): Chapter 1. (See note 22)

[25]Thompson (1979). pp. 8–9. (See note 22)

[26]Kenyon, J., ed. (1992). *Collecting for the 21st century. A survey of industrial and social history collections in the museums of Yorkshire and Humberside Leeds,* Yorkshire and Humberside Museums Service. p. 51.

[27]Clavir, M. (2002). Preserving what is valued: museums, conservation and First Nations. p. 203. UBC Press.

[28]Throsby (2001). pp. 33, 67–68.

[29]Throsby (2001). pp. 82–83.

[30]Throsby (2001). pp. 82–83.

Throsby, D. (2003). Determining the value of cultural goods: how much (or how little) does contingent valuation tell us? *Journal of cultural economics,* **27** (3/4) 275–285.

Epstein, R. (2003). The regrettable necessity of contingent valuation. *Journal of cultural economics,* **27** (3/4) 259–274.

[31]For instance, Vaughan investigated what people felt was important about the role of museums and found that *conservation of collections* rated the highest of all for all categories of individuals in his sample. A consultancy survey for the Tower Armouries in 1985 by Mori found the same.

MORI, 1985. *Attitudes to museums and the armouries. Report on research conducted for the Royal Armouries.*The Royal Armouries.

Prentice, R., Davies, A. and Beeho, A. (1997). Seeking generic motivations for visiting and not visiting museums and like cultural attractions. *Museum Management and Curatorship*, **16** (1), 45–70. p. 53.

Vaughan, R. (2001). Images of a museum. *Museum Management & Curatorship*, **19** (3), 253–268. p. 258.

[32]Throsby (2001). p. 134. (See note 2)

[33]Fisher, P. (1997). *Art and the future's past.* Harvard University Press. p. 28.

[34]Thompson (1979). p. 31. (See note 22)

[35]Thomson, K. (2001). *Treasures on earth.* Faber & Faber. Chapter 7.

[36]Fisher (1997). p. 10. (See note 33)

[37]Ashley-Smith, (1999). p. 86. (See note 3)

[38]Ashley-Smith (1999). p. 96. (See note 3)

[39]Cheke, A. (2003). Treasure Island – the rise and decline of a small tropical museum, the Mauritius Institute. In *Why museums matter: avian archives in an age of extinction* (N. Collar, D. Fisher and C.Feare, eds). Bulletin of the British Ornithologists' Club Supplement, 123A, pp. 197–206. p. 197.

[40]A few examples of many others in NMDC (2003). *Too much stuff? Disposal from museums.* National Museum Directors' Conference. pp. 12–13.

See also Robertson, I. (1990). Infamous de-accessions. *Museums Journal* **March** pp. 32–34.

[41]Hampden-Turner, C. and Trompenaars, F. (1994). *The seven cultures of capitalism.* London: Piatkus. Chapter 1.

[42]Throsby (2001). p. 69. (See note 2)

[43]Websites: CCRN, 2003.

http://www.arts.uwaterloo.ca/ccm/ccrn/ccrn_colloq03.html

Demos *Valuing culture. An event held in the National Theatre Studio, London, on 17th June 2003.* Demos. http://www.demos.co.uk/catalogue/valuingculture-speeches/

[44]Website: *Culturelink.* Culturelink Network: Cultural policy database. UNESCO. http://www.culturelink.org/culpol/

[45]Website: *Die Bundesregierung. Die regierung. The Federal Government's cultural and media policy.* http://www.bundesregierung.de/en/News-by-subject/Culture-, 11019/Cultural-and-media-policy.htm

[46]RCMG (2004). *Inspiration, identity, learning: the value of museums.* The evaluation of the impact of DCMS/DfES Strategic Commissioning 2003–2004: National/ Regional Museum Education Partnerships. A report by the Research Centre for Museums & Galleries. DCMS.

[47]Jowell, T. (2004). *Government and the value of culture.* DCMS.

[48]This summary of changing attitudes to the value of culture in the UK is drawn from Pachter, M. and Landry, C. (2001). *Culture at the crossroads.* Comedia in association with the London Institute.

[49]Pachter, M. and Landry, C. (2001). *Culture at the crossroads.* Comedia in association with the London Institute. pp. 50–56.

[50]Pachter and Landry (2001). pp. 56–58. (See note above)

Forida, R.L. (2002). *The rise of the creative class: and how it's transforming work, leisure, community and everyday life.* Basic Books. Chapter 12.

[51]Pachter and Landry (2001). p. 60. (See note 49)

[52]Travers, T., Glaister, S, and Wakefield, J. (2003). *Treasure house and powerhouse: an assessment of the scientific, cultural and economic value of the Natural History Museum.* Natural History Museum.Travers, T., and Glaister, S. (2004). *Valuing museums: impact and innovation among national museums.* National Museum Directors' Conference.

[53]Kennedy, M. (2004). No lottery cash for V&A extension. *The Guardian.* 22 July.

[54]A search of the Heritage Lottery Fund website for heritage projects from 1994–2004, London and UK wide, revealed five projects to conserve or increase access to museum collections out of 146. Others were for buildings, to acquire objects or collections, for archives or for digitisation.

[55]Appleton, J. (2001). *Museums for the people: conversations in print.* Academy of Ideas.

[56]Throsby (2001). p. 163. (See note 2)

[57]A few of the sources of support for cultural values are economists such as David Throsby, Pachter and Landry's essay, a colloquium in Canada, an essay by the UK Minister for Culture Media & Sport and a consequent consultation paper, statements by the Dutch Minister for Culture, and other national statements to be found in the UNESCO Culturelink website cited above.

Gregg, J. (2003). Reframing the case for culture. Paper to *Accounting for culture: examining the building blocks of cultural citizenship. A colloquium marking the 5th anniversary of the Canadian Cultural Research Network and the 10th anniversary of the Department of Canadian Heritage.* Canadian Cultural Research Network. http://www.arts.uwaterloo.ca/ccm/ccrn/ccrn_colloq03.html

Pachter and Landry, 2001: pp. 71–79. (See note 49)

Jowell, T. (2004). *Government and the value of culture.* DCMS.

Holden, J. (2004). *Capturing cultural value.* Demos.

DCMS (2005). *Understanding the future: museums and 21st century life. Consultation paper.* Department of Culture Media & Sport.

van der Laan, Medy. (2003). *More than the sum.* Cultural Policy Letter 2004–2007. The President of the Lower House of the States General, The Hague, 3 November 2003.

[58]van der Ploeg, R. (2000). *A fortune to display: a consideration of the profits in cultural terms from the Collectie Nederland.* Introduction from cultural policy statement. Dutch State Secretary of Cultural affairs, 1999–2000. April 2000.

Poetry

By Saadi Youssef, translated from the Arabic by Khaled Mattawa

Who broke these mirrors
and tossed them
shard
by shard
among the branches
And now ...
shall we ask L'Akhdar to come and see?

Colours are all muddled up
and the image is entangled
with the thing
and the eyes burn.
L'Akhdar must gather these mirrors
on his palm
and match the pieces together
any way he likes
and preserve
the memory of the branch.

11 Piecing together the fragments

'I'd rather see all this than a quarter displayed properly': said a visitor to the National Railway Museum's open store, The Warehouse. The consultants' concluding advice: *Market the mystery.*[1]

The four questions that opened this book set out the problem. People, when they realize the extent of the collections, wonder, what is all this stuff for? – unwittingly touching on a key issue for museums; one that has not been satisfactorily addressed.

The investigation of values showed that museums as a whole are most often defended on the grounds of the economic benefits that they can bring, from cultural tourism, area regeneration, skills and education, and the quality of life. The values of the collections themselves are harder to untangle but they lie in the essential foundations of culture and identity. This aspect of their value is appreciated more in some countries than in others. In the UK and the Netherlands in particular, museums are being challenged to justify their collections. In most other countries this is neither a very public nor a general issue.

The issues uncovered are diverse. Museums themselves vary, and they have different histories of acquiring their collections and different purposes. Political, economic, and social circumstances constrain what they do. Collections are also of very different types, and to a large extent their nature determines the uses that are possible and desirable, from research to aesthetic appreciation. It is apparent from this overview that there will never be one universal answer to the best uses of museum collections. Rather, museums need to apply the same imagination and enthusiasm to using their collections that they do to their exhibitions and other programmes. They need to diversify what they offer to their audiences so as to use the whole of their resources.

Museums and collections in the future

Thanks to national museum bodies and international ones, such as ICOM and its international committees, there is a general expectation of what should be the role of a museum in the twenty-first century. It will be an outward looking organization that is responsive and accountable to its public. It will be aware that the views and interpretations it puts forward through its exhibitions are only one way of seeing the issues and topics that are addressed, and that its audiences bring perceptions and views of their own. It will recognize the need to represent the interests and cultures of all of its varied audiences in its collections and in its communications. This viewpoint is more strongly held in some countries than in others, and there is a very wide range of principle and practice among museums, but still there is a general consensus around this perspective among museums and stakeholders alike.

When it comes to collections, there is no similar general perception of what they are for and how they can be used. In this research, the views and experience of many people have been gathered, via interviews, newsgroup discussions, and the invaluable consultation carried out by the UK Museums Association in 2005, *Collections for the future*. Many examples of collections uses have been found, including some unexpected and imaginative ones. In view of the range of imaginative and impressive activities that are going on with collections, it seems almost churlish to complain. But the results add up to a scatter of glittering fragments. There is lacking a general appreciation of the role of museum collections and there is no comprehensive approach on how to make use of them. Thus it is difficult to make the case for the proper care and management of collections.

What can museums do?

How can these issues be addressed?

Too much stuff?

There is the obvious question of disposal. Could not the collections be less but better, through disposal or transfer to more appropriate owners, not excluding private ownership?

The pressure to consider reducing the collections is by no means universal: it appears to be really only felt in the UK, the Netherlands, and sometimes in Canada. In the US, disposal of museum objects has long been a way of life.[2] Other countries, such as Sweden where the SAMDOK process was instigated, have acted in advance and reduced the rapid rate of collecting; in Australia, a considered review of archaeological collections, at least those in the state of Victoria, is under way.[3] But disposing of collections can later be regretted.[4] It would be a mistake to export a solution to countries that currently do not have a problem.

Addressing the question of disposal, experience from the *Delta Plan* in the Netherlands and the Glenbow Museum in Canada has underlined what we knew: that a proper process of disposal is costly and demanding.[5] Collections have to be fully documented first in order to confirm ownership so as to take properly based decisions. The due process of proper disposal and consultation then takes further effort. It is much more immediately cost effective to dispose of large objects than small ones. Large objects take up more space and are generally more expensive to preserve and handle, yet it is small objects that generally silt up collections and are the most difficult to make use of. These are practical considerations: but there is also the question, raised in Chapter 7: Memory and identity, of whether or not disposal would compromise the validity of collections because of bias due to a current cultural or political viewpoint. There are examples of this happening in the past both in the West and in other countries.[6]

The Glenbow Museum appears to have greatly benefited from their project, despite the cost. It freed substantial resources for the better care and use of the collections that they retained, and transferred others to more appropriate ownership. On the other hand, in the Netherlands, as the Delta Plan progressed and better information emerged, the perceived scale of the problem grew! There is no doubt that a Delta Plan style process of a proper review of museum holdings would result in much better information about what was in them and on their state of preservation, but it was costly and is perhaps best implemented case by case at individual museums or regional levels.[7]

Collections out and about

The answer articulated in 2003 for the Netherlands was to get the collections out of the stores into public places or other museums.[8] The Glasgow Open Museum approach shows how effective this approach can be.[9] This may be part of the answer, but large parts of the collections are not suitable for display. Who is going to be fascinated by a collection of small surgical instruments, a row of indistinguishable grey boxes with small dials and wires sticking out (instruments used in scientific experiments), or boxes of bones and potsherds? Will people of the countries from which ethnographic collections are derived be pleased that things that they value from their own cultures are dispersed in outreach displays throughout Western shops and airports? There are many other imaginative ways of exploiting collections for general benefit and enjoyment. Key to them is that the museum acts as a service to encourage and enable others to access and use the collections.

Collections centres

Collections centres are often seen as the answer. It will be much less expensive to store the collections in a remote place, in a dedicated building. It is unfashionable to express scepticism about collections centres but when this concept is properly thought through, many serious issues arise: loss of intellectual ownership, reduction in the possibility of access to and use of collections, and uncertainties about ongoing finance for such centres. Issues relating to collections centres are discussed in more detail in Chapter 4: Research.

There are benefits, especially for some types of collection – in particular archaeological collections. Collaborative storage may have advantages over a facility for a single museum. The Smithsonian Resource Centre and the store in London that is shared by three of the national museums there work well, largely because they are easy for museum staff to reach, and thus are very busy. The Science Museum's large objects store nearly 90 miles out of London worked less well because it was not visited much by curators – therefore it had to develop uses of the collections as a sort of low technology alternative museum. This may be a pointer to a solution.

Remote centres could simply exacerbate the problem. They might just transfer the problem – or challenge – to some unspecified 'others', and enable the museum to shuffle off its responsibility for making proper use of the collections that it has accumulated. It would be essential to consider first what the purpose of the collection was and who the users were. Local collections should surely serve local users.

However, there could be a future for collections centres as a sort of alternative museums. This would need to go far beyond simply providing facilities for researchers. Their entire purpose would be to serve access to and use for the collections by every sector of the public: academics, others in education, schools, people from families to the elderly. In Lincolnshire you will now find 'The Collection: Art and Archaeology in Lincolnshire': the Collection at the centre with planet museums (exhibition centres?).[10]

The fundamentals

Of course, it is obvious that properly managed collections are the foundation for any use – documentation, storage, preservation measures, and conservation. Museums should push ahead with digital documentation of their collections – at collections level, at object information level, ultimately with an image of each object as well. The electronic documentation should then be put online for public access.

It must be acknowledged that any solution requires resources: both initial capital and project funding, and also ongoing funding for staff, equipment, and premises.[11] But running the collections and making use of them cannot be considered as an optional extra. For example, at present, educational activities mainly use special handling collections with a semi-disposable status, because of the risk of damage. With will and training, the actual collections could be much more effectively used without compromising their preservation, perhaps by grading them or by developing alternatives to actual handling. But handling is sometimes seen as some sort of a magic experience, when providing a context to explain the objects and facilities to look at them closely without handling could be more effective.

More uses, more use

However, necessary though professional collections management is, it is far from being sufficient. It is the basis for action, not an end in itself.

Research has the potential to make the most comprehensive use of the collections and also to add to them, as a store of knowledge and information. Research use requires proper collections management, knowledge of what is available, and facilities for research at various levels. Many important questions need to be explored, for example, how much are collections used for research? How can non-academic interest groups be encouraged to make greater use of the collections? How can academic use be encouraged? What facilities would help these groups to use the collections as a resource?

In considering collections for *ongoing learning*, this study focused on post-school uses. There is scope for greatly increasing such use. Partnerships with further and higher education establishments and with local groups are ways in which educational uses could be developed. Awareness needs to be raised with course providers of the potential uses of collections in teaching. Resources would be needed, but there is a lot of interest in new ways of learning and teaching. Education funding could be drawn on, too; in general, this is well funded by governments. There are many questions that need to be addressed about using collections for education, starting with the potential role of objects in the learning process. How exactly could collections be made use of. Bring students to objects or objects to students? Use them in seminars or lectures or as a basis for coursework or private study? What sort of courses might benefit? Where can good case-study examples be found? By simply providing study rooms, even if only open one or a few days a week, as in the Norfolk example, users are drawn to the collections.

Creativity and collections came as a surprise. It was only a chance remark from a natural history museum director that alerted me to its importance. In his experience, about half the requests to access the collections were for artistic purposes. Poems alluding to objects illuminate and adorn this book. There is a wealth of examples of creative engagement with collections.

Of course, they are drawn on not only by designers and craftspeople interested in the ways that objects have been made but also by artists using collections as media for expression, in literature from the earliest of times, in films where the collections themselves are alluded to as the dark unconscious, in architecture, music, and new media (see Fig. 11.2). All that is needed for museums is to welcome the creative uses of their collections, to encourage and engage with artists, and to exploit available funding for artistic partnerships, since artists need income as well as inspiration.

Memory and identity depend in many crucial ways on objects, and museum collections play important roles. They may play a part in establishing national identity as in the National Museum of Ireland, where golden Celtic adornments are at the heart of the entrance display (with the struggle for independence in the next gallery). They may foster a collective *ésprit de corps*, for remembrance of relatives who have given military service. For people from countries once colonized wishing to reclaim their culture, museum collections are crucial and are highly valued. Museums need to supply the basic services of making known what they have and provide

Photo: S. Keene

Fig. 11.1 *The Darwin Centre of the Natural History Museum, London (2001). The vast majority of the museum's specimens are stored on site in South Kensington, where they are extensively used for research. This extension to Waterhouse's building houses the specimens stored in spirit. There is a public programme of visits, lectures, demonstrations, etc*

for visitors in a welcoming and supporting manner. There is a two-way process: museums can also play a valued part in capturing and storing the remembrances that make collections objects meaningful.

Finally, *enjoyment* (Fig. 11.1). Those who work in museums are privileged in being able to enjoy collections: that is why many of them choose these careers. It can be a lot of fun to tour collections as a visitor (though I have been reminded of the hazard of being trapped in a tedious trail from which escape was impossible). The effectiveness of open storage, designed with an eye to being visited, is debated: in some places it has been very successful, in others, less so. Similarly, conducted tours of stores have had mixed success. Demonstrated collections – functional objects seen working – are popular with some people. This use is on a collision course with preservation, though, and not only with the conservation profession: collections objects are popularly used as reference material for making replicas or models, and for this they need to be authentic. (See discussion in Chapter 3: Collections: Using functional objects). Here, new technologies, in particular ambient computing using local sound or light projection, or other alternatives to keyboards and screens, could be helpful in enlivening objects and providing information about them.

Digitization: what will it mean for museums?

Digitization could almost have been the whole basis for this study. These technologies could result in far-reaching changes on the ways that museums operate. They could lead them to become much more open to inputs from outside their ranks: knowledge brokers and facilitators of access rather than gatekeepers. Simply making public what is in museum collections would lead to greater demand for access and use, which in due course could have considerable effects on how museums allocate and prioritize their resources.

As well as the technologies of information science, there are those of ambient computing, where sound, images, and other media can be delivered via a range of new devices quite different from screens and keyboards. These lie behind many of the imaginative and entertaining techniques that Julian Spalding has admired in science centres and children's' museums.[12] Museums have hardly begun to explore these varied capabilities.[13] They could indeed be the key to the wider and better uses and appreciation of collections.

There is also the matter of the intangible heritage. Almost the only way of collecting these materials is in digital form. How will these materials be used: have museums appreciated the exacting preservation requirements?[14]

How could digital technologies serve each of the uses reviewed so far? There are many new and exciting opportunities to be explored.

A new focus on collections

Is the new emphasis on the people relegating collections from the central purpose of the museum to a backdrop? This is an anxiety often expressed in museums. But it doesn't have to be like that.

Why should the emphasis on people make the collections redundant? On the contrary, this is a great opportunity. The concern about how to justify collections is widespread, and there is a feeling that something has to be done. It seems to me that we do have the seeds of some important answers, as well as some new questions. If the focus moved to how best to truly make use of collections for people (those in the future as well as those now), then there would surely be another revolution in how museums function and are perceived.

By collecting so much stuff museums have turned themselves into different organizations without acknowledging this fact. Most current thinking is about their place- and visitor-based communication and interpretation role, but in their collections, they have now created a new sort of important resource that has to be used in completely new ways.

Mark Dion, the artist, is quoted as calling for the museum *'to be turned inside out – the back rooms put on exhibition and the displays put into storage'*.[15] Few would want to banish museum displays and exhibitions – but Dion is surely on the right track: let us find out what it would mean.

Collections as a service

A positive view of collections will start with the mindset that they are a public resource, not a private treasure to be jealously guarded. The museum's role is to provide the services necessary to achieve the proper use of this resource. The first step would be to bring the collections into a proper state of documentation and care and to publish the holdings on line (Fig. 4.3).

Working in collaboration

Key to success will be for the museum to stop seeing activities as valid only if it has originated them. The museum will act as one of the players in a network of other organizations and individuals that routinely draw on the collections as a resource for their particular activities. 'Use' does not imply physically handling objects: this particular activity will be rare. Conservators find many ingenious ways of enabling objects to be closely inspected without physically handling them. Intellectual access is equally important, and the rapidly developing technologies of virtual reality and 3D representation will increasingly be employed.

Fig. 11.2 *The Museum of Civilization, Ottawa (1989). The collections build-ing is sited beside the museum gallery building in view of Canada's Parliament Building across the Gatineau River, a symbolic link for the nation. It holds 3.5 million artefacts – most of the collections*

The organizations that will be players in this network already include schools and many local community groups. More opportunities will be created to visit and work with the collections. More universities and colleges will work with museums to include collections in their teaching and research. The responsibility rests with educational institutions also, and, education sector budgets may meet some of the costs of more intensive access to and use of collections. Useful precedents are already set by the Arts & Humanities Research Council and by other schemes in the UK to promote innovative teaching.[16]

Working with individuals

Individuals from outside the museum, too, are welcome and will be encouraged to access collections and objects, and also to contribute to infor-mation and knowledge about them. Natural history museums already benefit from the work of outside researchers, who identify specimens, catalogue collections, and publish on them. There could be similar work with other collections also.

Digital opportunities

In many ways this revolution is in step with the digital age. Information and digital technologies are certainly not the complete answer but they could be important to the solution. In particular, information technology facilitates the functioning of organizations as knowledge organizations: knowledge and information are key to the collections. Wider electronic technologies are key to enjoying them.

Measuring success

This is a challenge, since the number of people using collections in whatever way can never be more than a tiny fraction of those who visit museum exhibitions. The most important measures will be those of activities outside the museum, for instance publications by external researchers, rather than those of the museum itself. An example is for the fish collections in the Australian Museum.[17] If required, ways of measuring the reach of these uses could be developed by studying educational benefits, the ripple effect of visits (rather like secondary readership of publications), and by increased individual and community cultural capital. Such issues are discussed in Chapter 10: Values, and addressed by Holden in his 2004 essay.[18]

Difficult balances

Museums will have to perform some difficult balancing acts. They will continue to provide proper stewardship of the collections for the future as well as access and use for people today. It is too easy to use the possible needs of the future as an excuse for ignoring those of the present: both can and must be served. Collaboration also brings challenges. In accepting information and knowledge from outside people, museums cannot relinquish their responsibility to provide accurate and impartial information. This is highly prized by the public.

Is there a solution?

This book has a positive focus on generating a perception of the usefulness of collections and showing some ways in which this has been achieved. But I am mindful that there is a quite substantial volume of museum collections in store, certainly in the UK, and that it is inexorably growing.

What should museums do with all their stuff? This is the crunch point. Any solution has to be multi-dimensional: better collecting (let's get away from 'I am a curator therefore I collect'); review, and some disposal of the existing collections (dispersal to other museums? This is costly and doesn't reduce the quantity); collections centres, more like alternative museums; more uses by more people of more of the collections. Better understanding and information made public on what is in the collections underpins everything. But it is essential to generate greater use.

Conclusions

If museums allocated the imagination, resources and priority to using the collections that go into exhibitions there would not be a problem.

A passion for collecting things is apparently an almost universal human trait, but it seems that once we have the stuff we all wonder what exactly it is for. In countries where museums are not traditional, people often do not see the point of collections in museums. In contrast, in the West a museum is often used as the answer, but it is turning out that this merely escalates the problem.

When collections outgrow the ability of museums to use them and to support their proper stewardship, there needs to be a thorough review of what is there and what is needed. Careful use of centres that would evolve as alternative museums could be another part of the answer. But above all, there must be the commitment to make the collections used and useful.

This study has found many inspiring and diverse examples of collections being used and enjoyed. It has set the context for and has assembled evidence so as to encourage a perception that they are in fact a used and useful resource for now as well as for the future. Now we need a change of focus among museums – one that they would surely welcome – to wholeheartedly provide a service to make their collections a resource for all.

Notes

[1]Holdsworth, R. and Bryan, R. (2003). *National Railway Museum: Warehouse display report*. NRM: unpublished report.

[2]Malaro, M. (2003). Collections management and deaccessioning in the United States. *ICOM News* **56** no. 1.

[3]Steen, A. (1999). Samdok: tools to make the world visible. In *Museums and the future of collecting* (S. Knell, ed.), Ch. 17 pp. 196–203, Ashgate.

Deakin University: Cultural Heritage Centre. Research and consultancies: *Making room for the past: Determining significance in archaeological collections from historic sites.*
   http://www.deakin.edu.au/arts/centres/CulturalHeritage_Centre/research/making.room.php
[4]Sheriff, A. (2000). Zanzibar: Encapsulating history: the Palace Museum and the House of Wonders. In *Museums & history in West Africa* (C. Ardouin and E. Arinze, eds) pp. 155–163, James Currey.
[5]Van Dijken *et al.* (2001). *The Delta Plan for the preservation of the cultural heritage evaluated.* Ministry of Education, Culture and Science.
Janes, R. (2004). *Email correspondence.* 24 November – 4 December.
[6]Robertson, I. (1995). Infamous de-accessions. In *Collections management* (A. Fahy, ed.) Routledge. Sheriff, 2000.
[7]Van Dijken *et al.* (2001). (See note 5)
[8]Ministrie van OCenW (1999). *Culture as confrontation. Principles on cultural policy in 2001–2004.* Ministerie van Onderwijs, Cultuur en Wetenschap, Netherlands.
[9]RCMG (2002). *A catalyst for change: the social impact of the Open Museum. A report for the Heritage Lottery Fund.* Research Centre for Museums & Galleries.
[10]Website: *The Collection.* The Collection: art & archaeology in Lincolnshire. Lincolnshire City & County Museum.
   http://www.thecollection.lincoln.museum/
[11]Resource (2001). *Renaissance in the Regions: a new vision for England's museums.* Resource (now the MLA). Section 3.5.
[12]Spalding, J. (2002). *The poetic museum.* Prestel. p. 63.
[13]Geser, G. and Pereira, J., eds (2004). *The future digital heritage space: an expedition report.* Thematic Issue 7. DigiCULT. pp. 16–19.
[14]Keene, S. (2002). Preserving digital materials: confronting tomorrow's problems today. *The Conservator,* no. 26, 93–99.
[15]Corrin, L.G. (1997). *Mark Dion.* Phaidon, p. 17.
[16] Website: *AHRC.* Arts & Humanities Research Council. http://www.ahrc.ac.uk.
[17]Website: *Australian Museum Online.* Fishes.
   http://www.amonline.net.au/fishes/collectons/papers/index.htm
[18]Holden, J. (2004). *Capturing cultural value.* Demos.

Acknowledgements

I am grateful first to the Institute of Archaeology, University College London, for granting me six month's research time to concentrate on this book, and to my colleagues Beverley Butler, Paulette McManus, and Nick Merriman who took on my teaching work to enable this. I also thank the Pilgrim Trust and the University College London Research Leave Fund for providing grants that made it possible.

Many people have generously helped me by agreeing to be interviewed or by sharing their views and opinions with me and I am delighted to have the chance to thank them here. They include, among others, Max Barclay, Jim Bennett, Liz Graham, Francis Grew, Clare Harris, Beverley Hoff, Robert Janes, Stephen Johnston, Frances Keene, Xerxes Mazda, Nigel Moynihan, Pat Nietfield, Raghnall Ó Floinn, Frances Palmer, Cecilia Pardo, Cathy Ross, Ilka Schacht, Libby Shelton, Bill Sillars, Hedley Swain, Matthew Thomson, Peter Ucko, David Willey, John Woodward, and members of the Museums Association project, *Collections for the future*, especially Helen Wilkinson. For providing or assisting with illustrations, I thank Libby Sheldon and Sally Woodcock, and also Janet Knell, Helen Chatterjee, Hugh Kilmister, and others who have provided images of stored collections. Daniel Antoine and Libby Sheldon kindly provided accounts of their research for Chapter 4.

I am extremely grateful to those who have taken the time and trouble to read and comment on parts of the book: Nick Merriman, Paulette McManus, Beverley Butler, Alan Morton, Tom Keene and those who read the whole of the text and sparked major improvements: Frances Keene and Matthew Thomson. Derek Keene was a source of wise assistance and kind support. Of course, mistakes and deficiencies that still exist after all their invaluable advice, are mine.

Research method

The book is first and foremost grounded in many years of experience in managing very large and diverse museum collections in archaeology, social history, and science and industry. This gave me plenty of opportunity to reflect on the questions with which it opens.

Recent research for it was based on the published literature from the scientific and other disciplines that could inform what we do as well as that pertaining to museums. Books and monographs are referenced as far as possible in preference to articles, as they represent developed ideas and are easier for others to consult.

Interviews or discussions were conducted with colleagues working with collections in several countries. I corresponded with many others by email. Membership of the Museums Association's working party on the uses of collections, part of its excellent project to develop a view on this very topic for collections in the UK, was invaluable. Matthew Thompson and Frances Keene kindly acted as my research assistants in China, Vietnam, Laos, Croatia, and India.

Not least, this work is the product of the resources that are available on the internet. I was able to find articles and reports that I would never have come across if I had used only print publication and conventional media. Email conversations were held with colleagues in a number of countries. And, museums are now publishing their activities so comprehensively well via the web that an impression can be gained or facts checked in moments for countries from Afghanistan (the Kabul Museum) to Zimbabwe (National Railways Museum).

Interviews and visits

Chippenham Museum & Heritage Centre. Interview: Assistant Curator. 14 June 2004.

Nordisk Konservatorforbund, DK. Conference discussion, *22 October.* Course, Storage. Held in Sorø, Denmark, 18–22 October 2004.

Deakin University, Melbourne. Email correspondence and interview: I. Schacht, PhD candidate. Project: *Making room for the past: determining significance in archaeological collections from historic sites.*, 21 October 2004.

INTERCOM-L. Email correspondence. Discussion group. 19 November – 4 December 2004.

Janes, R. Email correspondence. 24 November – 4 December 2004.

Museum of London. Interview: H. Swain, Head of the Department of Early London History. 1 June 2004.

Museum of London. Interview: Curator, Department of Early London History. 11 June 2004.

Museum of London. Interview: C. Ross, Head of Department of Later London History. 3 December 2004.

Museum of the History of Science, Oxford. Seminar in the course, MA in the History of Science. Attended 27 October 2004.

MUSEUM-L. Non-displayed collections: is this an issue? Newsgroup discussion. Archived: November – December 2004. http://home.ease.lsoft.com/archives/museum-l.html

National Museum of Ireland. Interview: N. Moynihan, Director, Museum of Natural History. 6 April 2004.

National Museum of Ireland. Interview: R. Ó Floinn, Head of Collections. 6 April 2004.

Natural History Museum. Interview: Curator. 9 July 2004.

Royal Academy of Music. Interview: F. Palmer, Curator of Collections. 9 June 2004.

Science Museum. Interview: X. Mazda, Curator. 19 August 2004.

Smithsonian Institution. Email correspondence: P. Nietfeld, Collections Manager, National Museum of the American Indian, Collections Resource Centre. 30 June 2004.

The Tank Museum. Interview: John Woodward, Director. 11 June 2004.

The Tank Museum. Interview: David Willey, Head of Collections. 27 June 2004.

Thomson, M. and Keene, F. Interview and email correspondence: 22 July 2004 – 25 February 2005.

University College London, Institute of Archaeology. Interview: E. Graham. 16 June 2004.

University College London, Institute of Archaeology. Interview: B. Sillars. 17 June 2004.

University College London, Institute of Archaeology. Interview: P. Ucko, Director. 15 June 2004.

University College London, Institute of Archaeology. Seminar: A. Reid. 14 December 2004.

University College London, Institute of Archaeology. J. Bennett, *Museum of the History of Science, Oxford..* Seminar: *The uses of collections: science history collections.* Institute of Archaeology, University College London. 20 March 2003.

Copyright and permissions

Quotations

Poem: *The Pitt-Rivers Museum, Oxford*. Reprinted by permission of Sll/Sterling Lord Literistic, Inc. Copyright © 1972 by James Fenton.

Poem: Rubbish theory: i.m. Denny Hickey. Copyright © Bernard O'Donaghue; reprinted by his permission.

Poem, extract: *Beowulf*, trans. Howard D. Chickering. Reprinted by permission of Anchor Books.

Poem: *Place du Jour de Balle, Brussells*. Copyright © John Fuller. Reprinted by permission of pfd.

Poem: *Poetry*, by Saadi Youssef, translated from the Arabic by Kholed Mattawa. English language translation copyright 2002 by Kholed Mattawa. Reprinted from *without an Alphabet, without a face* with the permission of Gray Wolf Press, Saint Paul, Minnesota.

p. 86: Quotation from J. Baudrillard, *The System of Objects*, trs. J. Benedict. Verso. Reproduced by kind permission of Verso.

p. 95: Quotation from Vietnam Veterans Memorial Collection. Reprinted by permission of the National Parks Service.

p. 38: Quotations from *Museums & history in West Africa*. © West African Museums Programme, 2000. Reprinted by kind permission of James Currey Publishers.

Images

Fig. 1.2   Image: Conservatoire des Arts et Metiers: © F. Keene and M. Thomson.

Fig. 2.1   Image: the Petrie Museum of Egyptian Archaeology. © University College London. Published by kind permission of the Petrie Museum.

Fig. 2.4   Image: War Remnants Museum. © F. Keene and M. Thomson.

Fig. 3.1   Image: the Science Museum. © Science Museum. Reproduced by permission.

Fig. 3.3   Image: whale vertebrae. Published by permission of the Canadian Museum of Nature.

Fig. 3.4   Image: the Science Museum. © Science Museum. Reproduced by permission.

Figs. 4.1, 4.2   Images: © Libby Sheldon.

Fig. 4.3   Image © the Museum of the History of Science, Oxford. Reproduced by permission. www.isin.org.

Fig. 5.2   Image: the store of the Marischal Collection. © University of Aberdeen.

Fig. 6.1   Image: the Science Museum. © Science Museum. Reproduced by permission.

Fig. 6.4   Image: the Pitt-Rivers Museum, Oxford. © Oxford University. Reproduced by permission.

Fig. 7.1   Image: published by permission of the Grant Museum of Zoology, University College London. Sound guide text from *The Sculpture of the Grant Museum*. Reproduced by kind permission of The Grant Museum, UCL, and the artists. © Ann Byrne and Dan Smith.

Fig. 7.3   Drawings reproduced by kind permission of the artist. Copyright © J.E. Knell.

Fig. 8.2   Image: the Science Museum. © Science Museum. Reproduced by permission.

Fig. 8.4   Image: the Canadian Museum of Nature. Published by permission.

Fig. 9.1   Image: the Horniman Museum music gallery. Published by permission.

Fig. 9.2   Image: Canadian Museum of Civilization website. Image © Canadian Museum of Civilization, no. D2005-6152, from www.civilization.ca

Fig. 9.3   Image: Australian Museum website. © Australian Museum. Reproduced by permission.

Fig. 10.1   Image: © the Science Museum. Reproduced by permission.

Fig. 10.3   Image: Himalayan Mountaineering Institute, Darjeeling. © F. Keene and M. Thomson.

Fig. 11.2   Image: Canadian Museum of Civilization no. S89-1713. Image © 1989 Harry Foster. Reproduced by permission.

Index